Ezgi Başaran is a Turkish journalist who made her name covering the Kurdish conflict – reporting 'on the ground' in the fight between ISIS, the YPG (People's Protection Unit), the PKK (Kurdistan Workers' Party) and the Turkish state. After accepting an offer to write a daily column on Turkish foreign affairs, she became the youngest ever editor of *Radikal*, the biggest centre-left news outlet in Turkey, and the first woman to hold the role. After facing government censorship when covering the breakdown of the Kurdish talks, she resigned and *Radikal* was shut down – an event which made headlines worldwide. Başaran is now coordinator of the Programme on Contemporary Turkey at the South East European Centre (SEESOX) at St Antony's College, Oxford University, where she explores the bridge between journalism and academia. In 2017 she was awarded a prestigious Dulverton Scholarship for her upcoming MPhil in Modern Middle Eastern Studies at Oxford University. She has written on Turkish domestic politics and her comments have appeared in major international media, including the BBC, the *Financial Times*, *The Economist*, the *Wall Street Journal* and the *Washington Post*. Her book *Barış Bir Varmış, Bir Yokmuş (Once upon a Time Peace)* was published by Doğan Kitap in 2015.

'Başaran writes that "the new Turkey" under Erdogan's Justice and Development Party (AKP) is "rushing headlong towards an authoritarian regime and a new, darker Middle East after the hope of the Arab Uprisings". The solution to what is happening in the Middle East is "directly related to Turkey's 40-year-old Kurdish problem and how the Turkish government chooses to deal with it".

Başaran's survey of Kurdish history is both familiar and instructive... It is a fascinating, frightening story, journalism bringing all the connections together... Now the Turkish–Kurdish war goes on, Gülen is ready for his extradition and ISIS appears to be free to stage its suicide attacks in Turkey... Watch this space. And read this book.'

Robert Fisk, *Independent*

FRONTLINE TURKEY

*The Conflict
at the Heart of
the Middle East*

EZGI BAŞARAN

I.B. TAURIS
LONDON · NEW YORK

Published in 2017 by
I.B.Tauris & Co. Ltd
London • New York
www.ibtauris.com

ISBN: 978 1 78453 841 5
eISBN: 978 1 78672 280 5
ePDF: 978 1 78673 280 4

A full CIP record for this book is available from the British Library
A full CIP record is available from the Library of Congress

Library of Congress Catalog Card Number: available

Typeset by Tetragon, London
Printed and bound in Sweden by ScandBook AB

MIX
Paper from
responsible sources
FSC www.fsc.org   FSC® C007584

For Memo and Deniz…

Contents

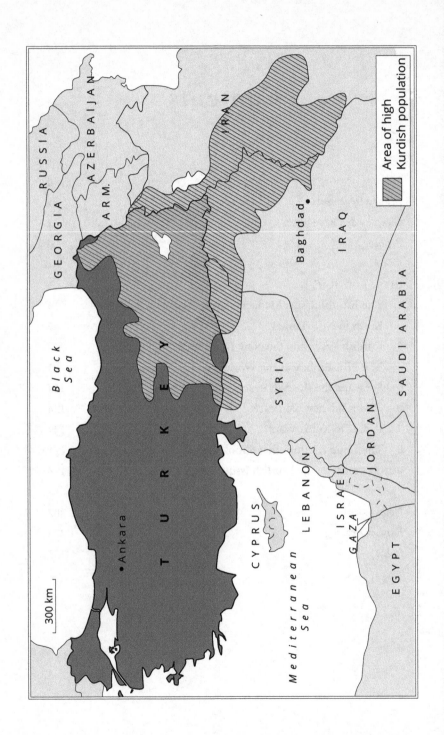

Acknowledgements

I came to Oxford with a broken wing. However, sometimes the best opportunities arise from unfortunate and unexpected developments. At Oxford University, I have benefited tremendously from being among distinguished scholars from all around the world. I would like to thank each and every one of those at St Antony's College who made me feel at home at a time when I felt like I had none. I will never forget the friendship and support that Othon Anastasakis, Kalypso Nicolaïdis, Timothy Garton Ash and Eugene Rogan have lent me. I would also like to thank all those kind people at the European Studies Centre at St Antony's College, who have become my family over time.

A very special thanks to Ingrid Cranfield, Sarah Terry and Apostolos Doxiadis for their help in getting my ideas down as precisely as possible on paper. I also would like to thank my editor at I.B.Tauris, Tomasz Hoskins, who was one of the first people to see the idea behind this book.

Thanks to my mother Yelda Başaran and my in-laws Gürsu and Hulusi Karlı for always being there to lean on.

And last but not least, thanks to the two incredible men who own my heart forever: my husband Mehmet Karlı and my son Deniz Karlı.

You are my mind and soul. This book is dedicated to you, as always.

Glossary and Key Players

ABDULLAH ÖCALAN (APO): Leader and founder of the PKK and the KCK. Imprisoned for life on İmralı Island, Turkey, where he has been held since 1999.

CEMIL BAYIK: Co-chair of the KCK, along with Besê Hozat.

HDP (HALKLARIN DEMOKRATIK PARTISI): The Peoples' Democratic Party, the main Kurdish political party in Turkey.

İMRALI DELEGATION: A group which consisted of HDP MPs Sırrı Süreyya Önder, Pervin Buldan and İdris Baluken, who shuttled between İmralı prison, Ankara and Qandil Mountain during the peace process.

KCK (KOMA CIVAKÊN KÜRDISTAN): The Kurdistan Communities Union, an umbrella organization of Kurdish entities, including the PKK and the PYD.

KRG: Kurdish Regional Government (Iraq).

MIT (MILLÎ İSTIHBARAT TEŞKILATI): National Intelligence Organization.

MURAT KARAYILAN: Former chair of the KCK and acting chief of the HPG (People's Defence Force), the paramilitary branch of the PKK.

PJAK (PARTIYA JIYANA AZAD A KURDISTANÊ): Kurdistan Free Life Party (Iran and northern Iraq).

PKK (PARTIYA KARKERÊN KURDISTANÊ): The Kurdistan Workers' Party, founded by Abdullah Öcalan. It has been waging an armed struggle against the Turkish state since 1984.

PUK: Patriotic Union of Kurdistan (northern Iraq).

PYD (PARTIYA YEKÎTIYA DEMOKRAT): The Democratic Union Party, established in 1993 in Syria by Kurdish activists and influenced by Abdullah Öcalan and the PKK.

QANDIL MOUNTAIN: Headquarters of the PKK in northern Iraq.

SALIH MUSLIM: Co-chair of the PYD, along with Asya Abdullah.

YDG-H (YURTSEVER DEVRIMCI GENÇLIK HAREKETI): The Patriotic Revolutionary Youth Movement, the youth wing of the PKK, which has been actively initiating urban warfare in the Kurdish region of Turkey since the end of 2014.

YPG (YEKÎNEYÊN PARASTINA GEL): People's Protection Unit, the armed militia of the PYD in Syria.

Preface

Three years ago, if I had been asked to choose three words that defined me, I would unhesitatingly have said *woman, journalist, Istanbulite* – in that order.

Now, I find myself struggling with two of these three descriptions, although they have been part of me since the year I began studying journalism at university. I still proudly call myself a journalist and an Istanbulite, but now I find myself in a strange position: these words are rapidly becoming old labels rather than having a tangible meaning.

I never thought of taking a break from journalism, nor did I want to. For that matter, I never wanted to leave Istanbul, the city I passionately love.

When the liberal-left newspaper *Radikal*, of which I was editor-in-chief, was shut down in March 2016 in a government crackdown, pursuing a decent journalistic career in Turkey became not only impossible but also very dangerous. Having already been offered police protection at the beginning of that year, I knew I was on the brink of a forced break from the newsroom. It was at this time that I came to St Antony's College at Oxford University as an academic visitor. Since then, I have immersed myself in the world of academia with the curiosity and inquisitiveness of journalism, while also attempting to build a much-needed bridge between these two crucial pillars of intellectual activity. At Oxford, I have benefited tremendously from being among distinguished scholars from all around the world. This book relies on my interviews, reports and fieldwork of the last seven years and was written during my time at Oxford, where I had to watch in great sorrow as some of my close colleagues lost their jobs, had to leave the country for their own safety and that of their loved ones or ended up in jail on incomprehensible charges.

My knowledge and experience regarding Turkish and Middle Eastern politics come directly from the field. From the very beginning of my journalistic career, I reported from conflict zones and places in which political turmoil erupted from time to time: northern Iraq, Iran, Pakistan, North Ossetia and Malaysia, as well as south-east Turkey. During this period, I was fortunate to be able to interview many prominent figures in Turkish and Kurdish politics.

As I began writing in spring 2016, the violence in Turkey's Kurdish conflict had reached a 40-year high. The two-year peace process between the PKK – the Kurdistan Workers' Party, an armed militia which Turkey, the US and the EU regard as a terror organization – and the Turkish government had collapsed the previous summer, and the situation in my home country had become extremely volatile. Since early 2016, Turkey has suffered not only the PKK insurgency in the south-east but also major ISIS attacks in its cities. As if the spillover from the Syrian quagmire had not been enough of a security issue, a botched coup attempt on 15 July 2016 left more than 200 casualties, and in its aftermath more than 100,000 people from the state bureaucracy, judiciary, military and police were purged, almost 200 media outlets shut down and thousands arrested. A month later, Turkey launched its biggest military intervention in Syria since the war began. The main objective of this intervention, given the code name Operation Euphrates Shield, was to drive ISIS and Kurdish fighters away from Turkey's borders. After retaking the towns of Jerablus, Dabiq and al-Bab, Turkey, a member of NATO, was confronted with Kurdish militias in Manbij, who were backed by coalition forces led by the US, also a member of NATO.

After the collapse of the Kurdish peace process, Turkey's relationship with its Western allies sank to an all-time low, since Turkey was attacking the Syrian Kurdish militias closely linked to the PKK, and the PKK in turn were collaborating with militias on the ground in Syria. Turkey could not persuade the US either to push the Kurds out of Manbij or to exclude them from an operation to free Raqqa from ISIS control; on the contrary, President Trump approved the arming of the Syrian Democratic Forces (SDF), led by the Kurds, to enable them to seize the ISIS stronghold in Raqqa.

This dealt a major blow to Turkey's relationship with the US and NATO. While Turkey was going through a deep period of turmoil, a constitutional reform package that would give President Erdoğan more executive power and suspend all checks and balances was won in a referendum by a razor-thin margin.

The publication of this book therefore comes at a time when Turkey, whose geopolitical position is crucial for the West, is transforming politically, socially and militarily and making, breaking and cutting across conventional international ties. Turkey's Kurdish conflict lies at the heart of this change and will continue to affect its domestic politics, civil and state institutions, social fabric and foreign policy.

In the current climate, reinstating a peace process with the Kurds would be a huge undertaking. Yet I firmly believe it is the only thing that would set the country on the path to a stable democratic future, a society at peace with itself and a status worthy of respect on the international scene.

My reasons for this belief – and the challenges and aspirations for Turkey and the Kurds – are elaborated in depth in the book you are about to read.

INTRODUCTION

He came home, went to open his bag, and froze. On it, resting just above the zip, was a piece of human flesh. He was lucky. It was only the bag that belonged to him, not the burnt, blackened charcoal scrap.

You share the nausea he felt. But do not let it blind you. Now more than ever, we must open our eyes and see what is happening around the world.

What I am going to tell you could very easily have been your story. And reading it here makes you one of the lucky ones.

＊

On 10 October 2015, 20-year-old Kadir,[1] a dark-haired, bearded young man with a constant smile who had graduated from one of the best high schools in the country and enrolled as an undergraduate in the sociology department of Boğaziçi University – the best academic institution in Turkey – boarded a night bus from Istanbul, along with five friends. They arrived in Ankara around 7.30 in the morning. It was a beautiful sunny day, atypical of October in the capital. Kadir and his friends collected their banners with left-wing slogans on them and strolled to the main train station, where a peace rally was to take place. The rally had been organized by a group of pro-Kurdish and leftist activists, and aimed to urge the Turkish government to return to the process of forging peace with its own Kurds.

Göksel,[2] another university student, similar in appearance but a bit older than Kadir, was already there with his flags and banners. The place buzzed with the enthusiasm of the young people gathered to demand peace for their country.

Around 8,000 people showed up in front of the 1930s art deco stone station building. Göksel and Kadir decided to find a place where they could do the *halay* – a line or circle dance found throughout Turkey, especially in the south and the south-east, which is also performed as a political statement.

A few minutes after they had started dancing and chanting slogans, there was a deafening bang. 'Don't worry,' said one, trying to soothe the others, 'it's probably a stun grenade.' Seconds later, the ground shook with another loud noise. Kadir looked up at the sky and saw 'things' flying. What were those 'things'? Steel balls the size of shrapnel – and human flesh.

The moment before people realized that a bomb had just exploded, the air was filled with cries and screams. Some shouted the names of their friends; some called for their mothers, as small children instinctively do; and some just groaned loudly with pain.

Kadir and Göksel each grabbed their mobile phones to reach out to their family.

'Mama, there was an explosion at the railway station. I am OK. I may not have reception in the next few hours. Don't worry,' texted Kadir. Göksel had to take a selfie to assure his mother that he was alive, but his mother looked at the photo and thought that Göksel had lost his legs, because the photo only showed his upper body, as most selfies do. While she cried at home, her son was facing the bloody reality, walking among scattered human limbs and ripped banners, fluttering in the wind, with peace slogans on them.

Along with other people who had survived the double explosion, Göksel helped the wounded to the ambulances. He searched for his friends in the piles of bodies. He did what he could. And then, like a ghost, each went home.

It was only afterwards that they were able to grasp the horror of the attack.

Göksel took off his navy cardigan, which had come through the day unscathed, though covered in a fine grey dust.

Kadir laid his bag in front of his legs, as if wanting to shed the burden of the day, to unlive what he had lived.

And there they were. On the shoulder of the navy cardigan. On the front pocket of the bag. On each, a scrap of human flesh that brought home to them as nothing else the cruelty of the world they live in today. A scrap that will haunt them throughout their lives.

Kadir and Göksel were survivors of an ISIS attack that wrought havoc on Turkey. Two suicide bombers, one of whom was part of an ISIS cell from the south-east of the country, caused bloodshed on a scale that, to some, was Turkey's 9/11. It was the biggest terrorist attack the country had suffered since its founding. It killed 102 and wounded 391.

What Kadir and Göksel went through was similar to the experience of Indian air stewardess Nidhi Chaphekar at Brussels Airport in March 2016. In the minutes following the ISIS attack, she sat down on a bench, clothes torn, her shocked face covered in dust and blood. Her photo became iconic, representing the innocent across the world – those who suffer from the display of Islamist extremism in the capital cities of well-ordered, thriving countries.

The horror that Nidhi, Kadir and Göksel suffered was no different from what people in the *Charlie Hebdo* office or the Bataclan concert hall in Paris went through when ISIS members decided to take lives in the most brutal of ways.

This could be my story. Or your story.

There are many ways to look at the ISIS phenomenon, and one of them must include the new Turkey, which, under the Justice and Development Party (AKP), is rushing headlong towards an authoritarian regime and a new, darker Middle East after the hope of the Arab Uprisings. This book aims to offer an alternative point of view, focusing on a possible solution as well as the roots of the problem. The solution to what is happening in the Middle East, I argue, is directly related to Turkey's 40-year-old Kurdish problem and how the Turkish government chooses to deal with it.

It is also my task in this book to interpret and lay out the complex tapestry of Turkey's Kurdish history, which lies at the very heart of the Middle East. Without understanding the Kurdish problem, it is impossible to get the measure of what is going on in the Middle East or to fumble a way towards peace in the region. That is what makes the Kurdish story so important.

'Boots on the ground' and the Turkish Triangle

Since the summer of 2015, at the time of writing 685 people have been killed and more than 2,000 wounded in 269 separate terrorist attacks in Turkey. The most ferocious 15 of these attacks were perpetrated by ISIS and the rest were by the PKK, the violent leftist Kurdish group that has been waging a bloody campaign for Kurdish autonomy inside Turkey since the 1980s.

This is Turkey now. A brand new one, as the ruling AKP likes to call it. The new Middle East, on the other hand, is a far more grisly arena, where a proxy World War III is taking place in front of our eyes. Syria is worse than anything we have seen in recent history. How we ended up here is a complicated matter that requires thorough analysis, sincere discussion and self-criticism by all parties involved.

It is true that all the regional powers in the Middle East have been and still are concerned about ISIS and its stronghold in Syria, but they do not always rank their concerns in the same order as the Western powers.

The US, with the bitter memory of the Iraq war still very much alive, did not want to become militarily involved in the Syrian crisis in the early days, when obliterating ISIS would not have been too difficult, especially after ISIS besieged the Iraqi city of Mosul in June 2014. Several strategies adopted by the US to tackle the problem, such as training and equipping rebel groups, without having 'boots on the ground', have proved to be a dismal failure.

While there was a consensus among policy makers that there needed to be 'boots on the ground', no one could agree whose boots they should be. To unravel the intricate web of fighting ISIS is a task we will struggle with for decades, but here is a crude simplification:

The Saudis and the Gulf states see Iran as a greater threat than ISIS, and they had already diverted their energy towards Yemen, where what they believed to be an Iranian-backed coup was taking place. The Iraqi government has no control over the Shi'i militias, which fuel the sectarianism in the region that gave birth to ISIS in the first place. Syrian opposition forces, of whom a considerable portion are radical jihadists, see Assad as a bigger threat than ISIS. As for Russia, fighting ISIS means supporting the dictator that is Assad. And Turkey unfortunately sees the Kurds having an autonomous land near its border as a bigger threat than ISIS.

The Iraqi Kurdistan leadership appears to be sandwiched between Turkish pressure and 'kinship pressure'. While dallying frequently with Turkey, it cannot simply abandon its brothers fighting under the flags of the PKK and the PYD – the latter a Syrian Kurdish group that fights both ISIS and Bashar al-Assad – as dictated by the Turkish government. On the other hand, those Kurds have proved to be an ally of the US.

I argue here that if the Turkish government had not intentionally built an explosive triangle of ISIS, Kurds and Turks, this wrangle over priorities and divergences of interests would be more manageable.

To figure out how Turkey finds itself in this situation, we need to look more closely at its identity paradigms, its coordinates on the map and, of course, its dramatis personae. It is not an attempt to hide in the nook of country exceptionalism but an endeavour to lay out the blueprint of the AKP's Turkey, its approach to Kurdish conflict and the consequences of that approach for the region.

Confused? You are not alone

Turkey's neo-liberal, Islamist ruling party the AKP had great aspirations when it came to power in 2002. It mended a broken financial system – by religiously following an IMF recipe – and turned a shrinking economy into a blossoming one, while restarting discussions about joining the EU. Because of the EU accession process and its pledge to eliminate the military's tutelage, the AKP received support from Turkey's intelligentsia and the West. According to the AKP's national and international proponents, it was a flawless combination: a pro-business party which was developing its own Islamic middle class while adhering to the basics of a democratic system. Unlike their predecessors, or the so-called secular establishment, they were not detached from the majority of the population, who were conservative Muslims. For this reason, the AKP's Turkey had become an archetype for consonance between Islam and democracy.

On the other hand, the EU accession process was, it seems clear now, just another tool used by the AKP and its leader, Recep Tayyip Erdoğan, to gain approbation both within and outside the country. 'Democracy is like a train,' Erdoğan had once let slip, 'and you get off once you reach your destination.'

To get to its ultimate destination, the AKP formed a tacit alliance with an Islamic network led by an imam from Anatolia called Fethullah Gülen. Gülenists were followers of Sufi Islam who had been investing in education to raise their so-called 'Golden Generation'.

On top of building a global empire of Gülen schools, the movement has also infiltrated the Turkish judiciary, bureaucracy and police since the late 1980s. Initially, for the first decade of the AKP's rule, Gülenists formed the backbone of the bureaucracy, lending the AKP a helping hand in its struggle with the secular establishment. When Erdoğan began to consolidate his position in the government from 2011 onwards, a power struggle erupted between his party and the Gülen movement. Former partners became bitter foes. The 15 July 2016 coup attempt – when F-16s attacked the capital city and the parliament building – was the final skirmish in this battle.

Erdoğan's AKP conceived a different authoritarianism that brought about a new kind of state–society relationship, spiced up with political Islam.[3]

Power became simultaneously more personalized and more populist. This new authoritarianism had democratizing potential, but it could also become, as one analyst has stated, 'more oppressive than any other regime Turkey has previously experienced',[4] especially for those who did not fit into the alliances Erdoğan relies upon, such as secularists, leftists and Kurds. True, the 15 July coup was botched, but an attempted coup can only take place in a country where the democratic institutions are enormously eroded and social harmony is strained. Although the nuisance in society is the product of the failed Kurdish peace process, this was caused by the erosion of the very democracy that was supposed to protect all Turkish citizens. Ironically, the AKP was the first government to seek a genuinely political solution to the Kurdish issue, but in the end it destroyed it.

This book tracks the sequence of events from the emergence of the AKP to that of the Turkish–Kurdish peace process. It also reveals a very little-known aspect of the unrest – the feud in the AKP–Gülen movement – which revolves around the Kurdish issue. As human memory is fallible, the chronology followed in this book may clarify events and essential issues for anyone interested in looking at the Middle East and conflict resolution from another perspective. The story of Erdoğan's deeds in the context of the peace process can also serve to demonstrate how a populist strongman can instrumentalize people's hopes to maximize his own individual power.

The consequences of the collapse of this Erdoğan–Kurdish peace process affected not only Turkey but also the EU and the US. The key variable that determines Turkey's relations with the Middle East and the West is and will be the Kurdish issue. With the Syrian war, the Kurdish issue has just become a global one.

Syria, and the Collapse

On the 100th anniversary of the 1916 Sykes–Picot Agreement that partitioned the Ottoman Empire, the Syrian civil war and the emergence of ISIS marked a shake-up of the old world order and became a matter of national security for the Western world – it was a perfect symmetry, as if to remind everyone that today's Middle East is the product of World War I. When the war in Syria first erupted, Turkey's leadership was adamant that it would be only a matter of months before Bashar al-Assad was ousted. In 2012, President Erdoğan bragged that he would go to Damascus and pray at the Umayyad Mosque. This did not happen.

Turkey's Syrian policy has proven to be an epic failure, which has brought Turkey into conflict with its Western allies and stifled the global fight against ISIS. Overconfidence and frivolous neo-Ottoman and pan-Islamist aspirations aside, the main reason for this failure of policy has been the Kurdish issue. When it became apparent that Assad was not going anywhere any time soon, Turkey's main objective in Syria shifted to obstructing Syrian Kurds, led by the PYD (Democratic Union Party / Partiya Yekîtiya Demokrat), in their bid to form an autonomous region in the north of Syria called Rojava ('Western Kurdistan' in Kurdish). Indeed, from the end of 2013 to the start of 2015, Turkey saw no problem in having an open-border policy for the jihadists in Syria. Not surprisingly, this turned the country into a hub for jihadists from all around the world, including ISIS recruits. This has caused huge security vulnerabilities, not only for Turkey but also for Europe as a whole.

According to the *New York Times*, the vast majority of American ISIS recruits used Turkey as a staging post,[5] while the BBC reported that at least 1,000 British jihadists and thousands more Europeans are believed to have evaded police and intelligence surveillance to cross into Turkey and reach ISIS territory.[6]

Turkey's policy was not directly to help ISIS but rather to suppress the Syrian Kurds. Why would Turkey prefer jihadists as neighbours, rather than Kurds, who had lived side by side with them for hundreds of years? For the very simple reason that the PYD / YPG was ideologically affiliated with the PKK and that an autonomous Kurdish region in Syria would serve as an example for the Kurds in Turkey.

If Turkey had made peace with its Kurds *and* helped the Syrian Kurds fighting ISIS rather than fighting them, there might have been a viable plan for a truce in Syria, and both Turkey and the Middle East would now be safer and stronger.

Turkey's peace process with the Kurds had collapsed in the summer of 2015, mainly owing to the expansion of the Syrian Kurdish cantons next to the Turkish border and President Recep Tayyip Erdoğan's ambitions to create an executive presidency for himself. It was exactly at that time that things in Turkey started disintegrating, exacerbating the turmoil in Syria.

A year later, following the botched coup, Turkey launched a military operation in northern Syria on 24 August 2016. The offensive was primarily aimed at preventing the PYD from moving to the west of the River Euphrates, and was not against ISIS, as initially proclaimed. Indeed, ISIS had vacated Jerablus – a city in northern Syria – before Turkish forces and the forces of the Free Syrian Army set foot there.

Around the same time, President Erdoğan started to express an irredentist rhetoric regarding the Middle East, where an international proxy war was taking place. He made constant references to the 1920 National Pact (Misak-ı Millî) as an aspiration, and repeatedly called the 1923 Treaty of Lausanne – which ended World War I and settled modern Turkey's borders – a failure. The Treaty of Lausanne marked the point at which Turkey had disclaimed the rest of the Ottoman lands and settled with the borders of today.

As so often with Turkey, the explanation for its present is to be found in its past. Misak-ı Millî was a national political declaration that was adopted at the last meeting of the Ottoman parliament as a reaction to colonial occupation. Mustafa Kemal Atatürk and his comrades defined the borders of a new Turkish state arising from the ruins of an empire. Their ideal map was slightly different from the one ratified in Lausanne. It showed Mosul, Sulaymaniyah and Kirkuk belonging to what would be called Turkey, the argument being that these three now Iraqi cities were Kurdish and Kurds and Turks were inseparable.

Mustafa Kemal – the founder of modern Turkey – was a realist leader above all. Although he used Misak-ı Millî as a call to arms against occupying powers, when the war in Anatolia ended in 1922 he did not allow yet another struggle in the south-east. He and his fellow founding fathers of Turkey accepted the deal they got in Lausanne and also agreed that the fate of such Misak-ı Millî cities as Mosul would be decided later by the League of Nations. But the first Kurdish uprising in 1925 weakened Turkey's hand at the League of Nations. 'Turks were told, "Kurds don't want to be with you." Turkey's warring strength was limited; so Mosul was left to Iraq by the terms of a treaty signed in 1926. And the chapter was closed.'[7]

'The status quo will change somehow,' President Erdoğan said in a cabinet meeting he chaired in October 2016. He pointed at the map. 'We will either leap with moves forward or we will be bound to shrink.'[8] Turkey's military presence in northern Syria was an indication that references to Misak-ı Millî were more than internal politics.

Turkey's leadership was rekindling an old endeavour that had failed. And the government is now channelling the internal legitimacy that it garnered after the coup – using legal means gained through the declaration of a state of emergency – and moving against not only the followers of the Gülen movement but also against academics, journalists and Kurdish politicians.

'We are Kurds; spending time in jail in Turkey is our folklore'

Selahattin Demirtaş, the co-chair of the main Kurdish party in Turkey, is the most popular Kurdish politician ever. He was once dubbed 'the Kurdish Obama' by the Western press because of his inclusive campaign during his presidential bid in 2014. I had met him in London days before his arrest. He knew it was coming. 'We are Kurds; spending time in jail in Turkey is our folklore,' he had joked. In truth, it was far from funny. A one-time presidential candidate and peace negotiator is now waiting to be tried for terrorism. There is a photograph that Demirtaş kept in his smartphone archive, which was taken some 20 years earlier, during the ceremony marking his graduation as a barrister. Two of his colleagues from Diyarbakır Bar Association helped him put on his robes – Fırat Anlı and Tahir Elçi. Elçi was murdered and Anlı is in jail. So is Demirtaş himself. That photo may be one of the best depictions of a failed peace process. Arresting these leaders was, no doubt, a symbolic blow to the Kurdish movement, but it carries the risk of further radicalizing an already alienated Kurdish youth.

Similarly, curbing the Kurdish presence in Syria by military means not only laid waste to any possibility of reconciling Turkey's Kurds with the government, but has also threatened any stability that remained in Turkey's fraught relations with Europe and the US.

In Turkey's thinking, the PYD is equal to the PKK, which the EU and the US have designated a terrorist organization. However, the US supports the PYD's armed militia, the YPG, in its fight against ISIS. Similarly, the EU is giving a platform to PKK-related activists, who are both diminishing the legitimacy of Turkey's Syrian policies and eroding the country's international image. The more hawkish Turkey becomes in its Syrian policies, the more risk there will be that this in turn will adversely affect Turkey's relations with the West. The road from a failed peace process to the brink of becoming a failed state has proved to be short for Turkey.

✳

As a journalist, I have been following the Kurdish issue for more than a decade, during which time I have interviewed almost all of the prominent figures who have shaped the course of the Kurdish movement in Turkey. These interviews composed the backbone of this book. Some of the people I talked to have either died naturally or been killed. Some went up to the mountains and joined the PKK, while others are in jail. Some continue to make plans to fight ISIS or liberate Kurds from persecution at the hands of authoritarian regimes. Ultimately, in telling the story of the Kurdish problem and the Kurds, in the context of almost a decade and a half of AKP rule in Turkey, this book argues that this long-standing issue has the power to either make or break the country.

All the while during the writing process, a song by a famous Kurdish singer from Turkey kept coming into my mind. 'How Will You Know?' seemed to capture the essence of the book:

> I was a young tree, I fell down,
> I was a tempest, I calmed down,
> I have been tired, very tired.
> How will you know what I have been going through?
> I come by destroying concrete walls

I come by ripping of steel
I come by destroying my life
How will you know what I have been running away from?
In the skies, stars are fading now
My mother is calling me now
I have a lover, she is suffering now
How will you know why I have been drinking?
I was a fountain; I turned into blood,
I became a roadhouse,
I made a mistake, I have become wasted.
How will you know why I have been silent?[9]

The song was written by Ahmet Kaya, who had to flee Turkey after receiving death threats. In 1999, he won the 'Best Singer' title at the Entertainment Journalists' Society annual awards. When he came up onstage, he said, 'I have composed a Kurdish song. Now, I am looking for a brave producer and a brave TV channel to broadcast it. I know there are some among you who could.'[10] The audience of celebrities and musicians showed their disapproval by booing and throwing forks and knives at him. He died of a heart attack only a few months after going into exile.

As a Turk born and raised in the western part of Turkey, it took me half my life to really know what Ahmet Kaya and the Kurds had been going through since the foundation of the Turkish Republic. It would be impossible for anyone not born in the Kurdish region of Turkey to fully comprehend the depth of agony conveyed in Kaya's 'How Will You Know?'

And yet we all need to know now. We need to know why the Kurdish fountains turned into blood and why the young saplings on both sides were felled. We all need to know how opportunities for peace have been exhausted by government policies. We need to know how and why so many on all sides lost their lives.

How will *you* know?

In the pages that follow, I will try to tell you.

ONE

The Kurdish Issue
Made in Turkey

The Kurdish Insurgency

'Why do you call it the Kurdish problem?' an American novelist had once asked me, trying, genuinely, to grasp the subject. 'It is like calling a person a headache.' When I think about the Kurds in Turkey, it is never my head but my heart that aches. There are around 30 million Kurds in the world, primarily in Iran, Iraq, Syria and Turkey. The majority of them – 14.7 million – live in Turkey.[1] And they have a problem. Even acknowledging the fact that Kurds have a problem was a huge step for Turkey to take, one which took decades. Thus the term 'Kurdish problem' does not disturb them; on the contrary.

Many people draw comparisons between the Irish Republican Army (IRA) and Kurdish violent separatist group the PKK, which was founded in 1978 on the premises that the Kurds of Turkey have long been persecuted by the state, that Kurdistan – divided into four countries: Turkey, Iraq, Syria and Iran – was colonized by regional ruling elites and that it should be first liberated and then united.[2] Between 1969 and 2010, the Northern Ireland conflict claimed 3,568 lives.[3] In Turkey, 35,576 people have died in clashes between the Turkish army and the PKK since the 1980s.[4] The Kurdish conflict – or problem or issue, call it what you will – is one of the most violent and long-standing intrastate conflicts in the world today.

There is a plethora of descriptions regarding the Kurdish problem, many of which reflect the political and strategic position of the person or group making them. For the majority of Kurds, it is a plight that befell them as a consequence of demanding their birthright from the state. They were Kurds, they were squeezed and they wanted to be recognized as a distinct population living in Turkey. Simply put, they wanted to be who they are. On the other hand, for the Turkish government, the Kurdish problem was a case of terrorism, embodied in the PKK's deadly assaults on Turkish soldiers and police officers, predominantly in south-east Turkey. For some, solving the Kurdish problem means giving up Turkey's land to Kurds so that they can build their own state. For others, Turkey will only truly be unified if the Kurdish problem is solved.

Undoubtedly, the Kurdish issue is a political problem that demands a political solution. It is rooted in the demand for Kurdish self-determination, which has been denied them since the fall of the Ottoman Empire, something that led to the birth of the Republic of Turkey. It is not only about Kurdish ethnicity, nor is it about diminishing or eradicating PKK violence. The PKK is not the cause of the problem, but emerged as a consequence of it. Nor can the unrest in the Kurdish region or the PKK's emergence be explained solely as an issue of economic underdevelopment, as many politicians in Turkey have characterized it since the 1960s. It is true that areas where mainly Kurdish people live are less developed than the rest of Turkey. Even at the beginning of the millennium, GDP per capita in Diyarbakır was little more than half the national figure.[5] However, this underdevelopment is hardly the main reason for the Kurdish insurgency.

So, what lies at the core of the Kurdish problem? For the answer, we need to return to the founding of the Republic of Turkey.

Turkey's nation-building project, which dates back to the 1920s, grew out of a notion that the non-Muslim population, and the Muslim and non-Turkish population, should be clamped down on and assimilated. Compared with other ethnic minorities in Turkey, such as the Lazis, Circassians, Bosnians and Arabs, Kurds as an autochthonous people occupy a different place in society. Having lived together in a particular region for a very long time, they have developed a distinct set of interrelated economic, historical, cultural and geographical features. Thus, they possessed all the necessary requirements for being a nation. They were neither leaving their land, nor were they abiding by the Turkish state's assimilation policies. They were Muslims and had fought effectively side by side with the Turks in the War of Independence in 1919.[6] Kurds had a certain awareness that they were different from other minorities in Turkey. This self-awareness could not only be attributed to the size of their population. There were several other reasons for it.

According to the renowned political scientist Professor Hamit Bozarslan of L'École des hautes études en sciences sociales, whose specialist expertise is on the Kurdish issue, one of those reasons was the establishment of regiments called Hamidiye by the Ottoman state in 1846.[7] The Hamidiye regiments consisted of Kurdish tribes and were assigned to combat Armenian rebels, and their actions enabled the Kurdish tribes to have local authority in the region. 'They were keen to preserve their own autonomy rather than defending the state's interests, [and] later became the most fervent supporters of the Kurdish challenge to state authority.'[8] The abolishment of the Hamidiye regiments by the Young Turks – a political reform movement which desired to replace the Ottoman monarchy with a constitutional government – and the fall of the Russian front in World War I left Turks and Kurds pitted against each other.[9]

The second reason for the heightening of the Kurds' self-awareness as a distinct population was the claim that they had been promised the right to self-determination in south-eastern Turkey, where they predominantly lived. According to Andrew Mango, Atatürk was vocal about Kurdish rights during the War of Independence and said that certain Kurdish-speaking counties might be allowed to govern themselves in accordance with the constitution.[10] This is a long-running argument in Turkey, one that involves politicians rather than historians. On the other hand, historical evidence has been unearthed that could potentially prove the Kurds right. A protocol signed on 22 October 1919 in the city of Amasya between the national independence movement led by Mustafa Kemal Atatürk and the Istanbul government of the Ottoman Empire was kept secret from the public until the 1960s.[11] The first article of the protocol 'accepted the principle of Kurdish autonomy and recognized the national and social rights of the Kurds'.[12]

Abdullah Öcalan, the founder of the PKK, after a meeting with his lawyers in İmralı prison, had commented on this protocol in 2009:

> Currently the press is discussing the Amasya Protocols of 20–23 October. Of the protocols, three are known and two are still being kept secret. The second protocol, of 22 October 1919, signed by Mustafa Kemal, also contains ethnic and social rights of Kurds. […] What is more, there was a plenary [held in parliament] on 10 February 1922. A friend from prison wrote to me and told me that there were 237 votes for and 64 votes against Kurdish autonomy.[13]

The Treaty of Lausanne, which concluded World War I in Anatolia and led to the foundation of the Republic of Turkey, signified the end of the Kurdish nationalists' hopes and laid the foundations for the division of lands where Kurds mainly lived among four different countries: Iran, Iraq, Turkey and Syria. There was no mention of a Kurdistan. This ended the political bargaining for self-determination and the alliance between the Kurds and Mustafa Kemal, which would give rise to hostilities for the next nine decades. Kurds were let down not only by the new successor to the Ottoman Empire in Lausanne but also by Great Britain, which had at first encouraged an independent Kurdistan but then opposed the idea in order to appease Turkey.[14] Although the Kurdish people are not on the whole familiar with the details of these protocols or the Treaty of Lausanne in full, they know and talk about the fundamental unfairness perpetrated against them during the foundation of the Republic of Turkey. Emine Ayna, a Kurdish politician, articulated that feeling to me:

> They [the government] talk about giving Kurds cultural rights, but that is not the same as shared administration. Think of a company led by a partnership of five families. What if one of the families says, 'This is my company; you are employees here'? If we built it together, then we must govern it together.[15]

Kurds revolted against the Turkish state 28 times between 1923 and 1938, all the uprisings being quelled with heavy bloodshed and considerable overkill. The Kurds were revolting not only against the nationalistic Turkish state but also against its secularization. The ending of the caliphate by Mustafa Kemal meant that an important feature that bonded Turks and Kurds together was gone.[16] It was no coincidence that the first major uprising in 1925 was led by a Kurdish religious leader, Sheikh Said. He was hanged at the direction of the Independence Tribunal in Diyarbakır, founded earlier that year to prosecute individuals fomenting uprisings. Following Said's revolt, the Turkish government began to perceive Kurdish ethnicity as a threat to national sovereignty and gradually adopted policies to weaken it.

An unspoken Turkification project had been initiated. According to that project, '[t]ribes of eastern Turkey were purely of Turkish origin and their language was a corrupted Turkish owing to their geographical closeness to Iran, and they should be called Mountain Turks.'[17] By the end of 1924, one year after the declaration of the new republic, all Kurdish madrasas (an Arabic word for educational institutions) were closed, and publications in languages other than Turkish were prohibited. The Republic of Turkey's first attempt at resettling the Kurds started in 1926 with a law that authorized the Internal Affairs Ministry 'to settle nomadic tribes'.

A 1927 law was more precise, demanding 'certain people of the east be displaced and resettled in the west' ('*Bazı eşhasın şark menatıkından garp vilâyetlerine nakillerine dair kanun*').[18] With that law, 1,400 locally influential Kurdish landlords were displaced. The displacement policy continued until 1936, only to be revived in 1980 and again at the beginning of the 1990s. Between 1927 and 1936, the number of displaced Kurdish people was 2,774. Another law that entered into effect in 1936 forced 25,831 Kurdish people from the cities of Tunceli, Erzincan, Bitlis, Siirt, Van, Bingöl, Diyarbakır, Ağrı, Muş, Erzurum, Elazığ, Kars, Malatya, Mardin and Çoruh to leave their houses and start a new, more 'Turkified' life in Western Anatolia.[19] However, the attempts to dissolve Kurdish identity never worked, instead causing a great backlash among Kurds, who suffered ever more forceful suppression by the Turkish governments. According to Andrew Mango, the Kurdish areas were too inhospitable to attract newcomers, and a voluntary migration to richer provinces outside the Kurdish area followed the forced deportation. Coupled with a high birth rate, the government's plan of displacement and resettlement had little effect on the ethnic map.[20]

In 1937–8, the Turkish state carried out a series of operations in Dersim, a mainly Kurdish and Alawite city in south-eastern Turkey, where an uprising of 'bandits' and 'looters' had been going on for some time. The military operations were brutal beyond words. A lieutenant who had taken part expressed his remorse about the Dersim operation in his memoir: 'I beg my readers to excuse me. I shall not write this page of my life.'[21] One of the pilots, Sabiha Gökçen, stepdaughter of Mustafa Kemal Atatürk and the first Turkish woman to fly a combat plane, also maintained her silence. She had returned home from Dersim as a heroine. But for what? There had been no mention of a Dersim operation in the press, nor was there a statement from the government as to why Gökçen had received a medal of honour.[22] In her memoir, she talked about Dersim very briefly: 'I will not go into the reasons for and consequences of the Dersim operation. What I and my friends tried to do in this operation was to carry out a duty given to me by my country.'[23]

This state-perpetrated atrocity was kept from the public for a long time and then denied by the Kemalists, secular nationalists who were devoted to Mustafa Kemal's foundational ideology, implying that such cruelty could not have been inflicted during Mustafa Kemal's time. However, the accounts of witnesses tell a different story. Hüsamettin Cindoruk, a Turkish politician and a lawyer who had worked for Celâl Bayar, the prime minister of Turkey at the time of the Dersim operation, remembered a conversation:

> I was Bayar's lawyer for 25 years, so I had the chance to ask him about Dersim. What he told me was exactly this: 'The Republic [of Turkey] had achieved total control over the country except in Dersim. Neither police nor gendarmerie could go into Dersim. They could not even collect taxes. The nature of its geography had enabled such resistance. We issued countless warnings and

passed laws to overcome this situation, but to no avail. In the end, Atatürk told us to hit Dersim, so we hit it. We annexed Dersim by annihilating it.' So, people who are saying that Atatürk did not know what was going on in Dersim because he was ill are not telling the truth.[24]

The National Pact (Misak-ı Millî) was the manifesto of Turkey's War of Independence. The six-article text advocated not only for Turkish national identity but for that of all Ottoman Muslims.[25] However, this did not prevent the fledgling Turkish state from treating Kurds as a threat to the National Pact or as a group of bandits whose 'illogical' demands for a national identity should be crushed. The government had shaped its policies through that lens, ironically giving birth to a socio-economic crisis characterized as the 'Kurdish problem', which is now as old as the republic itself.

Persecution of the Kurdish identity has endured throughout the modern era in Turkey, regardless of the political party that has been in power, with only a few exceptions, as in the era of former president Turgut Özal. He acknowledged the Kurdish problem and had ideas for a liberal solution, such as forming a federation. He once famously said,

Kurds are not a minority. Turkey is like a little America, because we are the successors of an empire. What if Mustafa Kemal had called it the Ottoman Republic instead of the Turkish Republic? Then we would all be Ottomans, right?[26]

In terms of the Kurdish issue, he was way ahead of both his predecessor and his successors. It was he who orchestrated the 1993 PKK ceasefire through Jalal Talabani, the then leader of the PUK (Patriotic Union of Kurdistan) in northern Iraq.[27] He also planned an amnesty for the PKK guerrillas if the ceasefire held. But his aspirations for solving the Kurdish issue met with strong resistance from the army, and he died of a heart attack in April 1993 before he could realize any of his plans.

His sudden death sparked notions of conspiracy, implying dark forces within the state might have poisoned him because of his plans regarding the Kurdish issue. Abdullah Öcalan is a fervent believer in this conspiracy theory. He has even claimed that Özal was about to meet him and proceed with peace negotiations on the day he died. Özal's long-time aide supported Öcalan's claims during an interview in 2012.[28]

It is a common saying in Turkey that the ruling parties and the structure of the administrations change but the real authority running the country remains the same. The 'real authority' in this context could be defined as the Kemalist base, comprising the military and the bureaucracy. Turgut Özal and his contemporaries tried to act outside the scope of that establishment on the Kurdish issue, but to no avail. Because the main component was the army, the machinery was designed in such a way that military methods alone could provide the ultimate solution. This machinery, unsurprisingly, condoned the cultural and social persecution of the Kurds as a sanctioned state programme.

Why? Why do the political elites of the country prefer a military solution to negotiations with the Kurdish movement? The plain answer to that should be, as Professor Feroz Ahmad points out, that they see the Kurdish issue as a challenge to the unitary state, a challenge that would lead to separatism.[29] Behind this idea lies the 'Sèvres syndrome'. Turks fear that the Western world holds a grudge against the nationalists once led by Mustafa Kemal, who, it is argued, will always try to find a way to dismember Turkey via the Kurdish issue and Armenian irredentism, something which they could not achieve during the Sèvres Treaty talks of 1920. In Turkey one frequently hears statements such as *The Western world is plotting against us, They want to carve up our land*, or *We are surrounded by enemies*, which obviously do not contribute to the solving of the Kurdish issue.

There is a counterargument among secular elites which identifies the Turkish state's treatment of Kurdish identity as 'intentional neglect', rather than assimilation. According to them, Ottomans did not have a tradition of assimilation; there were already diverse ethnic and religious groups living on their own. When the Republic of Turkey was founded, a nation already existed, and therefore the leaders of the burgeoning republic did not have to resort to means such as assimilation.

In his famous speech 'Nutuk', on the tenth anniversary of the Republic of Turkey, Mustafa Kemal had coined the motto *Ne Mutlu Türk'üm Diyene!* (How happy is the person who can say, 'I am Turkish'!). Adherents of this argument claim that Mustafa Kemal had been using the term 'Turk' as a noun, not an adjective defining the word it preceded. Professor Metin Heper of Bilkent University, author of *Devlet ve Kürtler* (*The State and the Kurds*), defends this position:

'Turk' is a generic, nominal word, which does not refer to any ethnicity. When you say 'Turkish nation', it covers Bosnians, Kurds, Turks, Armenians and Greeks, even though they have their own identities, in addition to being part of the Turkish nation. Yes, between 1935 and 1938 there were 17 Kurdish uprisings. But from 1938 until the 1960s there were none. Why? The answer cannot be 'Because the Kurds were assimilated', since, after the 1960s, insurgency on the Kurdish side started again. If a state wants to assimilate a certain group, it does not take a break. It continues. Therefore, I offer a different explanation for the Turkish state's approach to the Kurds. It is not assimilation but intentional neglect. The state banned Kurdish names, not because it denied their identity. On the contrary, it acknowledged their Kurdishness very well. Precisely for that reason, it insisted that they accept, first and foremost, being a part of the Turkish nation rather than being a Kurd.[30]

At this point, it is important to note that most people who proudly call themselves Kemalists, mainly the people of western Turkey, do not condone atrocities and assimilation programmes directed at the Kurds. They simply ignore or deny that there are any. They do not believe that Kurds were deliberately persecuted as a state policy. Nor do they believe that the Dersim massacre took place. They see Mustafa Kemal Atatürk as someone who saved the people of Turkey, especially women, from the backwardness of Islam and gave them the right to vote and stand for election. No doubt Mustafa Kemal did all these things. However, as in all revolutions, there were excesses in the case of the Kemalist revolution and Kurds were on the losing end of those excesses. Therefore, it would jolt them painfully out of their comfort zone if they were to acknowledge the authoritarianism and ruthlessness of the Kemalist era.

Nevertheless, a Kurd living in the south-east would find this position selfish and irrelevant. For a Kurd, the difference between 'intentional neglect' and 'assimilation' is pedantic and almost trivial.

The Kemalist regime was a success on social, political and cultural levels, but it also aimed to neutralize diversity, mark a rupture with the Ottoman past, intensify ethnic and religious differences and rewrite history. It was, on the whole, a success for Turkey, but certainly not for everyone in the country.

The founding of the PKK and the Turkish left

In order to follow the intricate details of the Kurdish problem, it is essential to identify the basic actors involved. There are five main strands of activity and influence that determine the nature and course of the problem. First and foremost is the Turkish state: in order of influence, this consists of the armed forces, the National Intelligence Organization (MIT) and the elected government. Second is the outlawed leftist Kurdish organization, the PKK, the armed wing of the movement. The third is the legal political party (with various different names over the years), the activists, NGOs and intellectuals that surround it, and the civilian wing of this movement. It is crucial to note that, unlike the relationship between Sinn Féin and the IRA, where the IRA was born out of the political party Sinn Féin in the Northern Ireland conflict, it was the PKK that had first taken the stage; the political party followed. Thus, the PKK always had a greater say than the civilian wing over what steps should be taken. Fourth is the Kurdish diaspora in European countries, which consists of former PKK members who fled Turkey for fear of incarceration. And last but not least is Abdullah Öcalan, the overall leader of the movement.

Abdullah Öcalan, born in 1948 in Siverek, a town in Urfa, south-east Turkey, went to a boarding high school in Ankara which provided vocational education on land registry and cadastral surveying. After working for a while as a registrar of title deeds, first in Diyarbakır and then in Istanbul, he took the exams and managed to get into Istanbul University's Faculty of Law. Upon enrolment, he applied to be transferred to one of the most reputable social science institutions in Turkey, Ankara University's Faculty of Political Science, known as Siyasal ('Politics') for short. Siyasal was the place where many of Turkey's leftists studied and its social movements surfaced. Abdullah, nicknamed Apo, had become involved in politics, despite his upbringing in an ordinary peasant household where there was anything but a politically charged environment. He joined an association called the AYÖD (Ankara Higher Education Association), which was influenced by the Marxist–Leninist and Maoist movements.[31] However, before Öcalan became a public figure, there was already a solid Kurdish leftist movement, which had a close-knit relationship with the Turkish left.

The affinity between Turkey's leftists and the Kurdish movement goes back as far as the beginning of the 1960s. The PKK arose out of the mobilization that the Turkish left had created in the 1970s, and there was close comradeship between the two political movements for 20 years, until the PKK became an independent entity with a mission to influence Turkey's political scene.[32] It was a Marxist–Leninist comradeship of oppressed classes and oppressed people acting against state-sponsored nationalism.[33]

The Revolutionary Eastern Cultural Hearths (Devrimci Doğu Kültür Ocakları, DDKO for short), founded in 1969, is considered to be the first Kurdish leftist organization to have promoted an independent Kurdish state and Kurdish language, and in that sense represents the first departure from the Turkish left.[34] In the 1970s, violence was considered a just means of achieving political aspirations for many of the Turkish leftist groups, such as Dev-Genç, Devrimci Yol and Halkın Kurtuluşu. However, while claiming that violence was legitimate, these groups did not espouse it as a strategy but only as a last resort when all other options were exhausted.

The PKK had differed from such groups and from the Turkish left in that sense. Immediately after its founding, it had invoked armed struggle, first against other Kurdish organizations and later against the Turkish armed forces. According to Öcalan, who had fled the country in July 1979, the elimination of other Kurdish organizations was essential for the PKK to rise as the sole defender of Kurdish rights. In 1974, Öcalan, along with several friends – later called Apocular ('followers of Apo') – had decided to form a Kurdish leftist organization detached from the Turkish left, in Tuzlucayir, a suburb of Ankara.[35] But it was not until 27 November 1978 that the PKK was officially formed. The PKK's founding is considered the 29th and last Kurdish uprising in Turkey.

Like that of many militant groups, there is more than one version of the PKK's history. One is that mentioned above. Another is that it was founded by Öcalan in Fis, a small village in Diyarbakır. Yet another version, promulgated by those who were part of the core group when the organization was forming, claims that 'the PKK was established between 1974 and 1978 by Kurdish nationalists and that Abdullah Öcalan was not a significant figure at that time'.[36] There is also a conspiracy theory put forth among certain groups in Turkey that the Turkish National Intelligence Organization (MIT) and/or the 'deep state' – composed of high-level elements of intelligence, the military, security, the judiciary and the mafia – actually founded the PKK. Although there is evidence that MIT could have infiltrated the PKK on several levels and at different times in the past, there is no convincing or sound argument to indicate that either MIT or the deep state was the founder.

Tarık Ziya Ekinci, who was an influential member of the Revolutionary Eastern Cultural Hearths and was arrested along with the Kurdish author and intellectual Musa Anter after the 1971 coup, responded to this allegation. He believed that the only involvement of MIT in the PKK had been to appease the insurgency:

Since the emergence of the Kurdish problem, MIT has talked to Kurdish leaders on behalf of the state and has made promises. I remember how Musa Anter was taken away from prison one day. He was out for a while, then he came back. 'Where have you been, Musa?' I asked. 'I took care of some business,' Musa replied. 'I sat down and told them [MIT officials] everything. After we get out of prison, we will be able to talk to them and resolve things. He [MIT officer] said that he would ensure our friends are discharged as soon as possible.' They did nothing, of course. They took him, ordered him food and detained him for a few days. They did the same to Öcalan over the years. This is a state tactic.[37]

Şerafettin Elçi, a leading political figure in the Kurdish movement until his death, mentioned a similar encounter with a 'Colonel in MIT' in the mid-1970s.

'We would like the incidents to calm down. So we want to know and understand what the Kurds want,' said the Colonel. 'That's easy,' replied Elçi. 'Let them air TV and radio programmes in Kurdish, let them publish their newspapers and magazines and let them have free speech; that's all.' The Colonel replied, 'Şerafettin Bey [Mr Şerafettin], you can be sure that we would give you those rights if we knew you would be satisfied with them, but we have concerns. If we give you those rights, you will gradually ask for more rights, leading to separation.'[38]

What the Colonel said to Elçi not only reveals the futility of such encounters but also sums up the Turkish state's approach to the Kurdish problem. The hostility of the PKK had taken firm root in the hostile soils where this approach had been sown.

At its founding, the PKK numbered 162 members, of whom five had a university degree, 24 were undergraduates, 83 were either teachers or graduates of a training school, 48 were high-school graduates and two had primary-school education.[39] None of them had had any experience in another Turkish leftist organization before joining the PKK, except for Kemal Pir, who was a Turkish socialist. It is also important to note that the founding members' education levels were higher than the average for Turkey back then. This contradicts the

Turkish government's long-time conviction and propaganda that the PKK is a bunch of ignorant, uncivilized, uninformed thugs. This propaganda was useful in masking the real reasons behind the Kurdish issue and framing the emergence of the PKK as a sporadic incident that did not reflect the sentiment of the rest of the Kurdish population.

Shortly before the 12 September 1980 military coup, PKK leaders fled the country along with Öcalan and went to Syria, where they set up a military camp, which would continue to exist until 1999. There they established relations with the Palestine Liberation Front and received military training. That was when the PKK decided that it was crucial to be on good terms with other Kurds in the region, which 'required an understanding with the KDP (Kurdistan Democratic Party) of Iraqi Kurdistan, despite its political conservatism and its defeatist aim of autonomy rather than independence'.[40] The leader of the KDP, Masoud Barzani, agreed to sign a protocol with the PKK in July 1983 which allowed the PKK to use northern Iraqi territory.[41]

Among the core group that founded the PKK, 44 were executed by the organization itself, while 36 were 'purged' and forced to leave. Only three of the PKK members who now dominate the organization from their base in Qandil Mountain in northern Iraq were present at the beginning: Duran Kalkan, Cemil Bayık and Mustafa Karasu.

Cemil Bayık, who is the co-chair of KCK, an umbrella organization of Kurdish entities including the PKK, joined the group while he was an undergraduate at Ankara University. He adopted the alias Cuma when he was in Syria's Bekaa Valley with Abdullah Öcalan. He is considered a hawkish type and known for his ties with Iranian and Syrian intelligence and also with the Iranian Kurdish party PJAK (Kurdistan Free Life Party).

Duran Kalkan, born in 1954 in Adana, is the highest-ranking PKK member in Qandil who is of Turkish ethnicity. He graduated from the humanities department of Ankara University. Kalkan was among those who, at a meeting in the city of Urfa in November 1979, decided that the PKK should have an armed wing. He was also one of those who went to the Bekaa Valley to meet Öcalan and receive military training. Thereafter, he served the organization in northern Iraq and Germany and then settled in Qandil, where he has lived ever since.

Mustafa Karasu was attending Ankara University when he joined the PKK. He was arrested and spent many years in Diyarbakır Prison No. 5, a place that was infamous for torturing Kurds after the 1980 junta. His route in the organization was similar to that of Kalkan and Bayık: Bekaa, Europe, ending up in Qandil. It should be underlined that these three figures are known to be devoted to Abdullah Öcalan.

Beyond a certain point, it was irrelevant who actually founded the PKK, even to the Turkish state, since what mattered was the inexorable rise of the recruits, who numbered in the thousands. The initial support had come from impoverished Kurdish towns such as Doğubayazıt, Hakkâri, Cizre, Nusaybin, Midyat and Diyarbakır in the mid-1980s, just at the time when the party initiated armed struggle. What many of the Kurds who either supported or joined the PKK then wanted was simply to be recognized as Kurds.

The PKK was not initially established to promote Kurdish nationalism in classical terms. The widely spoken and written language of the organization has always been Turkish.[42] The PKK first targeted other Kurdish organizations and feudal landlords in the region. The initial ideological structure of the Kurdish movement was Marxist–Leninist, as set out in a booklet called 'The Revolutionary Road to Kurdistan: A Manifesto'. There are traces of theoretical knowledge of the Turkish left in this document. Öcalan said, in his speech to the first congress of the PKK in 1978, 'We did not actually start this movement by vigorous agitation and distributing propaganda in a booklet. We started it via verbal propaganda in small student units, on table tops, at local meetings.'[43] This manifesto also featured formulations of certain aims beyond the Turkish left's horizon, such as the independence of Kurdistan. This is exactly where the Turkish left and the Kurdish left parted company, which led to the formation of the PKK. In the Kurdish region, the majority of political activists thought armed struggle was a valid course of action under the circumstances.

Şerafettin Elçi explained those circumstances in the context of his own personal story:

> The Kurds did not willingly resort to arms. Some people who had never held a gun in their lives and avoided violence were in prison for years just because they expressed their views. I am one of them. When I was a minister in 1979, I served two years and three months in prison just for saying, 'Kurds exist, and I am Kurdish myself.' The earth came tumbling down for no other reason than because I gave voice to a sociological reality. You cannot question why people take up arms and head for the mountains[44] under such circumstances. I always outlawed violence in my party and in person, but if it were not for the armed struggle, it would not have been possible to put the Kurds on Turkey's agenda and make Kurdish identity a topic for discussion. This armed organization announced a ceasefire several times. If the state had had the desire to solve the problem peacefully, they could have taken advantage of those times. On the contrary, they virtually swept the Kurdish problem under the carpet. The issue came back on the agenda only when guns started firing. That is why such a perception is very widespread among Kurds.[45]

On 12 September 1980 came the most ferocious *coup d'état*. It determined the fate of the leftist movement in Turkey – a fate that would differ for Kurdish and Turkish leftists. As journalist Ruşen Çakır pointed out, in the years following the 1980 junta, the Kurdish movement rose from the ashes and became a prominent political actor, not only in Turkey but also in the wider Middle East.[46] Concurrently, the Turkish socialist left, once an important force, shrank and vanished from the political scene. Disappointment and a sense of defeat prevailed, since many of the actors of the Turkish left had either disappeared or been jailed. It was after this that the PKK decided that the only way to accomplish its goals was through guns. The fraternity between the Kurdish and Turkish left had gradually been eroded. Young Kurds had lost interest in Turkey-wide socialist projects and focused more on Kurdish identity and the Kurdish issue. However, close ties between legal Kurdish parties and Turkish parties of the left have continued to this day.

After the military takeover of 1980, Diyarbakır Prison No. 5 became a place in which to crush the Kurdish activists with the use of unspeakable torture that included electric shocks, Palestine hanging,[47] beating with a plastic hose, pulling teeth and being forced to eat faeces. The late Felat Cemiloğlu remembered one of his experiences while there:

> One day I was told to stand on one foot. After a while I collapsed. This meant I had to be punished. They made me open the lid of the sewage near the wall and take a handful of excrement and put it in my mouth.[48]

Cemiloğlu had spent eight months in Diyarbakır Prison No. 5 on a cooked-up charge that he had given money to PKK members. When he was finally allowed to go back to his cell, he extracted all his teeth, which were already loose because of severe beatings. 'I had washed my mouth out but no matter how hard I tried, I felt the smell. I couldn't bear it.'[49]

As Murat Paker, a professor of psychology at Bilgi University put it, 'In Diyarbakır prison they wanted to crush Kurdishness.'[50] The roads to civil resistance were not only blocked once again for the Kurds but also strewn with unconscionable dangers and barbarities.

A high official of the PKK explained to me the initial decision to take up arms:

> We did not take up guns to defeat the Turkish army or destroy the state. We did so to defend our existence and rights as Kurds. If we had been given our rights, what would we have needed guns for? The PKK's approach is to force the Turkish Republic to solve the Kurdish problem.[51]

A more draconian state had risen from the 1980 junta. Its first attempt to curb Kurdish culture was to prohibit the Kurdish language in 1983. From then on, all things Kurdish were, in effect, banned. Martial law was imposed in the region, followed in 1987 by a state of emergency rule that would last until 2002. Not only had living in the region become intolerable, but so had travelling to western Turkey. Kurdish author Şeyhmus Diken explained in his book what it meant to be an ordinary citizen from Diyarbakır:

> When we drove to the west of the country with our car plate numbered 21, which showed that we were from Diyarbakır, we were stopped by the police and searched. We thought that changing our plate would save us from this misery. But no, every time we had business in any government office, we were treated badly. We learned to police ourselves, concealing signs that would indicate our Kurdishness and thus irritate the government. That was what being from Diyarbakır was like.[52]

Kurdish cities and towns were renamed. By 1986, 2,842 out of 3,524 villages in the region had new Turkish names.[53] Prisons had become a second home for Kurds, and were the places where the PKK and the Kurdish movement were revived for the second time. A poignant story by the influential Kurdish writer Musa Anter (Ape Musa) shows how arrests and prisons played a role in the Kurdish movement. It was the beginning of the 1990s. Musa Anter bought a bowl of rice pilaf from a street vendor in front of the AKM (Atatürk Cultural Centre) in Taksim and began to eat it. The vendor boy, who realized that his customer was Musa Anter, yelled in Kurdish at the other pilaf vendors lined up ahead of him, 'Ape Musa hat!' ('Uncle Musa is here!'). Quickly, they all pushed their stalls towards him, and as Ape Musa finished his pilaf and headed to a shuttle bus, they accompanied him in a convoy, holding up the traffic. Ape Musa kissed them all on the forehead, and got on the bus. Astonished, the driver asked, 'Uncle, how are you related to all these guys?' He replied, 'They are all my sons.' The driver persisted, 'Uncle, are all your sons rice pilaf vendors?' 'No,' explained Ape Musa, 'these are only the ones I have here. The others are in jail, there and over there.'

In a climate of fierce government suppression, the PKK returned to Turkey and its main target became the Turkish state, starting in

August 1984 with an assault on Turkish security forces in the Kurdish towns of Eruh and Şemdinli. The clash between the PKK and Turkish forces, which used all the tools of conventional warfare, continues to this day. As part of the government's counterterrorism policy, a village guard system was created, which by 1993 had supplied almost 35,000 villagers with arms to fight the PKK.

Meanwhile, on the PKK front, the rules of the game were changing too. The 1991 Gulf War added to the PKK's military strength. After Iraqi Kurds were given an autonomous region, the PKK started using the territories under their control and acquired heavy weaponry. The establishment of Qandil Mountain and adjacent lands as the headquarters of the PKK dates back to that period. From then on it 'began to act more like an army rather than guerrilla bands'.[54] 'The leadership endorsed carnage and showed a willingness to even sacrifice its own rank and file to prove the PKK's ability to act forcefully.'[55]

The PKK was ruthless, but so was the government. Between 1984 and 1999, 5,828 Turkish security officials, 5,390 civilians and 19,786 PKK guerrillas were killed.[56] Around 4,000 villages were evacuated from 1987 to 1995. According to the Human Rights Research Commission of 2014, 386,000 villagers were relocated, but many scholars estimate the number to be closer to 4.5 million.[57]

A 1996 report by the Republican People's Party's (CHP, the main opposition party) East and South-Eastern Turkey Commission claims that between 1993 and 1995, on the orders of local police chiefs and village guards, thousands of Kurdish people were displaced from their houses because of an alleged link to the PKK. The same report also revealed that people's vacated houses, fields and barns were burnt down and their lands confiscated by the state. The government had been oblivious to the needs of those forcibly displaced, such as for healthcare, education and shelter.[58]

The presence of Turkish soldiers and gendarmerie had become constant, their numbers rising to more than 200,000. There were extrajudicial killings of Kurdish businessmen and activists. The disappearance of hundreds of Kurdish people has been deemed a human rights violation by the European Court of Human Rights, which has also issued a condemnation of the Turkish government. Every Saturday, mothers of those who disappeared in the late 1980s and 1990s, the so-called 'Saturday Mothers', gather in central Istanbul's Taksim Square to remember and remind others of their sons and daughters. Undoubtedly, both Turkish and Kurdish civilians were victims of the relentless battles between the two parties.

In the mid-1990s, the PKK announced a new programme, according to which women became a crucial part of the PKK insurgency and a generator of the cultural revolution that was dreamed of by some in the Kurdish region. By that time, the PKK had realized that it needed to attract international attention to the Kurdish issue to achieve any of its goals. It used the only method it knew worked: violence. The PKK embarked on a spree of collective protests and bombings of Turkish commercial interests, mainly in Europe. But the real shift in the organization's policy came about after Abdullah Öcalan was arrested and sentenced to life imprisonment in İmralı. Although his arrest was greeted by mass protests and in some cases attempts at self-immolation by protesters, there were also serious defections from the organization.[59] According to the Turkish armed forces, the PKK's guerrilla force had been reduced to 6,000 from around 50,000,[60] even though Öcalan continued to communicate with the high cadres of the PKK through his lawyers.[61] Öcalan's arrest represented a shift in the PKK's rhetoric and ideology, as he stated in 1999: 'A broad struggle for brotherhood and sisterhood, peace and democracy must be the foundation of all activities inside and outside the country. We want real peace and real democracy for Turkey.'[62]

The evolution of the PKK

Occasionally my Western colleagues, trying to make sense of the PKK's violent actions, which seem to contradict its rhetoric, have asked me things like *What is the PKK doing? What is the point it's trying to make?* My first simple response is usually that there is no logic in war. But then I point out that it is a complicated organization, both in structure and in culture. It differs from other militant insurgency groups as much as it does from any political party.

A major transformation occurred in the early 1990s, when Öcalan spoke passionately about the participation of women in the Kurdish movement. 'The twenty-first century must be the era of awakening; the era of the liberated, emancipated woman,' he wrote. 'This is more important than class or national liberation. The era of democratic civilisation shall be the one when woman rises and succeeds fully.'[63] As the liberation of women had become one of the fundamental discourses of the PKK, joining the organization meant the unleashing of Kurdish women from patriarchal family and gender roles. The PKK leadership's rhetoric was that the more women fight, the more they become liberated. In 1990–1, women from universities and from both rural and urban areas joined the PKK in huge numbers. By 1993, women represented 3.1 per cent of the mountain team of the PKK. The number of women recruits steadily increased over the years.[64] As of today, women make up 40 per cent of the PKK's armed and political structure.

From the late 1990s, and particularly after Öcalan's arrest, the PKK pledged freedom, democracy and cultural rights to the Kurdish people. It has evolved ideologically from merely demanding an independent Kurdish state to promising democratic autonomy within Turkey's borders. But it has not ceased using violence. While adopting the tactics of civil disobedience campaigns and political lobbying, it started at the same time to use suicide bombers to gain international attention. This may look like an irreconcilable dichotomy, but pursuing dual strategies has been common throughout the PKK's history. More interestingly, these contradictions have not caused the organization to lose social ground and support – because even when it shifted its methods from violence to civil disobedience or changed its discourse and ideology, one thing remained the same, namely being a fierce advocate of Kurdish identity and rights.

The continuing denial by the Turkish state of Kurds' rights had helped the PKK retain legitimacy and relevance in the eyes of the people.[65] 'They say that if the PKK goes away, the problem will be solved. The PKK is not a problem. It is a power that was born as a result of a problem,' said Duran Kalkan in an interview given to Firat News Agency in February 2013:

> You solve the problem, and the PKK will no longer be the current PKK: if you don't solve the problem, you won't change the PKK, no matter what you do. There is a limit to what the PKK can do. It is the state, the government that has the responsibility for generating a solution. The rulers of the PKK have no ambition to govern Turkey or Kurdish society.[66]

Years of violence, ferocious attacks, collateral damage involving civilian victims and tens of thousands of deaths have failed to erode the wish among most Kurds for the PKK to endure. No matter what its ideology or methods, the group has been seen as a defender of the Kurds against the state. Its raison d'être is alive and well, and will remain so as long as the Turkish government pursues its current policies.

Thomas Friedman once wrote in his *New York Times* column that 'just trying to figure out the differences among the Kurdish parties and militias in Syria and Iraq – the YPG, PYD, PUK, KDP and PKK – took me a day.'[67] He was right. It is indeed hard to follow Kurdish politics, since there are so many groups and there is much fragmentation on the political spectrum and in every part of Kurdistan. The PKK occupies a special place on the scene in that sense, because it has a tendency to rename itself, establish umbrella organizations and found new political entities. It does so first out of a desire to reinvent and adapt the organization through different ideological phases. Second, it wishes to accommodate as many people as possible within the movement. It is difficult to involve non-violent activists and public figures in an armed group, but easier to do so through different assemblies and organizations. That is why Öcalan gave decorative names to new organizations, many of which are not even remembered today. But this aspiration caused confusion and an eruption of abbreviations that failed to serve the purpose. The PKK renamed itself first as KADEK (the Freedom and Democracy Congress of Kurdistan) and then as KONGRA-GEL (the Kurdistan People's Congress), before eventually returning to being the PKK, since the other names did not stick with the constituency. In 2005, the PKK formed another executive and legislative organization called KCK (Koma Civakên Kurdistan, which means Group of Communities in Kurdistan), which included Iran's and Syria's Kurdish organizations of the same ideology, the PJAK and the PYD, respectively.

In his meetings with officials of the main Kurdish party, the HDP, during the peace process in February 2014, Öcalan offered a brief explanation for his founding of the KCK:

> They say that the National Intelligence Organization [MIT] founded the KCK. I told Mr Emre [Emre Taner, former chief of MIT] that we needed another organization, because the PKK is illegal. I wanted the KCK to be the legal branch.[68]

In addition, he believed that his dream of a democratic confederalism could be realized through an umbrella organization like the KCK. This was an ideology he had derived from political theorist Murray Bookchin's work.[69] According to the rationale for the KCK, which Öcalan had written,

> The democratic confederalism of Kurdistan is not a state system, it is the movement of the Kurdish people to found their own democracy and organize their own social system, it is the expression of the democratic union of the Kurdish people, who have been split into four parts and have spread all over the world.[70]

The Turkish government interpreted the KCK as the 'urban structure of the PKK' and launched a campaign of arrests of acting mayors, academics, lawyers and journalists in 2009. In the two years that followed, 4,000 people were arrested or detained in this anti-KCK operation, many of them supporters of the legal Kurdish party BDP (the former HDP). The government's aim was to 'obstruct the continued socio-political institutionalization of the Kurdish movement and to prevent Öcalan's democratic confederalism from taking shape'.[71]

Criminalization of Kurdish politicians was not a new tactic: it had been used against the movement since the 1970s. Moderate Kurdish politicians were not allowed to become part of the political process. The People's Labour Party (HEP) was banned, as were its predecessors. Leyla Zana, the first Kurdish woman to be elected to Parliament in 1991, caused a furore by speaking in Kurdish at the end of her parliamentary oath and was imprisoned for ten years as a result.

In 1995, HADEP (People's Democracy Party) was formed. Its leader and members were constantly harassed by the police and judiciary apparatus until the constitutional court decided to shut the party down in 2003 on the grounds of their organic link to the PKK. The DTP (Democratic Society Party), which was led by Ahmet Türk and Aysel Tuğluk, was established in 2005, only to experience the ill fate of its predecessors four years later. The DTP, which had 20 deputies in parliament and 99 mayorships in the Kurdish region, was closed down in 2009. Many of these acts were not justifiable in the eyes of the European Court of Human Rights, which concluded that the closures were in breach of the Convention. However, the government's persecution of the Kurds added to its negative image and served only to bolster the PKK's position, rather than diminish it. It is fair to say that the PKK, despite its own violent actions, owes much of its popularity to the Turkish government. Kurdish political parties also enjoyed a fair share of that popularity, despite state harassment. In 2014, the BDP (Peace and Democracy Party), the predecessor of the HDP, received the majority of the votes in the region, becoming the largest party and being rewarded with 97 elected mayors.

The Öcalan phenomenon

It is impossible to grasp the true significance of Abdullah Öcalan for the Kurdish people and movement without walking on the streets of Diyarbakır, Hakkâri or Şırnak. Similarly, it is impossible to discern people's boundless devotion to him without seeing his posters hung next to Sheikh Said's in most of their living rooms or hearing five-year-olds shrieking in Kurdish, 'Biji Serok Apo' ('Long live President Apo'). 'Do you know what Kurds think when they think of Öcalan?' a Kurdish politician once asked me. Answering his own question, he went on,

> I didn't exist. My identity was rejected. I was ashamed to say that I was Kurdish. I was in danger of losing my language. I was being ill-treated. I was being ostracized. I was deprived of a national consciousness. I felt like a vacuum in space. Now I no longer feel like that. And that's all thanks to Öcalan.[72]

For more than a decade now, the PKK has been governed by 'The Leadership', that is, Abdullah Öcalan. He is referred to not as 'the leader' but as 'The Leadership' (Önderlik), a very unusual usage of the word in the Turkish language. Loyalty to Öcalan in the Kurdish movement is never publicly questioned and criticizing him can only be done off the record, behind closed doors, in discreet murmurs. Öcalan's political, ideological and organizational leadership is not open to discussion in the PKK. In 2005, the party statute made him unassailable: 'The highest ideological and theoretical organ of the party is The Leadership. The Leadership determines the party's strategy, mentality and notional policies. The PKK considers comrade Öcalan and his thoughts as its own and accepts him as The Leadership.'[73]

In the same statute, 'to make Leader Apo's life and freedom his or her own life's purpose' is cited as the first task of a PKK member. It is out of the question for the Kurdish movement to even think about challenging Öcalan, let alone replacing him. As he has not been elected to the position of 'The Leadership', he cannot be replaced through any democratic process.

In the early days of the formation of the PKK, Abdullah Öcalan was just one of the founders, one of the 'older brothers'. He was in fact one of the oldest, better educated and more articulate than the others, but did not possess any significant, distinctive trait that would elevate him to the position of undisputed leader. He did not even speak

Kurdish, only Turkish. Öcalan himself acknowledged this in 1987: 'I had neither held a gun in my hand and been a militant nor wandered among the crowd. But my fierce loyalty to organizational tasks made me a constant powerful figure.'[74]

The cult of personality is very common in the leftist tradition of the twentieth century, where the PKK has its ideological roots. Vera Eccarius-Kelly, author of *The Militant Kurds*, finds similarities between the PKK and the Peruvian Maoist organization Shining Path (Sendero Luminoso) in that sense, since both groups relied on the inspiration of an omnipotent leader who enforced a rigid system of hierarchy and control.[75]

There were two pivotal events that cast Öcalan in that role. The first was the evolution of the PKK as mainly an armed organization, rather than a political party, despite its name. Ensuring the adherence of recruits to the PKK required a steady figure and an irrefutable hierarchy. Öcalan becoming 'The Leadership' met that condition. His reference to the guerrillas who lost their lives as the only ones – other than himself, of course – epitomizing the true Kurdish revolutionaries stemmed from this commitment. Even though the organization is governed by a personality cult and lacks an internal democratic process, self-criticism is customary, in accordance with its Marxist–Leninist origins. The minutes of PKK Congresses over the years show that criticism bordering on hostility among the members is commonplace. Only Öcalan was exempt from this institutionalized self-criticism. Many of the high-ranking guerrillas, including those who currently lead the PKK from Qandil, had to go through that process of expressing self-criticism (*özeleştiri vermek*, in PKK jargon) and paying for it in one of the PKK prisons, either in the Bekaa Valley or in Qandil.

The second incident that made Öcalan a larger-than-life figure was his arrest in February 1999. Until 1998, he was based in Syria, but after Turkey's pressure on the Syrian government to extradite him, Öcalan fled to Kenya, where he was captured. This turned him into a self-sacrificing hero in the eyes of the Kurdish people. Now he was no longer just the chief of an insurgent organization but also the leader of a social, cultural and political movement. When I asked Murat

Karayılan, one of the highest-ranking members of the PKK, why they had built the institution of 'The Leadership', he replied,

> Look, we have a party culture, a collective culture. It took a long time, but finally it has been established. Whatever the joint decision is, everyone sticks to it now without raising any objections. However, this should not be perceived as a culture of obedience. If the decision has been discussed at length, why should anyone raise an objection, right? This is a new practice among Kurds. What was the trouble with the Kurdish movement for years? Not being able to pull together. That is why we unite so strongly around The Leadership. All the Kurdish movements were internally fragmented and weakened. The PKK is a synthesis of it all; it is a governance structure born out of all the fragmentation.[76]

For the Kurdish people, however, 'The Leadership' has a more emotional meaning than the pragmatic explanation given by Karayılan. Fırat Anlı, acting mayor of Diyarbakır, who served time for being a member of the PKK in 2009 and later, in 2016, after the peace process failed, elucidates why Öcalan is held in such affection among the Kurdish people:

> Öcalan is a phenomenon. He is almost like a mythological character for a considerable number of Kurds. He is extremely influential. Let's not forget that hundreds of people set fire to themselves for him and thousands of others went on hunger strike when he was arrested. That is why, no matter what, Kurds will always accept that 'The Leadership must know something if he has made this decision.'[77]

Kurdish activists went on hunger strike to protest for Öcalan every time he was kept in solitary confinement and his communication with his family and lawyers was cut off by the government. The latest of those strikes was in 2012. Several of the 500 strikers had sent me inconsolable letters from prison, explaining their vain attempt to be heard. One of them said,

We have been on an irreversible hunger strike since 12 September 2012. We are doing this because a nation is being ignored once again, a nation in the person of Abdullah Öcalan, whom thousands of people refer to as the voice of 'our will'. The only means of achieving social peace in this land is revoking his interdiction.

Another wrote,

The fact that the state turns a blind eye to our demands for the right to receive education in our mother tongue and to the right to freedom of the leader of PKK is a red line for the Kurdish people. A lot of my friends in prison went on hunger strike because of that. If any harm comes to them, it is the government that should be held accountable.

On the 68th day of the strike, the government let Abdullah Öcalan see his brother, ending a month's isolation. Through his brother, Öcalan requested that the strike be ended, 'since it had achieved its purpose'.[78] It was only then that hundreds of people called an end to the strike.

According to Abbas Vali of Boğaziçi University, an Iranian Kurdish scholar, if it had not been for the erroneous policies of the state, the PKK might never have elevated him to such a high level:

For the Kurdish intelligentsia and political actors, Öcalan was always Öcalan. Yet his imprisonment made him a recognized leader of the Kurdish people. You can imprison a political leader, but you cannot put the leader of a political movement behind bars.[79]

It took the Turkish government a long time, but in the end it realized that Öcalan can be demonized, fought militarily and even captured, but he can be neither ignored nor disregarded. It used to be deemed a crime to address Öcalan by the title 'Mr'. Many Kurdish politicians and activists were fined on the charge of endorsing crime or praising a criminal, until in 2013 the European Court of Human Rights ruled such utterances to be freedom of speech. It was in the same year that the latest peace process began. From banning Mr Öcalan to making him the main negotiator for peace, the government had taken a giant step in terms of recognizing the nature of the Kurdish problem. At least, this was what many of us enthusiastically reckoned in the spring of 2013. 'Serok Apo' ('President Apo' in Kurdish), as he was known among the Kurds on the street, 'The Leadership' to the Kurdish political movement, and 'the master terrorist' to the Turkish government, was about to call for peace on 21 March 2013, the day of Newroz.

The peace process starts

Newroz, a celebration of the new year in Kurdish and Persian culture, usually resonates with clashes in south-eastern Turkey. Celebrating Newroz was effectively prohibited until 2000, because it was a symbol of Kurdish identity and, like all expressions of Kurdish identity, was not welcomed by the Turkish state. But this time it was different. Newroz would be celebrated and a new era would begin. We, the people of Turkey, would vault over the bitterness of history, over all the ills we had done to one another in the past 30 years, and land in a bright new future. Newroz 2013 would be remembered as the day Turkey's Kurdish problem was solved and the armed conflict between the PKK and the Turkish government came to an end.

The then Turkish prime minister, Recep Tayyip Erdoğan, announced during a TV interview that MIT had started a dialogue with Abdullah Öcalan, who, after his capture in 1999, had been imprisoned for life on İmralı, an island in the Sea of Marmara. The Turkish public learned of the peace process through Erdoğan's words, which were uttered in such a nonchalant way as to raise doubts about whether he was aware of the importance of the news he was giving. Erdoğan, known for keeping a tight grip on public sentiment, was certainly aware, and his nonchalance was premeditated. Knowing that what he was saying had the potential to stir huge public resentment, he decided to wrap it up in such a way as to suggest that it was routine procedure for the

Turkish government to meet a man who had been portrayed as the greatest enemy of the state.

The meeting was not something new, but it certainly was not 'routine procedure'. Encounters constituting quasi-negotiations between Öcalan and various Turkish governments had been taking place since 1993, usually through MIT or Turkish army officials. Former prime ministers of Turkey Süleyman Demirel and Necmettin Erbakan and the former president Turgut Özal had contacted the PKK leaders at various levels.[80] From the time of Abdullah Öcalan's capture in 1999 to 2006, only officers of the Turkish army had sat across the table from Öcalan on behalf of the government. From 2006 onwards, MIT took over this role. What made the 2013 initiative special was that this time it had been made known to the public from the start and elected politicians were involved.

Two days after his announcement, Erdoğan vowed to 'drink poison hemlock' if necessary to pursue the peace process,[81] implying he was ready to go ahead regardless of the political costs. In the following weeks, the public learned that a letter from Abdullah Öcalan, who for decades had been called a 'baby killer' and a 'master terrorist', would initiate the process. The letter would be read by Kurdish MPs to a gathering in Diyarbakır and broadcast live throughout the country.

It would have been impossible even to dream of such an event 20 years earlier.

What was all the more surprising was that there was no public backlash, except from the leader of the nationalist party, MHP (Nationalist Action Party), then the third-largest party in the parliament, which did not have much of an impact. The CHP, which had positioned itself to be the sole defender of Mustafa Kemal Atatürk's ideology and representative of the secular nationalists, saluted the attempt by the ruling party, the AKP, to solve the Kurdish problem.

Here we were, a country exhausted by a violent conflict that had lasted since the 1980s and claimed almost 40,000 lives, making peace at last. It was what the majority of the country imagined, believed and genuinely wanted. A poll conducted in the spring of 2013 revealed that 81.3 per cent of the respondents thought that a solution to the

Kurdish problem would work for everyone's happiness.[82] Another poll, publicized by Prime Minister Erdoğan himself, revealed that 64 per cent of the people answered 'yes' when asked if they supported the peace process.[83] Erdoğan, notorious for living by the polls he receives weekly, was overjoyed. 'These numbers will skyrocket after Newroz,' he claimed in the same interview.

On 20 March 2013, a day before Newroz, I had arrived in Diyarbakır, feeling naively cheerful. I had walked the streets of Diyarbakır in anticipation of finding Kurds' feelings that matched mine, and had bumped into Tahir Elçi, chairman of the Diyarbakır Bar Association. I could see that he was as excited as I was.

'I think this time we can do it,' he said with a bright smile. 'We are closer to peace than ever before.'

We gave each other high-fives like two teenagers.

✳

At night, prominent journalists, directors of NGOs, politicians and activists were all gathered in a fancy five-star hotel called Liluz ('tulip' in Kurdish). As we were on the eve of a day that would be remembered in Turkish history, we needed to talk.

Our host was the owner of the hotel, Şahismail Bedirhanoğlu, a wealthy Kurdish businessman and the chair of the South-East Businessmen's Federation (DOGÜNSİFED). He was known to be a moderate Kurd in terms of ideology, a supporter of Kurdish rights and yet also a good servant to the AKP government. He had been walking a tightrope, trying not to upset either side. Therefore, he was more than happy for negotiations to begin between the PKK and the Turkish government, which would save him from having to choose his words carefully, one breath at a time.

Fifty of us were sitting around big dinner tables under ostentatious chandeliers in the top-floor lounge of the Liluz. The topic of conversation was obvious: the new Kurdish peace process – or the Solution Process, as the AKP government liked to call it – and what Abdullah Öcalan's letter to initiate the process would look like. It was around

9 p.m. when we heard that the co-chair of the main Kurdish party, the HDP (People's Democratic Party), Selahattin Demirtaş, had just received the letter from İmralı through MIT mediators.

'This is surprising,' Demirtaş had said to fellow party members who were present in the room.

'Surprising in a good way or a bad way?' I asked Sırrı Sakık, one of the HDP MPs at the Liluz dinner.

'I haven't the slightest idea,' replied Sakık. 'Only three people have read it: Selahattin [Demirtaş], İdris [Baluken] and Sırrı [Süreyya Önder], and they will read the letter to the crowd in Diyarbakır tomorrow. "Surprising" is the only word we could get out of Selahattin.'

Mere common sense dictated that if, in that letter, Öcalan were calling on PKK guerrillas to fight the Turkish forces to the death, that would indeed be surprising in the context of a peace process, but of course there was no way that the Turkish government would let that letter reach the hands of the Kurdish movement. Therefore, Öcalan's letter should be regarded as 'surprisingly positive', I reckoned. But how?

To understand Öcalan's mood, I went over to talk to a man who had known him for decades and had just returned from visiting him in İmralı prison. A month before Newroz, the Turkish government had let two Kurdish politicians converse face to face with Öcalan on the framework of the peace process. Ahmet Türk – a prominent figure in the Kurdish movement – was one of the two.

The last time he and Abdullah Öcalan had met was in June 1993 in a town called Bar Elias in Lebanon. Öcalan, Türk and Jalal Talabani – the then leader of the PUK (Patriotic Union of Kurdistan) in northern Iraq – had all shaken hands and announced a ceasefire by the PKK against Turkey. Because the Syrian government had decided to close down the PKK bases in Lebanon, Öcalan had demanded that, if the Turkish government was to end its 'policy of annihilation of the Kurdish people and military operations', the ceasefire would be indefinite. However, the ceasefire never led to a negotiation process, since the Turkish government continued its anti-PKK operations.[84]

Almost 20 years later, the two politicians had met again, this time in a prison under the heavy surveillance of the Turkish government,

and talked about a peace process. I sat down with Ahmet Türk at the
dinner table in the Liluz to learn what he had made of his visit to İmralı.
Türk, a tall, slim man with a grey moustache and a hunchback that
hinted at his long-time involvement in challenging Kurdish politics,
spoke calmly, as he always did.

'He [Öcalan] has not changed much. He thinks as quickly as ever,
and jumps from one topic to another, his eyes alight with fire. I am
very hopeful this time,' Türk said:

> We will get rid of that terrorist stigma on Kurdish politics. From
> now on, our resistance will be a civil one. Our Turkish socialist
> friends should try to understand us. We are not 'selling them out'
> to the AKP. But we have gone through so many hardships. We have
> suffered a lot. Now there is this opportunity and we want to take
> a shot at it. Nobody should blame us for trying.

Kurds are known to be proud of their loyalty on different levels:
loyalty to their neighbour, comrade and cause, whatever the context.
On a night like this, on the verge of a peace process, Ahmet Türk's
mention of 'socialist friends' and his apologetic stance about negotiating with the AKP government were symptoms of that obsession
with loyalty. Kurds would rather continue to suffer than be accused
of 'selling out'. But why would Kurds, or anyone, be considered as
selling out friends by choosing peace over war? The answer is that
the AKP government had already become increasingly authoritarian
regarding civil liberties and Kurds negotiating with an authoritarian
government perturbed many in the leftist intelligentsia. According to
this perspective, no good or peace could come out of this government,
and by negotiating with it, Kurds were not only legitimizing the AKP
internationally but also breaking the ranks of a possible resistance that
might emerge against this authoritarianism. The Kurdish movement
was aware of these arguments and perhaps agreed with them to some
extent. Nevertheless, they had to take their chances, not only because
they owed it to their people, who had lost tens of thousands of sons
and daughters, but also because there was a hope, however slight, that

the process of resolving the Kurdish issue would set the government on a democratic track.

✳

On 21 March 2013, I was one of the million people who had gathered in the Newroz arena in Diyarbakır, a city in south-eastern Turkey considered by the Kurdish movement as the capital of 'North Kurdistan'.

It was as hot as hell but it felt like heaven for the crowd, all of whom wore something red, green or yellow, traditional colours of the Kurdish movement. We were about to hear 'The Leadership' speak.

There were banners in Kurdish and Turkish, all addressing Öcalan. One of them read *Savaşta da Barışta da Seninleyiz Ey Serok* (We are with you at war and in peace, President). After several songs and rounds of *halay* dance, HDP MPs Sırrı Süreyya Önder and Pervin Buldan went up on stage. Önder was to read the Turkish version of Öcalan's letter, while Buldan read it in Kurdish.

Somewhere in the middle of the letter, it became obvious that the target audience of the letter was not those Kurds who were filling the Newroz arena, but the ordinary, conservative Turkish people who make up the majority of the country. In his years of fighting it, Öcalan had come to know the Turkish government very well. Hence, he believed he needed to help it prepare public sentiment for the peace process. That was precisely the reason he made several references to Turkish–Kurdish kinship under Islam in the letter.

However, the most compelling part of the letter was the call for an end to armed struggle:

> Witnessed by the millions of people who heed my call, I say a new era is beginning; an era where politics gains prominence over weapons. We have now arrived at the stage where we should withdraw our armed forces outside the borders. I believe that all those who have championed this cause are sensitive to the possible dangers of the process. This is not an end, but a new beginning. This is not abandoning the struggle – we are initiating a different

struggle. The creation of geographies based on ethnicity and a single nation is an inhuman fabrication of modernity that denies our roots and our origins.

Nobody was expecting that the Turkish public would embrace Öcalan as a peacemaker. The best possible outcome would be not to have any negative reaction. That never happened.

Nevertheless, there were mixed feelings on the Kurdish side. The letter had come as a shock, because the Kurdish audience had been expecting an announcement of a ceasefire but not a declaration of the end of armed struggle. *What have we gained that makes us ready to give up the armed struggle?* they wondered. But mostly they kept the shock and the frustration to themselves.

Both Turks and Kurds opted to wait and see how the process would develop, because we were an exhausted nation longing for peace. Years of war had turned us against one another. Kurds and Turks had long been finding joy in one another's agony, seeing the other's mourning as though it were a wedding, and a wedding as a cause for mourning. We had lost our humanity. How were we to heal that wound in the east and west of Turkey now? A peace process, a likely disarmament, meant people would no longer get hurt. This was a good start. And then we could try and mend one another's wounds too. That was what the majority of a nation contemplated in the spring of 2013.

If only we had known.

✳

'Naivety is the new realism,' say some of the contemporary optimists. It did not work for us. We were naive, but the reality did not match up. After two years of a stumbling but somehow working peace negotiation and a ceasefire with almost no deaths on either side, the peace process collapsed in June 2015. This failure created its own masterpieces of mayhem in the country.

Among the hundreds of civilians who lost their lives was a person who was very dear to the democrats of the country. He was the one that I had optimistically high-fived on the day before the peace process began.

✳

Tahir Elçi was a democrat, human rights activist and a relentless optimist. He was one of the founders of the Turkey Human Rights Foundation. He had defended the Kurds who had been forcibly displaced or whose relatives and friends had been lost or killed since the mid-1990s.

Elçi is gone now – assassinated on 28 November 2015 in the district of Sur, on a small historic road next to the one in which we had exchanged our hopes for the future two years earlier.

'We don't want guns, clashes and military operations here. This is a historic area, which has been the cradle of many civilizations.'[85] These were his last words. He was caught in a gun battle between Turkish police and the PKK's youth wing (YDG-H), which began right after he had given a press conference. Previously, on a TV show, Elçi had said that, even though he denounced violence, he would not call the PKK a terrorist organization, which had got him into trouble with the government following the collapse of the peace process. He had subsequently received countless death threats on social media and faced trial on charges of disseminating terrorist propaganda.

His death epitomized everything that had gone wrong with the Kurdish peace process and how abruptly the political climate could return to one of conflict and hostility.

TWO

Kurds in New Turkey

Sunnis, Muslims and Turks

Four key people have held sway over Turkey since the closing years of the second millennium: Mustafa Kemal Atatürk, Recep Tayyip Erdoğan, Fethullah Gülen and Abdullah Öcalan. To juxtapose them is unfortunate for several reasons, which I will explain in a moment.

The first of these was the founder of the Turkish Republic and the constructor of modern Turkish identity. The second has ruled Turkey since 2002, initially as prime minister and currently as president. The third is an Islamic cleric from Anatolia and the leader of a global religious network, which goes under the names of the Gülen movement, Cemaat or Hizmet. Fethullah Gülen was once an ally but is now a sworn enemy of Erdoğan. In March 2016, the Turkish state authorities designated the movement a terrorist organization, with Gülen labelled chief terrorist. And finally, the fourth is the undisputed leader of the Kurdish movement. Of these four protagonists of recent Turkish history, two are presidents, one dead, one living, who employed social-engineering mechanisms to build the Turkey to which they aspired. Mustafa Kemal utilized such mechanisms to wipe out the cultural and structural remnants of the Ottoman Empire and found a modern, Westernized Turkey. Ironically, Recep Tayyip Erdoğan has been using the same methods to overlay a 'new Turkey' on Mustafa Kemal's foundations.

According to Erdoğan, two of the named figures are very dangerous terrorists, who are enemies of the Turkish state. One, Öcalan, is imprisoned for life but continues to be the ultimate decision maker regarding the fate of millions of Kurds living in south-eastern Turkey. The other, Fethullah Gülen, is in exile in the US state of Pennsylvania, but still exerts great influence over millions of his disciples and Turkish schools scattered around the world. He is also accused of orchestrating a coup attempt on 15 July 2016, which killed more than 200 people.

Two crossed fault lines stretch across Turkey. Along one are the state-proclaimed terrorists, Abdullah Öcalan and Fethullah Gülen; along the other are two ideological social sects constructed by Mustafa Kemal and Tayyip Erdoğan. The feud between the followers of these four individuals is bitter, yet the accusations of each group against the others in fact carry more truth than bluster. Following Turkish politics or even leading an ordinary life in Turkey feels like being part of a political thriller. How did we end up being this country? To answer that question and make sense of this psychodrama, we need to look at the antecedents of today and understand the ongoing influence of these four men upon Turkish society.

Mustafa Kemal was a visionary and a revolutionary. His methods of attaining his vision of a secular Turkish nation were top-down and therefore had unexpected outcomes on two fronts: religion and ethnic identity. The building of a Turkish republic was, for him, a struggle towards modernization, secularization and centralization, which created an inevitable tension between Turks and Kurds and between political Islamists and secular groups.

The modernization of what we call Turkey now dates back to the Tanzimât period of the Ottoman Empire, between 1839 and 1876. Mustafa Kemal continued the modernization that the Tanzimât (literally 'reorganization') had begun with great vigour. During the late Ottoman era, a renewal from within was promoted among Islamists, which enriched the Islamist ideology until the Republic of Turkey was founded and began to meddle in the religious sphere. Subsequently, Islam gradually evaporated from urban life and became confined to the provinces. This was not in fact the main goal of the state, which initially cared little about the presence of Islam in public but still wanted to have total control over it.[1] The Turkish form of secularization can be simply described as state-controlled religion. Its aim was not to remove Islam from the state structure, because Islam would help to build a homogeneous, unified nation. And so it did.

However, Islamist discourse in Turkey lost its urban character, richness and quality and developed into a strict parochial piety, closely entwined with a rigid nationalism. The contribution of the Republic's Kemalist ideology to that loss of substance cannot be overlooked. Nevertheless, when we say Kemalism, it should be well understood that there are different types of Kemalism in Turkey: leftist, nationalistic, conservative and liberal. State-promoted Kemalism is the key to understanding the resurgence of a reactionary Islamism in the 1990s. That kind of Kemalism is nationalistic rather than leftist, conservative rather than liberal, and it gave birth to its own elite. The main traits of the Kemalist elite are Western positivism and secularism, which were derived from the French *laïcité*. They believe Islam hinders development and hence should be kept in the closet for the sake of the country's well-being and advancement. The Turkish military took on the role of guardian of Turkish secularization and defender of Kemalism, which led to several coups against the Islamists, as well as against the leftists.

After Turkey's regime evolved into a multiparty system in the 1950s, Adnan Menderes came to power as Turkey's first democratically elected prime minister. He pursued policies that gave leeway for Islam to exist in the public and political sphere. Menderes's story is infamous in Turkish political history. As he grew increasingly authoritarian in his second tenure, he was ousted by a *coup d'état* on 27 May 1960 and hanged on charges of violating the constitution. It is noteworthy that the Kemalist opponents of President Erdoğan have likened him to Adnan Menderes, implying a similar end is inevitable.

After Menderes, Necmettin Erbakan, founder of several Islamic parties and later deputy prime minister and then prime minister of Turkey, emerged as a prominent political figure promoting Islamism and the ideology of the Muslim Brotherhood. He advocated a return to sharia law and argued that only purity of Islam could save Turkey morally. Erbakan's 1969 manifesto of the religio-political movement National Vision (Millî Görüş) proclaimed an anti-Western, anti-Semitic Islamist approach to daily and political life. He argued that secularism was incompatible with justice and morality. Erbakan and his National Vision were highly influential and paved the way for other nationalistic Sunni parties and politicians to emerge, including Recep Tayyip Erdoğan and his party, the AKP (Justice and Development Party). In the eyes of the Kemalist state and military, Erbakan was a threat with his constant endorsement of an Islamist regime. He experienced several military coups throughout his career, the first in 1971 and another in 1980.

Both the 1971 and 12 September 1980 coups were mounted with the aim of curbing leftist movements in the fear that the communism of the Cold War era would spread to Turkey. The military, believing also that 'a controlled Islamism'[2] would be an antidote to communism, enforced mandatory religious classes in schools, increased the number of Imam Hatip schools – originally founded as vocational schools to raise imams for the state – and allowed Imam Hatip graduates to be appointed to the bureaucracy. The meaning of being Turkish, then, evolved into being Sunni – but not Sunni in terms of other Middle Eastern cultures. A Turkish Sunni identity was a state-invented fusion of nationalism and Islam, designed in such a way that it would not merge with other Islamist movements around the world and become a challenge to the republic. Precisely for that reason, while at the same time using Islam as a weapon against communism, the state, for example, banned the wearing of the hijab at the universities, fearing that Islamists influenced by the Iranian revolution would use it as a symbol and call for a revolution in Turkey.

In 1983, Turgut Özal and his centre-right Motherland Party (ANAP) won the first elections after the coup. Özal was not an Islamist but nor did he perceive Islam as a threat, believing that constant persecution would only lead to a reactionary and degraded version of Islamism. He made strenuous efforts to lift the hijab ban, but could not prevail over the military's hard line. However, he opened more Imam Hatip schools and gave support to religious businessmen in Anatolia who wished to engage in manufacturing, which resulted in the formation of a new religious bourgeois in the following two decades.

Fethullah Gülen and his moderate Islamist movement blossomed during that period, when the state's attitude towards Islamists was intentionally relatively lax. Gülen founded a nationalistic religious movement derived from the teachings of the Kurdish Sunni Muslim Bediüzzaman Said-i Nursî.[3] Although Gülen was himself an imam, he wanted more than just to educate clerics for the state, and established Turkish schools in central Africa and Asia as well as in Turkey. He believed an Islamic transformation could be achieved only through education. The image he constructed for himself and for Islam seemed to be just what the Western world needed and aspired to in the post-Cold War era. So they embraced him, with his constant references to peace, interfaith dialogue and tolerance, despite the fact that his private sermons (*sohbet* in Cemaat jargon) were laden with anti-Semitic and racist remarks. His devotees served at all ranks of the bureaucracy, judiciary and police force and continued to report state matters to him regularly.

The Gülen movement has two layers. The first, lower layer consists of Fethullah Gülen's many followers, who believe essentially that he is the Mahdi, the Islamic version of a messiah. The second is the top echelon, which is known to operate as a secret network, nested mainly in the security apparatus and the judiciary, and aims to achieve its goals through Machiavellian methods, especially in Turkey. His followers in the civil service, judiciary, police and the army are more loyal to Gülen than to the institutions they work for. They take orders from the 'brothers' of the movement, rather than acting within the lawful chain of command.

The Fethullah Gülen phenomenon

Talking to one of his journalist followers, Fethullah Gülen once explained the grandiosity of his movement like this:

> Some people say that [the Cemaat] is such a big project that it could not have come out of an imam's head. I never said that these activities are my project or products of my mind. All of them are God's blessings.[4]

It was not the first time that Gülen had attributed messianic powers to himself. He never openly said that he was the messenger of God, but neither did he deny he was 'special', claiming that he occasionally talked to the Prophet Muhammad in his dreams.[5]

He was born in Erzurum, a city in eastern Turkey, in 1942, but 'several Gülen-linked websites state that his date of birth is 10 December 1938,'[6] the day Mustafa Kemal Atatürk died. Although they are not outspoken about this, many Gülenists, including Gülen himself,[7] think of Atatürk as akin to Satan, and consider his death as marking the birth of a messiah.

Gülen was one of five brothers and two sisters. His mother was a housewife and his father an imam like himself, and he started his religious education when he was five years old, but his enthusiasm for learning was limited to the Qur'an. He received his elementary school diploma through exams he took later, having left school after failing to pass them several times. In 1959 he became a cleric and was one of the founders of an 'association for fighting communism'.[8]

In the mid-1960s he joined the Nur *tariqa* ('spiritual path') in Izmir, where he was appointed a state cleric, but soon departed from the Nur and initiated his own Islamic movement while teaching Qur'an courses in a private institution in Kestanepazarı, Izmir. It was at the beginning of the 1970s that Gülen started building his follower base, comprising poor children who attended his Qur'an course. Following the 1971 junta, he was arrested on the grounds of spreading religious propaganda. He was released after six months and vindicated, thanks to an amnesty law passed in 1974.

Gülen always cautioned his followers to be patient until they could accumulate economic and institutional influence. Gülenists prospered in the education sector with their private prep schools, as well as in the news, entertainment and finance sectors. But their primary goal was to exert influence at national level. Therefore, they aimed to occupy as many posts as possible in the judiciary, police force and military. By the early 2000s, the Gülenists operated schools and businesses in more than 100 countries and had acquired considerable power in the Turkish state structure.

Gülen believes in takeover that is incremental and by stealth. One of his early sermons epitomizes this belief:

> You must move in the arteries of the system without anyone noticing your existence until you reach all the power centres [...] until the conditions are ripe, they [the followers] must continue like this [...] You must wait for the time when you are complete and conditions are ripe, until we can shoulder the entire world and carry it [...] You must wait until such time as you have got all the state power, until you have brought to your side all the power of the constitutional institutions in Turkey [...] Until that time, any step taken would be too early – like breaking an egg without waiting the full 40 days for it to hatch. It would be like killing the chick inside.[9]

These words were included in the indictment that charged him with toppling the secular state in 1999. Gülen, having received the news that a case would be brought against him, had already left the country and gone into self-imposed exile in Pennsylvania the same year. It was Gülen's moving to America that changed the face and extent of the movement.

His first application to stay in the US, for 'a preference visa as an alien of extraordinary ability in the field of education', was denied on the grounds that he was

> not an educator, and [...] certainly not one of a small percentage of experts in the field of education who have risen to the very top of that field. Further, the record contained overwhelming evidence that the plaintiff is primarily the leader of a large and influential religious and political movement with immense commercial holdings.[10]

Nevertheless, Gülen was granted a green card on the basis of three reference letters from US officials: former US ambassador to Turkey Morton Abramowitz and former CIA officials George Fidas and Graham Fuller.

His education business continued at full tilt in the US, although in a different fashion that was more acceptable. Unlike in many countries, including Turkey, where Gülenist schools are 'for-profit institutions' requiring 'startup capital to be secured from within the GM [Gülenist movement] community', the Gülen movement gained access to charter funding in the US and started operating around 150 schools with public money.[11] The movement's presence in North and sub-Saharan Africa is also an important part of its income and expansion strategy. There are more than 100 Gülen-inspired primary, middle and secondary schools, a hospital in Somalia, student dorms in Morocco, a university in Nigeria, the largest mosque in the southern hemisphere in South Africa and many branches of his global charity, the Kimse Yok Mu Foundation.

According to US sources, the movement's financial capacity was estimated to be between US$25[12] and US$50[13] billion in the form of schools and charities. It relies on *himmet* – the Arabic word for donations – from business people linked to the movement, and followers are said to give between 2 and 10 per cent of their wages every month to the movement through their 'brothers'. But it is mostly the education business that makes up the movement's opaque estate.

Gülen spent his money 'wisely', working with the best PR agents in the US and building a strong lobbying machine in the US, the UK and Turkey. It was this machine that helped the Gülen movement spread the idea that it represents moderate Islam, peace, democracy and interfaith dialogue. In 2013, *Time* magazine included him among the 100 most influential people in the world.

Gülen's earlier views reveal a different story. In his book *Fasıldan Fasıla* (*From Chapter to Chapter*), published in 1995, he explains:

> The Jewish tribe is very intelligent. This intelligent tribe has put forth many things throughout history in the name of science and thought [...] But these have always been offered in the form of poisoned honey and have been presented to the world as such. For instance, Karl Marx is a Jew; the communism he developed looks like a good alternative to capitalism at first sight, but in essence it is a deadly poison mixed in honey.[14]

In his book *Küçük Dünyam* (*My Little World*), which was allegedly confiscated in the mid-2000s by the movement itself after it had attracted attention, Fethullah Gülen

> [justifies] wife-beating, albeit as a last resort [...] Of Christianity, he writes that it has become perverted (*sapıtmış*), of America, that it is 'our merciless enemy' (*aman bilmeyen düşman*) and of Europe that it has a 'sadist mentality' that wants to crush Islam.[15]

These statements may be known only to a few people, since Gülen, especially since moving to the US, has become accomplished in portraying himself as a friend of the West, a friend with benefits.

The Gülen movement's infiltration into the Turkish state dates back to the late 1980s. His followers' presence was tacitly condoned by the Bülent Ecevit, Süleyman Demirel and Tansu Çiller administrations, even though he has always been considered a threat by the Kemalist establishment and the army. Ironically, the only administration that opted to keep its distance from the Gülen movement was Necmettin Erbakan's, since Erbakan's understanding of Islam at that time was not compatible with Gülen's.

The rise of the AKP and the 'new Turkey'

At the end of the 1990s, the lax attitude to political Islamism reversed. Necmettin Erbakan and his Welfare Party (Refah Partisi) rose to prominence in 1995 as an alternative for those who 'believed in civic religions, [who] are ignored and marginalized by the center parties, the underdogs of the cities'.[16] Following his victory at the elections, Erbakan formed a coalition with the centre-right Doğru Yol. He was the co-leader of the government when the military ousted him on 28 February 1998 on the grounds of his perceived Islamist agenda. This coup brought about a change of government without the army's taking power, and for that reason it is referred to as a post-modern coup.

Recep Tayyip Erdoğan and his AKP emerged from Erbakan's National Vision movement and gained momentum as a reaction to the 28 February coup. The founders of the AKP were of the view that Erbakan and his National Vision had to modernize themselves in order to win elections. In other words, they defended a new, more populist Islamism. After its establishment under the leadership of Recep Tayyip Erdoğan in 2001, the AKP won the majority of seats in parliament in 2002, beginning a period of one-party rule that was to last more than a decade.

The AKP's initial appearance and discourse was not Islamist. It positioned itself on the centre-right trajectory. AKP deputies repeatedly claimed that 'they have taken off their National Vision shirt'.[17] Indeed, in a 2004 speech, Erdoğan said that he was 'not an Islamist but a conservative democrat who believes in a secular state'.[18] The AKP did not impose an Islamization agenda until after its third period in office in 2011, instead pledging to pursue economic stability and growth, which resonated well with the public and consolidated its constituency of right-wing conservative Turks and Kurds.

The AKP's initial pro-EU stance also won the hearts and minds of the liberal intellectuals of the country, who had long been criticizing the exclusive nature of the state's Kemalist ideology. The backing of the liberals gave the AKP legitimacy where it most wished for it, in the intellectual realm, and put the Kemalist opponents in the position of advocating for a passé, illiberal Turkey under military domination, based on unfounded fears of Islamization. While Kemalists accused the AKP of having a hidden Islamist agenda, it was also criticized by certain influential figures in grass-roots Islamism, such as Erbakan's disciples, for not being Islamist enough, for rejecting its roots. In their view, the AKP had been set up by those 'who were broken by the 28 February coup and estranged from their Islamist background'.[19]

The argument of the 'true Islamists' went like this. The decade 1985–95 was one of revival for Turkey's Islamists. While they were intellectually productive and active in terms of organizing and structuring the movement, their ultimate goal was to win power. But their aspirations were crushed by the 28 February coup. That was when they realized that an Islamic revolution in Turkey was inconceivable, even if they managed to win elections as Erbakan had done. The majority of the Islamists lost their way and their purpose in life after 28 February and dispersed around the right wing of the political spectrum. The AKP came to power thanks to its ability to mobilize those scattered Islamists. Even though the founders of the AKP were those who had lost their appetite for Erbakan's National Vision, it would be unwise to overlook their Islamist background when analysing the party's rise and ascendancy.

As is well known, there are several approaches to gaining power. One is the top-down revolutionary approach. Another is the grass-roots, bottom-up approach. Nurcular (followers of Said-i Nursi), Gülenists and the founders of the AKP belong to the second group. Unlike Erbakan, who was constantly at odds with the state and the army, this group was inclined to be a part of the system, rather than fighting it. After former president Turgut Özal opened the doors of power to the religious groups and initiated economic reforms, the Islamists grew wealthier in terms of accumulating capital, which they invested in education and media, creating Islamist cultural capital that paved the way for the establishment of the AKP.

In its early days, the AKP received help from the Gülen movement, whose support, along with that of liberal public figures, enabled the AKP to be considered a moderate Islamist party in Turkey and around the world. However, the core founders of the AKP had not changed their ideology much from that of Natural Vision, and had certainly not evolved to be conservative democrats. According to Professor Yüksel Taşkın, author of AKP Devri: Türkiye Siyaseti, İslamcılık, Arap Baharı (Era of the AKP: Turkish Politics, Islamism, the Arab Spring), the AKP had tried to concoct a synthesis between Islamism and centre-right ideology, but failed.[20] That was why the image-making task of the AKP was handed to liberals and the Gülen movement.

Followers of the Gülen movement were part of the national structure long before the AKP came to power, and so guided the fledgling AKP members into the avenues of bureaucracy. But the real alliance stemmed from having a common enemy, namely the military. Restraining the military's presence in politics had become one of the AKP's main pledges. In 2007, the then chief of the armed forces, Yasar

Büyükanıt, delivered an e-memorandum in which he opposed the presidency of Abdullah Gul, one of the founders of the AKP and long-time comrade of Erdoğan.[21] The AKP and parliament rose up against Büyükanıt's intervention and – following a renewed election – elected Abdullah Gül president.

The attempt by Büyükanıt to shape government affairs provoked a war between the AKP and the military leadership and increased the AKP's support in the eyes of the democrats.

Just 46 days after the e-memorandum, a high-profile court case started against Ergenekon, which, according to the formal charges, was a terrorist organization consisting of secular nationalists in the deep state. They had allegedly plotted assassinations and bombings to oust the AKP government and had been exerting some influence in the Turkish political sphere for decades. Among the 275 defendants in the Ergenekon case were opposition MPs, academics, politicians, journalists and army officials, including the former head of the armed forces, General İlker Başbuğ, successor to Yasar Büyükanıt. Newspapers affiliated with the Gülen movement were filled with stories about appalling plans by the army and the secular establishment to tip the political status quo in their favour. On the other hand, skimming through the thousands of pages of the charge details showed clearly that evidence to back the claims against the defendants was, on the face of it, extremely ambivalent and vague. Nevertheless, the arrests continued apace.

In 2010, another high-profile case, called Sledgehammer (*Balyoz*), was initiated, which led to the imprisonment of 300 army officials, convicted of plotting a coup in 2003 against the AKP government. It was revealed soon afterwards that the majority of the evidence consisted of fabricated Microsoft Word documents. However, anyone who mentioned the weak evidence and inconsistencies in the charges was accused of defending the military leadership and the Kemalist establishment.

I was one of those accused, and was called names like 'coup lover' and 'soldier's bootlicker'. The name-calling did not bother me, but at a certain point the harassment from the government and the Gülen movement went far beyond the usual smear campaigns. Lists of journalists who were to be arrested were leaked in the media by unknown sources. My name was on that list because of my articles pointing out the inconsistencies regarding the evidence and because I had voiced concerns over the machinations of those trials. Compellingly, 'attrition of the Gülen movement'[22] had become a crime according to these charges. Two colleagues, Ahmet Şık and Nedim Şener, who had been working on the Gülen movement's infiltration into the police force, were arrested on charges of being members of Ergenekon's media wing. Next morning, the police came to our newspaper office to see if any of us had a copy of Ahmet's unpublished book on how followers of Gülen operate in the security forces. It was surreal and reminded us of the 1980s military junta period when leftist books were confiscated and burnt.

Ahmet and Nedim's arrests were a breaking point which drove many people in Turkey and the West to question why they and other similar cases were being pursued. In 2015, both Ergenekon and Sledgehammer defendants were acquitted of their alleged crimes. It must be stressed that these court decisions vindicating innocent people came only after the AKP–Gülen alliance had been broken.

The outcome of the Sledgehammer and Ergenekon cases not only shattered many lives but also blocked the possibility of unearthing the real deep state and military hegemony. The Turkish military's intervention into politics and the subversive activities of the deep state are no secret, but because these trials were organized primarily to constrain the opposition against the AKP and its counterpart, the Gülen movement, they failed to reveal the real threat and instead laid the foundations for the 'new Turkey' to which Gülen and the AKP aspired.

Kurds in the AKP era

What does the new Turkey have to offer the Kurds? The AKP was new. It claimed to be a victim of the Kemalist state and military domination, like the Kurds. It did not carry the baggage of past mistakes like the main opposition CHP (Republican People's Party), which is known as Atatürk's party. The AKP constantly mentioned the kinship of Islam, which they claimed would solve the decades-long rift in the public sphere. These notions captured Kurdish minds and support.

The state of the Kurds was ameliorated in various ways during the AKP's first and second terms, mostly owing to the EU accession process and the requirements of the Copenhagen criteria. The 22-year-long state of emergency, imposed in the aftermath of the 1980 coup in the south-east region, was lifted. A state-run Kurdish TV channel called TRT Şeş was launched. The ban on public use of Kurdish was effectively lifted, allowing prisoners to speak to their visitors in their mother tongue. Private courses in the Kurdish language and optional Kurdish classes in the universities were permitted. In anticipation of healthy economic growth and advancement, private hospitals and shopping centres were built in the region.

During the latest peace process, possible amendments to the definition of citizenship in the Turkish constitution were fiercely debated. I asked PKK leader Murat Karayılan if the phrase 'Turkish nation', which was in the constitution, bothered them. He answered in a way that summarized the arguments of both the HDP (the successor to the Barış ve Demokrasi Partisi [BDP, Peace and Democracy Party]) and the PKK:

> The phrase 'Turkish nation' does not bother us if it covers everybody who lives in Turkey. And if it does cover everybody, we would like that 'everybody' to be mentioned in the constitution. All should have equal emphasis and the constitution should represent all who actually make up the public. Nothing less, nothing more.[23]

More hawkish residents of Qandil, such as Sabri Ok, were more direct about what kind of definition would satisfy the Kurdish movement: 'If Turkishness is mentioned in the constitution, so should Kurdishness be. Or the constitution could avoid any reference to ethnicity.'[24]

Despite the discussions, no step was taken towards drawing up a new constitution, and the parliamentary commission appointed to come up with a draft dissolved as a result of irreconcilable differences among the political parties. Therefore, little was achieved in terms of reforms during the peace process. The ban on election propaganda in languages other than Turkish was lifted; the morning pledge of allegiance, which starts with the words 'I am Turkish, I am honest, I am hard-working', was removed from schools, and Kurdish names for villages and towns were reinstated. But these steps were too little too late and, as International Crisis Group director Hugh Pope told me, 'were given piece by piece, as if slicing a salami'.[25]

Did the AKP genuinely want to solve the Kurdish problem? Yes and no. As Turkey approached the 2000s, one thing was certain: the Kurds were not becoming Turkified, either through assimilation or through military oppression. While not continuing the state's long-term tactics to assimilate the Kurds, the pragmatic and clever Tayyip Erdoğan did not attempt to fulfil Kurdish demands either. The EU accession process was also a factor that pushed the government to seek a solution to the issue. The Copenhagen criteria that frame whether or not a country is eligible to join the EU lay down the prerequisites: democracy, the rule of law, human rights and respect for and protection of minorities, and the existence of a functioning market economy. The European Parliament had thus become arguably the most important player regarding Turkey's Kurdish question.[26]

Actually, the formula for solving the Kurdish problem was simple: 'satisfy the Kurds, convince the Turks,'[27] as Şerafettin Elçi once told me. Kurds can be satisfied under four conditions, he said: 1. give the Kurdish identity constitutional recognition; 2. allow education in their mother tongue; 3. allow the use of Kurdish in public spaces; and 4. give them autonomy in their region. The AKP did not come close to this formula. Those piecemeal reforms were usually made around election time and were aimed at gaining the votes of the Kurds rather than meeting their fundamental demands. They did not pass the test of sincerity.

Erdoğan is a successful implementer of neo-liberal principles. Inevitably, therefore, his attempts to grapple with the Kurdish problem were a by-product of that mentality, which had had serious adverse consequences. For example, by allowing Kurdish education in private schools, he was actually diminishing the government's responsibility to provide education in the mother tongue.[28] There is also nothing fair and egalitarian in saying, in effect, that only Kurds with enough money can learn Kurdish. The investments, gentrification projects and influx of new apartments in the region did please the Kurds, but 'the majority of the people don't forget about their rights because their stomachs are being fed'.[29] And they were in no mood to be deceived. The AKP made no major concessions regarding the military presence and security measures in the Kurdish region and did not attempt to rescind the anti-terror law, using it instead to put pressure on the Kurdish movement. As Cihan Tuğal rightly articulated, the AKP was very successful in dressing its authoritarianism in 'democratic' and 'Islamic' garb.[30]

Nevertheless, that garb occasionally slipped, revealing the real body inside. Consider Erdoğan's changing rhetoric towards the Kurdish issue, for example. In the year that the AKP came to power, Erdoğan had visited a plant in Kars where a Kurdish worker said, 'The Kurdish problem should be solved. We don't want to continue living in agony.' To this, Erdoğan replied, 'If you say there is a problem, then there will be a problem. But look: I am married to a woman from Siirt and I am happy. You have to change the way you look at things.'[31] In 2005, he made a breakthrough speech in Diyarbakır, saying, 'The Kurdish problem is Turkey's problem and my problem too.'[32] This speech was cited many times by AKP officials as proof that their party would solve the problem. 2009 was the year in which the words were turned into action. Erdoğan announced, 'Whatever you like to call it, the Kurdish problem or the south-east problem, we have now started to work on resolving it.'[33] Yet by 2011 there was a palpable change in Erdoğan's tone. 'There is no Kurdish problem in Turkey any more. I don't accept that,' he said in a meeting in Muş. 'My Kurdish brother has a problem, but there is no Kurdish problem.'[34] A month after the elections on 12 June 2011, he put the national Kurdish discourse back in its place: 'There is no Kurdish problem, but a PKK problem. We supported our Kurdish citizens more than anyone.'[35] By 2015, his statements were hardening to an astonishing degree. At the very time when there was an ongoing peace process, he asked, 'What Kurdish problem? There is no such thing. To say that there is means discrimination.'[36]

In the general elections of 2007 and 2011, the AKP got more votes than the Kurdish party, the BDP, in south-east Turkey. On the other hand, its electorate shrank over time, while the BDP's grew bigger. The AKP for a long time claimed to be 'the biggest Kurdish party', meaning that it appealed to Kurds more than any other political party. However, a 2015 study directed by Professor Mesut Yeğen told another story.[37]

Turkey is divided into seven geographical regions. South-eastern Anatolia and Eastern Anatolia are the two regions known to be home to the majority of the Kurds. However, if one looks at the Kurdish population city by city, certain cities in the South-eastern and Eastern Anatolia regions, such as Erzurum and Erzincan, do not have a considerable Kurdish population. This therefore places a caveat on the AKP's rhetoric.

According to Professor Yeğen's study, the HDP (successor of the BDP) received the biggest chunk of Kurdish votes in 12 cities in the 2014 local elections.[38] The same trend continued in the 7 June 2015 and 1 November 2015 general elections. Kurds who voted for the AKP in the cities were either uneducated or wealthy, whereas HDP voters were predominantly either educated or poor.[39] It is worth emphasizing that the majority of the Kurdish electorate call themselves religious and 75 per cent claim to perform their religious duties every day. 'Therefore, the perception that the AKP draws more votes from religious people and the HDP is for secular Kurds is not correct,' according to Professor Yeğen.[40]

So, what did the Kurds gain in the AKP era, other than the by-products of a larger neo-liberal policy?

Under the Kemalists, it was the state that defined who was a proper citizen. Now the definition is in the hands of the new state ruled by the AKP, or, more accurately, by President Recep Tayyip Erdoğan himself. Although the respective ideologies of these groups seem to be opposed to each other, the use of the state to control the public has remained the same. That is why members of the AKP are occasionally called by Kurdish politicians[41] and the intelligentsia Islamist Kemalists and its leader Tayyip Erdoğan an Islamist Atatürk. Kurds are the ultimate victims of centralized statism, be it Islamist, neo-liberal or Kemalist, since both movements share the view that Turkey should be governed as a monolithic Turkish country, sidelining anyone and everyone who does not conform to this Turkishness. They differ only in the way in which they characterize a true citizen. In the eyes of the Kemalist elite, such a citizen would be secular, Westward-looking and indoctrinated by Kemalist education. To the Islamist AKP, the criteria are being a Sunni Muslim, promoting the *umma*, showing off his or her religious practice for the world to see and being taught in Imam Hatip schools – which have now grown into a front in the Islamization of education. Unsurprisingly, Kurds have not benefited from the actions and perspectives of either of these national powers, let alone been embraced and included with their own identity intact.

THREE

Kurdish Peace and the New Deep State

Who will govern the new Turkey?

It was after the constitutional referendum of 2010 that the term 'the new Turkey' was first coined. A government-affiliated think tank compiled a report in which it said that 'Society bought the ideal that is the New Turkey with 58 per cent [in support]. The referendum process had gone beyond a confidence vote for the AKP and become a vote of approval for a New Turkey plan.'[1] The 2010 referendum brought several changes to the constitution, such as lifting the ban on general strikes; the creation of an ombudsman to resolve disputes among citizens; and the restructuring of the constitutional court, allowing individual petitions to the constitutional court and enabling the trial of those involved in the 12 September 1980 coup. However, the most important of the changes was the restructuring of the Supreme Board of Judges and Prosecutors, a major overhaul that gave a greater say to the government in the appointment of judges. This marked the beginning of total control over all branches of the government by Erdoğan. It is fair to say that the consolidation of the AKP's power was complete after the referendum and the 2011 general elections.

However, there was a small problem, which Erdoğan tacitly tolerated: the Gülen movement's influence in matters of state. He and his party relied on the movement to surmount the obstacles put up by the military and the secular establishment in the form of cases such as Ergenekon and Sledgehammer. However, the more the AKP relied on the Cemaat's auspices at the level of national government and in the fight with the military, the more it lost executive control to the group. Erdoğan had realized this after the 2010 referendum and started to look for ways to curb Cemaat's presence in the judiciary, the bureaucracy and the police force. But it was too late. Once the common enemy of the secular establishment and the army had been stifled, the alliance between Gülen and Erdoğan turned into a power struggle over who would rule the country.

The Gülen movement's cadres were more educated, articulate and experienced in national matters, and had done all the dirty work of subduing the army. They strongly believed that they had the right and the capability to lead the country and make the ultimate decisions on all critical matters. Erdoğan, on the other hand, felt betrayed and had no intention of dealing with another kind of tutelage just when the military had been wiped off the stage. A fierce fight began at all levels of the bureaucracy, the judiciary, the police force and business life.

After Erdoğan declared that a bill was on its way to close down Gülen's prep schools in November 2013, the Gülen movement leaked tapes on 17 and 25 December 2013 that revealed a corruption scheme involving AKP ministers, an Iranian–Turkish businessman, Reza Zarrab, Erdoğan and his son Bilal Erdoğan. The so-called '17/25 operation' revealed US$17.5 million in cash, which was confiscated by the police at the residences of the son of state-owned Halkbank's director and former interior minister Muammer Güler. According to the prosecutor, the money was being used for bribery. The police detained 52 people and accused 14 of bribery, corruption, fraud and gold smuggling, among them four ministers and their family members. Much later, Zarrab got arrested in the US on charges of evading sanctions against Iran through the scheme that had been revealed by the 17/25 December investigation. He is currently awaiting trial in New York.

Erdoğan called it an attempt at a 'civilian coup' and ordered the arrest of the prosecutors and police officers involved in the operation. Although he asserted that the leaked tapes were forged, there were experts' reports claiming their authenticity. After a tape of a phone call allegedly between Erdoğan and his son Bilal was disseminated through Twitter, Erdoğan took out his anger on the social media giant and blocked it in Turkey for 24 hours. Shortly afterwards, a round of trials began, in which Fethullah Gülen was accused of being a terrorist and his followers of aiding a terrorist organization to overthrow the AKP government. Newspapers, TV channels and enterprises affiliated with Gülen were shut down, and journalists and businessmen were arrested. This time, the AKP was using Gülen's tactics of elimination against Gülen himself. The indictments aimed to defame and ostracize anyone close to Gülen. Just as the fabricated Ergenekon and Sledgehammer cases had failed to expose and penalize the real deep state, these Gülen cases also failed to unmask the unlawful organization of his followers in government institutions. But the AKP were in an impossible situation, as they were the ones who had put Gülenists into key positions as a shield against the secular state. A lawful purge of the Gülenists who were more loyal to Gülen than to the state would have to involve the AKP echelon that had given them ground in the first place. This would reveal the true nature of the AKP–Gülen alliance, which Erdoğan could not afford to be made public.

The Gülen movement and Kurdish peace

It is a much less known fact that the first and most major disagreement between the AKP and the Gülen movement was over the Kurdish issue. The Gülen movement's idea of handling the Kurdish issue did not involve a negotiating table,[2] but had two main perspectives. First and foremost, armed violence should be minimized. Second, the very strong organizational structure of the Kurdish movement should be dissolved and the Marxist–Leninist ideology should be challenged, using an educational mechanism like the movement's private prep schools all over Turkey and its Turkish schools in Africa and Central Asia.

The different approaches to the Kurdish issue were actually emblematic of Gülen's and Erdoğan's original ideologies. For example, the leaders of the Nur movement – the *tariqa* (school of Sufism) from which the Gülen movement stemmed – were also unhappy about Erbakan's contact with the Kurds.[3] According to Gülen, Erbakan was pushing the boundaries of nationalistic conservatism by advocating that the Kurdish problem could only be solved under the umbrella of Islam. In fact, Erbakan had a much more sensible understanding of the Kurdish issue compared to the Kemalist centre-left and centre-right parties. When I interviewed him several weeks before his death, he revealed his thoughts on the Kurdish issue. 'In south-east Turkey, certain individuals in public office tyrannized the people. They even got pleasure from this,' Erbakan said.

> I tried to warn the then Prime Minister, Süleyman Demirel, in the years leading up to the 1980 junta, that policies like village evacuation were antagonizing the people of the region. But he did not care and failed to investigate. Certain Turkish racists felt animosity towards the Kurds. These atrocities in the region were the consequence of that animosity.[4]

Erbakan, while admitting animosity towards Kurds, was careful not to describe it as a systematic practice by the state but rather to put the blame on 'certain Turkish racists'. However, even in this he was ahead of his peers.

During this period, the Gülen movement was silent and concentrating on establishing a presence in the region through schools, non-governmental organizations and charitable foundations. The Gülen movement's first educational institution in the Kurdish region dates back to 1988. The number doubled every year up until 2014. But the real increase began in 2003. The presence of Gülen-affiliated schools and foundations soared concurrently with the AKP's rule. The average rate of increase in students had been 3.3 per cent year on year, but then jumped to 8.5 per cent after 2002. Before the AKP's tenure, the Gülen movement was only establishing prep centres and private schools, but then it started to open centres where low-income students could receive free tuition.[5]

The late writer Cemal Uşşak used to be part of the Nur *tariqa* in his undergraduate years but then joined the Gülen movement, where he become a prominent figure. He told me that they were oblivious to the agony of the Kurds because they were having their own battle with the establishment as a religious movement. According to Uşşak, the Gülen movement then made up for their indifference in the last decade and built a strong network in the Kurdish region, which he thought was a very good deed (although this is not something everyone agrees on):

> When you visit our movement's study groups, prep school and Kimse Yok Mu Foundation[6] [a global aid organization linked to Gülen] you will find that people are happy with the aid they are receiving. But if you ask the PKK and its followers, the Gülen movement is assimilating them. This is outrageous.[7]

'Assimilation' may not be the right word, but the Gülenists did not establish themselves in the region solely to aid the poverty-stricken Kurds. They wanted to enforce their way of solving the Kurdish problem, which did not involve negotiating with the PKK.

When a journalist, Mustafa Akyol, once asked a high-profile Gülenist if they approved the latest 2013 peace process, he received the following response:

> We have reservations. Hocaefendi [Fethullah Gülen] believes that, while peace with the PKK is a good initiative, the state should also have Plan B, C, D and even E. Because he thinks that the PKK is not that trustworthy, and that there are ill-intentioned powers in the region that may interfere in the process.[8]

With hindsight, Fethullah Gülen proved to be right. Many ill-intentioned powers did interfere in the process, although none was as influential, forceful or traceable as the Gülen movement itself. Its interference actually went as far back as the campaign in 2009 to arrest Kurdish activists, academics and mayors. They were accused of being members of the

KCK. Hatip Dicle, acting co-chair of the Democratic Society Congress (DTK),[9] explained how the scheme worked back then:

> The impetus behind the KCK operations was the Gülen movement's elements in the police and the judiciary. But the AKP government was also involved in these operations. After we had won 100 mayorships in the 2009 local elections, they came up with the idea of these operations, just to terrorize us.[10]

The idea that the Gülen movement masterminded the KCK operations is shared not only by the Kurds but also by the AKP government. 'It was the Gülen movement that staged the KCK trials,' said Muhammed Dervişoğlu, Undersecretary of Public Security and Order, to Abdullah Öcalan in one of the İmralı meetings in 2014.[11]

Since the Gülen movement was fervently opposed to negotiating with the PKK, the second strike against the AKP government is acknowledged to have been the leaking of a tape of the Oslo talks in 2011, in which Hakan Fidan (later head of the National Intelligence Organization, MIT), in conversation with PKK officials Duran Kalkan and Murat Karasu, referred to Abdullah Öcalan as 'Sayın [Mister] Öcalan'. The leak came at a time when then prime minister Erdoğan was vowing that the Turkish government would never be involved in direct talks with PKK officials. The recording was first released by pro-PKK news agencies, but then was withdrawn from its website. It was later revealed that the website had been hacked and the tape planted by anonymous hackers.

Interestingly, the tape did not cause the belligerence that might have been expected. The main opposition Republican People's Party's accusation was related to the leak, not to the content of the tape, which showed obvious negotiations between the PKK and MIT. A CHP leader said, 'If the head of the intelligence service, whose job is to keep the state's secrets, is being tapped, it shows the situation of the rulers of this country.'[12] Yes, that situation was grim in terms of security and intelligence, but the content of the leak was also important. The Oslo talks had actually laid the groundwork for the latest peace process.

The Oslo talks

Since the earliest days of the PKK, interlocutors representing the government, who were either army or MIT officials, acted as backchannels in their negotiations with the organization. The first major negotiation process following Abdullah Öcalan's arrest, now known as the Oslo talks, began in 2005. It involved an international mediator, the MIT and four PKK officials – Adem Uzun and Zübeyir Aydar, who are still in exile in Europe, and Murat Karasu and Sabri Ok, who are based in the PKK headquarters in Qandil Mountain in northern Iraq.

The MIT team involved the then chief of the organization, Emre Taner, and his aide, Afet Güneş. Hakan Fidan, who later succeeded Taner as chief of the MIT, happened to be the main mediator in the peace process and attended the talks as 'the special representative to Prime Minister Erdoğan'.

The international mediation team, as we now know, comprised one Norwegian and one Briton, who were said to be experts on conflict resolution. Although the first contact between the parties was in 2005, face-to-face meetings only commenced in 2009. The MIT team that had been meeting with the PKK delegation in Oslo was also meeting with Öcalan in İmralı, keeping the two sides in contact via letters.

The then chief of the KCK, Murat Karayilan, explained to me how the Oslo talks had been designed:

> We were developing a strategy in this matter. It was more correct if issues were discussed with our leadership. If we had not pursued such a strict policy, then probably Öcalan would have been left outside of the process. To start at the beginning: there was an international institution acting as a mediator that insists on refusing to disclose its name. Let us say it was an institution within the framework of the United Nations. We first met them in 2005. After 2006, these meetings became systematic. They have solved many similar issues at an international level and, based on that, they imposed a couple of conditions. They said everything would be secret. It would be closed to the press. Only a very

narrow section of our administration would know this. They asked me who my most authorized staff were. I told them there were 11 people. They said, 'OK, nobody outside of this 11 should know.' After this, the talks began. They were indeed also speaking to the government. This international institution was shuttling between the two sides, carrying messages. After 2008, they took a delegation of our people to Oslo. That was when we recognized that they were operating on quite high authority. They were able to fly a private plane from Qandil. The first direct talks between our delegation and MIT occurred at that time.[13]

In one of the meetings in Oslo, the international body seemed satisfied with progress. Its representative said,

I congratulate both parties. It looks like the lights turned green at this phase of the negotiation, and we are happy to see that both parties believe the standstill should continue, because it will constitute the basis for a positive political negotiation process.[14]

According to Öcalan, he received a letter 'written by Sabri [Ok] and Zübeyir [Aydar]. He signed that letter and entered this process. It was the end of 2008, or maybe the beginning of 2009. He officially became part of the process proper.'[15]

However, things did not go as planned. In October 2009, as part of the agreement in Oslo, a group of 34 people from the PKK's Makhmur camp in northern Iraq came to Turkey on a bus from the Habur border gate. Eight of them were PKK fighters wearing guerrilla outfits 'who had not committed a crime'. They were met as war heroes by a chanting Kurdish crowd.

One of the eight was a woman called Elif Uludağ, who later sent me a letter from prison. 'I am a guerrilla and a mother,' she wrote.

That morning, I said farewell to my son, who was also a guerrilla. He was sad and concerned because I was going to Habur. I calmed him, saying, 'We will meet soon, because our going will bring peace. Then you all will come down from the mountain and we will dance freely on the soils we were born on.' Then I, along with the seven other guerrillas, took the bus to Habur. We were wearing guerrilla outfits because on the mountain we did not have anything else. The crowd in Turkey was euphoric, not because they had seen us, but because they had seen a window of peace. However [...] our outfits and the crowd's sentiments had become a huge problem. A short time later, all eight of us were arrested.[16]

According to many experts in conflict resolution, the Habur incident was a fiasco and should not have taken place. In my interview with Lord Alderdice, a British peer and expert in the psychology of terrorism and political violence, he told me, 'During a negotiation, moving too fast or too slowly can sometimes determine the fate of the talks. In the Habur incident, the government acted too fast. They should not have let that happen.'[17] The Habur incident caused a great backlash among the Turkish public and left the Oslo talks hanging in the air for months, though not destroying the process altogether. The negotiation between the parties carried on.

The Kurdish side had been asked to formulate their demands of the Turkish government. After dozens of meetings with PKK officials, Kurdish politicians and intelligentsia, the Kurdish side produced a memorandum that was given to Öcalan. In response, Öcalan came up with a road map and three protocols.[18]

The first of these protocols related to the representation of the Kurdish people in the constitution. For the amendment of the constitution, a commission should be appointed consisting of government officials and representatives of the PKK, the Kurdistan Regional Government (KRG), the EU, NATO and the UN. It was also recommended that, parallel to that, a Truth and Reconciliation Commission be set up, resembling the one that had been established in South Africa. The second protocol dealt with issues such as a permanent ceasefire, the withdrawal of PKK fighters from Turkey and the setting up of a Kurdistan security force in the region. The third protocol was in essence about the roles of Öcalan and the PKK cadre post-conflict.

The PKK was happy with how the process was unfolding. As Cemil Bayık, one of the hawkish members of the organization in Qandil, said during an interview, 'They have reached the end of armed conflict.'[19] And in response to this statement, the end date of the ceasefire, which had been set as 30 May 2010, was extended.

The mediators shuttled back and forth between the parties. The three protocols reached the hands of the government but, as Zübeyir Aydar, one of the parties to the talks, stated, the mediators could not find common ground. It was a general election period and Erdoğan had returned to his customary nationalistic rhetoric. 'There is no Kurdish question,' he proclaimed to an election rally in May 2011, which was received by the Kurdish side as an answer to Öcalan's protocols. On 12 June 2011, the AKP were elected, winning 46 per cent of the votes and becoming the majority party. The MIT envoy never showed up for the next meeting, which was supposed to take place on 15 June 2011.[20]

On 14 July, the PKK and army forces clashed in Silvan and a total of 13 soldiers lost their lives in disastrous circumstances. Twelve of the 13 soldiers were burned to death when grenades exploded in the forest. The PKK interpreted this 'encounter' as a 'conspiracy' or 'an attack on the peace process'.

The negotiating table that had been set up in Oslo was dismantled at the end of 2011, which reignited a war between the PKK and the Turkish army, one of the bloodiest since the 1990s.[21]

'Oslo was poorly designed, rushed and dirty,' said Hugh Pope, the Turkey/Cyprus project director of the International Crisis Group. 'It was a mistake to attempt to sign a protocol with the PKK without any reform of Kurdish rights and of Turkey itself, because the Kurdish party thought that a genuine resolution was on the way.'[22] Neither Turkey nor the political system was well prepared. The ending of the process led to a severe erosion of trust on the Kurdish side.

On the other hand, there was one particular striking detail in the Oslo talks that was later acknowledged by both the Turkish government and the Kurdish movement as an outright indicator of the Gülen movement's meddling with the Kurdish peace process. Following the leak of the Oslo talks tape in September 2011, there was an attempt on 7 February 2012 to detain Hakan Fidan, now the head of MIT, and former directors of the organization on account of their involvement in Oslo. 'MIT was suspicious that it was we who had leaked the Oslo tape in the first place,' said PKK official Zübeyir Aydar,

> but we asked them to run an investigation. When a lawsuit was filed against Hakan Fidan, they were convinced that we were not responsible for what happened. My personal conviction is that the Oslo records came out of MIT archives. I believe that they were taken from the MIT archives illegally and leaked.[23]

Following the attempt to detain the MIT chief, Abdullah Öcalan decided to contact MIT and recommence the peace process. 'The prosecutor mounted a coup against the National Intelligence Organization on 7 February,' he said.

> I sensed a coup there. I told the head of the prison that we should not leave Mr Hakan [Hakan Fidan, MIT chief] alone. I contacted him. The channel [of communication] opened again and the dialogue started. It was my duty to prevent a coup [orchestrated by the Gülen movement]. If they were successful in getting Hakan, Erdoğan would be next.[24]

So, the latest peace process was initiated in the beginning of 2013. However, a more arduous undertaking was ahead than any of the parties imagined.

Murder in the peace process

You negotiate not with your friend but with your enemy. Acknowledging this fact is a good start, although it doesn't help much with establishing at least a minimum level of trust as a basis for the process. Trust between the Turkish government and the Kurdish movement had already become corroded over the years.

Dewlet bi ker be ji xwe le meke (If the state is a donkey, do not ride him)[25] is a saying among the elderly in Kurdish villages. 'Never, ever trust the state,' they preach to the young, also quoting a famous statement by Seyit Rıza, who had led the 1938 Kurdish uprising in Dersim: 'I could not cope with your dishonesty and that is a lesson for me. But I did not kneel before you and that should pose a difficulty for you.'

Eleven days after the then prime minister Erdoğan declared a peace process had begun, news from Paris rocked the Kurdish movement, who were already suspicious that the government were poised to deceive them. On 9 January 2013, in Paris, three female PKK members were killed: Sakine Cansız, Fidan Doğan and Leyla Söylemez. These murders could have derailed the process almost before it started, because Cansız was no ordinary figure. She was among the core group who had founded the PKK. The peace process continued only because neither the Turkish government nor the Kurdish movement could point the finger at the other. The murder did not seem to serve any of them at the outset of negotiations. The only certainty was that it was meant to shatter the process.

French police arrested the hitman, Ömer Güney, shortly afterwards. Initially, Turkish officials portrayed the murder as an 'inside job of the PKK'.[26] However, there were serious gaps in the government's story. Although Güney had been acting as a PKK sympathizer for a year and working at the Kurdish Institute of Paris where the assassination took place, his family knew him as a strong Turkish nationalist. His passport also showed that he had visited Ankara shortly before the assassination.

A year later, in January 2014, a tape recording of Ömer Güney was leaked on YouTube. On that tape, Güney was heard rehearsing the murder verbally with two people who were claimed to be MIT members. He was explaining how he would enter the Kurdish Institute, where the three female PKK members including Sakine Cansız would be, and what kind of killing he planned. He also identified another target, the head of KONGRA-GEL, Remzi Kartal.

I knew that Kartal visited the Kurdish Institute in Paris, if only occasionally. I remembered that he had returned from Paris only a few hours earlier when I went to Brussels to interview him in April 2013. This meant that Güney must have been closely watching those who visited the institute in Paris, as well as the leaders of the organization who resided in Brussels.

Following the leak, the European wing of the PKK recognized that the tape was authentic. 'Five or six people who knew Güney have confirmed that the voice in the recording is his,' one of them told me. I rang Remzi Kartal to see how he felt when he heard he had been named as a probable target. 'I listened to the recording,' he said calmly. 'Ömer Güney says that MIT gave the instruction. Either that is true, or MIT should publicly disclose all the information they have about Güney and the Paris murders.'

In 2015, *Le Monde* newspaper ran an account of the 70-page list of charges by the Paris prosecution office regarding the assassination of Sakine Cansız and her two friends. The indictment involved the claims that had appeared in the Turkish press following the murders, as well as of the leaked tape of the conversation between Ömer Güney and two MIT officials. Another claim in the indictment was from the pro-government press, which said that Ömer Güney was in contact with a man named Kozanlı Ömer, who was known as a shadowy but influential imam of the Gülen movement.

The French prosecutor believed that MIT was involved in the murder in some way. It was the first time that the name of a foreign intelligence agency had appeared in an indictment in France. The relevant statement ran:

> There were several elements that created the suspicion that MIT might play a role in the planning and preparation of the assas-sinations. In fact, Ömer Güney's spying activity is now proven and it is known that he is secretly in touch with a lot of people in Turkey [...]. However, there is insufficient research to iden-tify whether MIT has officially committed these deeds with the approval of their superiors or whether they did so independently, to undermine or stultify the peace process, without the knowl-edge of MIT.[27]

The French prosecutor asked the Turkish government whether Ömer Güney actually worked for MIT and if he was in touch with Ankara. He could get no response at all. Immediately after being arrested, Güney had asked for the Turkish embassy in Paris to be informed, which was viewed as an 'illuminating' tip for the French prosecutor and the Paris law enforcement agency, and led to their belief that the murder was committed with the knowledge of the Turkish government. The prosecutor remarked in the list of charges that this strengthened suspicions about the government's hand in the events, but also mentioned that the Gülen movement's followers in MIT could have been responsible.

Does this all sound like a movie plot? Unfortunately, the Paris murders, which were one of the main reasons for the loss of trust during the peace process, were very real. So was Ömer Güney. Yet the Kurdish movement chose not to blame the Turkish government for the murders outright, instead tending to accept the argument that it was the Gülen movement that had orchestrated the murders to disrupt the Kurdish negotiations.

The KCK co-chair, Cemil Bayık, in an interview on 10 March 2015, said, 'MIT acknowledged the Paris murder, yet they said it was the Gülenists among them [who were guilty].'[28] Bayik also told another journalist that the head of MIT, Hakan Fidan,

had said that their official documents were used, that there were documents generated via the technology used inside the organization. They never denied MIT was uninvolved, but they said they didn't do it. It was committed by a certain group inside MIT, namely, Gülen movement members and neo-nationalists.[29]

One of the Europe-based heads of PKK, Zübeyir Aydar, talking to *Libération* newspaper, 'disagreed with the claim that the Turkish government is behind the assassinations'. He said he 'does not believe such a crime would serve the Turkish government. However, there are dark powers that want to sabotage the peace process.'[30] According to Aydar, those dark powers within the Turkish state can be defined as

'Green Gladio',[31] a nickname for a religious group acting as the new deep state and the perpetrator of the Paris murders, since the colour green is known to be a symbol of Islam. There was a consensus among Kurdish politicians that the religious group 'that had built a parallel state'[32] was the Gülen movement.

Following the Paris murders, the Kurdish movement thus pointed the finger at 'power groups' in Turkey that sought to impede the peace process. Even when Ömer Güney's tape came to light, MIT was never directly blamed by the PKK administration. MIT was criticized for its failure to control the 'powers' inside the agency, but the true blame lay at the door of the 'Green Gladio', 'the parallel state', and more explicitly the Gülen community. Had the lines of communication not been open between MIT and the PKK regarding these murders, it would undoubtedly not have been possible for the PKK to maintain their calm, given the horrendous nature of the incident, and they would surely have blamed MIT. It is fair to say that the MIT officials who had been deployed to communicate with the PKK accused the Gülenists of being the perpetrators. MIT and the PKK had clearly both reached the conclusion that the Gülen movement was doing its best to ensure that the Kurdish peace process would not work.

A peace process for the wrong reasons

Gülen's attempt to hamper negotiations with the PKK ironically accelerated a process involving the PKK, HDP and Öcalan on one side, and Erdoğan and the AKP on the other. Each of these parties had its own agenda when commencing the peace process, and restoring long-violated rights to the Kurds was not at the top of their list of desirable outcomes. There was no shared vision of where the process should wind up or even a common definition of the Kurdish issue.

The most obvious reason behind the attempt was that neither party had come to defeat the other militarily. This is reflected in the words of former commander-in-chief of the Turkish army İlker Başbuğ, and those of Murat Karayılan. In 2010, Başbuğ famously claimed ironically that 'We have finished PKK off five times since 1984.'[33] The PKK leader Murat Karayılan also acknowledged that there was no end in sight from fighting with weapons. 'We could not defeat the Turkish army,' he said, 'and nor could they vanquish the PKK.'[34]

From the standpoint of the AKP government, the confrontation with the Gülen movement – the battle with a parallel state, as they liked to call it – had just started. There were three critical elections due to take place: local elections in March 2014, the first presidential election in August later the same year and a general election in June 2015. Not only had the AKP government decided that it could not afford another battlefront, but it had also calculated that a sustained ceasefire meant more votes.

Scaling down the war footing was also an aim the PKK had pursued when sitting at the negotiating table. However, after the collapse of the process, the governing group of the organization resented this decision, saying that

> in the spring of 2013, we had been ready to deepen the concept of the People's Revolutionary War but had not been able to express this view to Öcalan, who had started a dialogue with the government, because we had respect and loyalty towards our leader.[35]

But it was not only a matter of 'respect and loyalty'. The Syrian civil war had just erupted and for the first time there had emerged an opportunity for an autonomous Kurdish state, which had to be fought for and led. This development degraded the fight in Turkey to second place in the priority list of the PKK, which made a negotiation process with the Turkish state all the more reasonable.

As for Öcalan, both the stakes and the rewards were high, depending on the outcome of the process. It could have led to a real peace, which would turn him from a terrorist chief into a Mandela-like peacemaker and be likely to accord him a more comfortable house arrest option, rescuing him from his then isolated situation in İmralı prison. This is why, after a channel for discussion with MIT had reopened, he had begun to devise road maps for both the peace process and a new Middle

East. 'Many in the PKK were skeptical of Öcalan's intentions,' says Gareth H. Jenkins, 'but, given the heights to which the organization had elevated him in its propaganda, once the dialogue had been embraced by Öcalan, the organization had little choice but to do likewise.'[36]

Many were concerned about whether the AKP was honestly interested in seriously considering the Kurdish movement's demands for equal rights. Or was Erdoğan using the peace process to buy time before the elections? Critics of the process expressed their apprehension, saying the PKK would exploit the process to gain more control and stock up arms in south-east Turkey. However, such arguments did not benefit the process at all, nor could they be called anything more than conjecture. At that time, I believed that looking for sincerity or goodwill in a leader involved in conflict resolution is futile. I thought that if the technical structure and framework of the process had been set right from the beginning, it might stumble and falter but it would continue to run. In one of our meetings, Jonathan Powell, former aide to Tony Blair in the Northern Ireland peace process, told me, 'The key in conflict resolution is to keep moving.' He likened the negotiation process to riding a bicycle. 'You need to keep pedalling to prevent it from falling,' he said.[37] Of course, pedalling in the wrong direction may keep the bike running, but eventually it will cause it to crash into a wall. The logical question would be why a government would steer the bike so that it crashes. This is where intentions can keep the bike going forward or make it swerve off course. If the parties at the table do not want a resolution and are just buying time to suit their own agenda, the bike hits the wall. Simple as that.

The latest peace process between the Turkish government and the PKK commenced with Abdullah Öcalan's letter at the time of Newroz and survived for almost two and a half years. The technical structure of the process was as follows. A delegation of elected Kurdish politicians from the People's Democratic Party (HDP, known at that time as the BDP) would act as interlocutors, conveying messages from Öcalan to PKK officials in Qandil and Europe and AKP officials in Ankara. Two agents from MIT, referred to as 'the officials' by Öcalan and the HDP delegation, would always accompany them during the meetings, which usually lasted five to six hours. Notes of the meeting taken by the HDP delegation were brought to Qandil and Europe in person and debated there with the high-ranking PKK officials. The minutes of each meeting between the HDP and Öcalan were also given to Recep Tayyip Erdoğan within hours of the end of the meeting.[38]

Öcalan had written three letters explaining the process, one for the HDP, its political wing, one for the exiled members of the PKK, and one for the high-ranking PKK officials in Qandil. Remzi Kartal, head of KONGRA-GEL (the Kurdistan People's Congress, a branch of the PKK) explained to me what was in these letters:[39]

> Our Leadership [Öcalan] started seeing MIT members in September 2012. By the time of the HDP delegation's first meeting on 3 January 2013, they had reached an agreement. These handwritten letters involve political aspects of that agreement. Actually, the whole thing started in Oslo. Every little detail had been debated in Oslo and it was in relation to those details that Öcalan wrote three protocols. The Turkish government never replied to the protocols. Now there is a new process, but it is just a continuation of the Oslo talks.

FOUR

The PKK Embraces the World

A day on Qandil Mountain

I took a pick-up truck from my hotel bound for a place that my government sees as 'the haven of evil'. A few hours' drive away from the south Kurdistan capital, Irbil, stands Qandil Mountain, where more than 5,000 PKK guerrillas and high-ranking executives live in a semi-nomadic fashion. After passing through several checkpoints managed by the Peshmerga of Iraqi Kurdistan's president Masoud Barzani,[1] we came to the 'PKK Medya Defence Area',[2] a place occupied only by PKK guerrillas. I was not the only journalist trying to reach Qandil on 25 April 2013. A horde of reporters from the Turkish mainstream media was flocking to PKK headquarters for a press conference to be held by the then KCK co-chair, Murat Karayılan.

The guerrilla standing at the virtual border of the Medya Defence Area was checking the journalists' IDs and press cards. 'Oh, even the Republic is here,' he said to my colleague in front of me in a jeering tone. 'We never thought the Republic would come all this way to visit us.' His play on words could only be understood by someone who knows the Turkish language and the Kurdish issue. The newspaper *Cumhuriyet* (Turkish for 'Republic') has been a defender of Kemalism, and its readership consists mainly of secular nationalists. The guard's remark also carried the idea that the Republic of Turkey, or Turkish state, 'had come all this way' to listen to their side of the story – which was unprecedented in view of the fact that the Turkish state had only 'visited' Qandil in the form of military actions before.

Could we have imagined something like this six or seven months earlier? In the past, it was a considerable challenge for a journalist to get to Qandil to interview PKK officials. You had to find at least ten mediators and references, and you had to do this as covertly as possible. Let's say you took care of that. But the Turkish government would nearly always find out about it, one way or another, and try to sabotage your meeting. If they did not find out about it and you succeeded in getting an interview with a PKK leader (which was usually Murat Karayılan himself), you would most probably be prosecuted. There were several cases when this became a reality. If neither happened, the interview transcript would sit in an editorial in tray waiting for a courageous editor to publish before it became out of date.

But now here we were, on Qandil Mountain, journalists from mainstream pro-government outlets such as ATV, A Haber, *Sabah*, *Habertürk*, Show TV, *Milliyet*, *Vatan* and CNN Türk and opposition media such as *Hürriyet*, *Radikal*, *Cumhuriyet* and *Birgün*. The last few days had been quite strange both for us and for the PKK people who were in charge of liaison with the journalists.

The average lifespan of a PKK guerrilla is about two and a half years.[3] Having said that, people whose main job was to stay alive now suddenly had to deal with the mainstream media's daily routines, such as meeting deadlines, wiring news, bypassing colleagues to get a scoop or finding the best light for a photo shoot. They were exposed to countless phone calls and dozens of questions.

'*Rojbaş*,' said one colleague to a guerrilla on the phone ('hello' in Kurdish). 'You have to arrange an exclusive interview with Karayılan!'

'Have to?' he asked, shocked. 'You will come to the press conference, right? What do you mean by an exclusive interview?'

'Where exactly can I find a wi-fi connection in Qandil?' asked another colleague.

'We don't offer that service,' the guerrilla replied. 'There is no 3G either. But believe me, our place isn't the only one that doesn't have these facilities.'

The absurdity of these dialogues was an offshoot of the mainstream media's decades-long ignorance about and belated interest in the Kurdish movement.

The encounter also suggested that a new era was beginning. Now the PKK had the chance to reintroduce itself to the Turkish audience, who had been indoctrinated by the state regarding the Kurdish issue. Even though the Turkish government kept an eye in the sky with its drones, it was the government itself that had enabled this meeting – not because it believed that it would be fair to demonstrate that the people on Qandil Mountain were also made of flesh and blood, but because it would be easier for them to pursue a peace process if the public ceased to think of the other side as the Devil. It seemed to be trying to correct the manipulative disinformation about the Kurdish issue that had prevailed for so long and was one of the main reasons behind the emergence of the PKK.

On that particular day, the PKK was to announce that it would withdraw its forces from Turkey to northern Iraq as part of the first phase of the peace process. Sceptics on both sides were suspicious of the organization's motives. From the Turkish secular nationalist perspective, there was a hidden agenda and the PKK had been promised self-rule in the Kurdish region in return for supporting Erdoğan's desire for an executive presidency. Kurdish sceptics asserted that Öcalan was making this huge concession because he was under government control in prison and 'selling the Kurdish cause for his own sake'.

However, neither was even part of the truth.

PKK and KCK leaders were ready not only to announce a withdrawal but also to make clear what the organization was and what it aimed to become. This was no trivial gain for the first phase of the peace process. The PKK engaged in this repositioning in order to become a political power that was not marginal or isolated.

As a prominent Kurdish politician put it at the beginning of the peace process, the movement strongly believed that 'they should disclaim the terrorist stigma from now on'.[4] Other than pragmatic, tangible demands like the right to education in the mother tongue, the PKK and the leaders of the movement also wanted to be taken off US and EU terrorist and drug-smuggler lists.[5] The atmosphere of the peace process was helping them reach their lofty goal of becoming a legitimate political power, not only in Turkey but also in Syria, Iran and Iraq. That was the underlying motive for the decision to meet the Turkish media, which had served as a vehicle to cover up state-inflicted atrocities in the 1990s. However, on that day in Qandil, there was no sign of a grudge, only sarcasm.

We had waited for several hours in a jerry-built place, since the PKK leaders had needed to change the press conference venue for security reasons and because of heavy drone surveillance. In the meantime, we were served lunch: chicken, rice and *çoban salatası*, a traditional Greek–Turkish salad with cucumber, tomato and onion. 'You can eat it. It is not poisoned or anything,' said one guerrilla as he put the food on our table. 'We don't stab people in the back like your beloved state does.' Without waiting for a reply, he continued, 'Plus, our chicken is organic. Real organic! Not like the ones you buy in your town markets for 30 Turkish lira.' Nobody really knew how to respond to these bitter jokes other than giving solemn half-smiles.

It was hard not to recall all those stories about these youngsters that I have listened to or read over the course of my career. A renowned Kurdish poet, Bejan Matur, had conducted interviews with former PKK guerrillas who mostly got caught, served time and then fled the country for a European city.

Kendal, from the city of Maraş, had learned how to play the flute at primary school. One day while he was playing the only song he knew, the teacher stopped him: 'That song is Kurdish. Never play that again.' He was startled. How can there be such a thing as a Kurdish flute? When he got back home, he asked his mother whether they were Kurdish or Turkish. 'We are Kırmanc,' she replied, not exactly knowing what that meant. Before finishing secondary school, he went up to the mountains:

> I was not a patriot. I did not know what socialism was either. So why did I join the PKK? I believe it was the Turkish regime that pushed us up to the mountains. If you grow up to armed

combat cars patrolling in your village constantly, you end up at the mountains.[6]

The son of a wealthy man, Rewan had lost his fingers and toes during a very cold winter night up there. His comrades had to 'slice' off the tips of his fingers in front of his eyes. He did not feel anything at the time, but the moment haunts him occasionally during his sleep. 'If it weren't for the PKK's violence, the name Kurd would not even be remembered,' he told Matur.[7]

I approached a group of guerrillas standing and watching the journalists from afar and tried to engage with them. *How is life here? How old are you? Why are you here?* I got one- or two-word replies. *Fine. Eighteen. For freedom. For my people, for the Kurds.* But when I dug deeper, their life stories had the same motifs, same darkness. A father beaten by the gendarmerie. A mother harassed by the police. A horrible teacher at school. A family member at the mountain. Several family members in jail. The urgency to hide one's language and identity. Social exclusion. Embarrassment. Anger. Resentment. One may think of these young kids as indoctrinated, brainwashed, and they very likely are. On the other hand, you can brainwash someone but you cannot inject them with those memories. They were very hurt, and it was their reality. When I was about to leave their side, one of them asked me why I was there. The presence of a load of journalists was confusing for them. 'To get to know you,' I replied. He smiled slyly. 'Well,' he said, 'you are late, *heval*.[8] A couple of decades late.'

Feeling as if I'd been punched in the stomach, I got on a truck that would take us to a meadow where the press conference was to take place. A plastic table covered with a PKK flag was set in a featureless clearing among the trees. Our bags were thoroughly searched before we neared the place, an act for which KCK leader Murat Karayılan apologized afterwards.

Karayılan and fellow PKK members Zeki Şengal and Hacer Zagros stood in front of a crowd of journalists who had come from Iraq, Iran, Syria and Turkey. Having a woman and a Yazidi next to the KCK leader for this historic announcement was a potential statement for the watching world that the PKK was led by women and by people of different beliefs. Karayılan started his speech by saying, 'I will now share with you our decision on how our guerrillas will leave Turkey and how the ceasefire will be restored in the following days.' He then went on to detail the steps to be taken:

1. Our guerrilla forces will withdraw by a route that they will decide. They will not withdraw without their weapons, since the route is dangerous, and there may be situations in which they need to defend themselves. There may even be wild animals, maybe wolves.

2. The withdrawal will start on 8 May 2013. It will be done discreetly and gradually, in line with the discipline of the guerrilla.

3. The forces from Turkey will come to northern Iraq. We expect the leadership of northern Iraq to respect that.

4. If an operation is mounted by the Turkish government, the withdrawal will cease and we will retaliate.

5. During the withdrawal, it is important that certain improvements are made by the Turkish government, such as an opportunity for our leader Öcalan to communicate with the world. These matters are mentioned in the letter that we have written to Öcalan and the government has also been informed.

6. To prevent any wrongdoing emanating from either side, an independent committee will monitor the withdrawal process.

After enumerating these points, Karayılan also mentioned that withdrawal was not an easy call for them to make but '[they] trusted Öcalan's trust in the government'.[9] Both the PKK and the HDP at the time insisted on a legal framework that would secure the withdrawal process. In this, they drew on a bitter memory. It was not the first time the PKK had agreed to withdraw from Turkey. The first withdrawal had happened in 1999 as a result of a quasi-negotiation with the Turkish military. Öcalan claimed that the former chief of the armed forces, İsmail Hakkı

Karadayı, and his successor, General Hüseyin Kıvrıkoğlu, had sent him messages in 1998–9 to curtail the war. The generals sought a ceasefire and wanted to gather the guerrilla forces in a single location so that a solution could be discussed. According to Öcalan, one of the generals said, 'If you declare that you have no intention of dividing the country and that you will renounce violence, then we can discuss everything.' Accordingly, in 1999, Öcalan declared a ceasefire and the guerrillas retreated. But things did not turn out the way they were supposed to.

A lawyer who had long acted on Öcalan's behalf, Cengiz Kapmaz, wrote about this incident in his book *Öcalan'ın İmralı Günleri* (*İmralı Journals*):

> According to Öcalan, for the Turkish state to take a step, the PKK should give an assurance. Therefore, a step that would enable a negotiation process should have come from the PKK. In Öcalan's mind, that step could be withdrawal. He shared this idea with his lawyers on 5 July 1999. He said that 'the cessation of hostilities and withdrawal could be a start. In practice, we can withdraw our forces to the south [northern Iraq] and then we can seek legal justification. That way, parliament's perspective may change.'[10]

Öcalan had planned the withdrawal to begin on 1 September 1999, and conveyed his message to the organization through his lawyers. What happened afterwards is recorded in Murat Karayilan's book, *Bir Savaşın Anatomisi* (*Anatomy of a War*):

> On 1 September, I had personally announced through our radio network the decision to withdraw. Two weeks later, there was tremendous chaos and panic among the guerrillas. Because we had not planned the withdrawal meticulously, the Turkish state saw it as an opportunity to attack. They planted ambushes and we lost serious numbers of guerrillas during the operation.[11]

A former PKK member who had defected from the organization when Öcalan was arrested claims more than 300 guerrillas were killed during that withdrawal and that this reinforced the mistrust of government promises.[12] Nearly six months later, on 16 February 1999, Abdullah Öcalan was captured in Kenya and brought to Turkey on a helicopter packed with Turkish commandos.

Karayılan had recalled that incident in order to explain why they were insisting on legislation:

> In 1999, our forces were ambushed while withdrawing. They all found themselves besieged in Amed [Diyarbakır]. They were killed after a ceasefire that had lasted five years. This time, for the withdrawal to be completed safely on both sides, the Turkish parliament should legislate for a commission to monitor the pull-out. That is what we want.[13]

He also mentioned that the Oslo talks had collapsed because of the lack of any legislation.

When the press conference in that Qandil meadow was over, only five of us from the Turkish media were allowed to go to another building in a barren area to conduct interviews with Karayılan, Zagros and Şengal.

The PKK's stance on peace negotiations was partly based on the fact that they would not want the armed struggle to end, since it would compromise their *raison d'être*. But PKK leaders disagreed among themselves, claiming that they were already engaged in politics and would continue with the political struggle even if they were to lay down their arms. 'How do I spend my days? I meet with political parties. I host guests coming from different places in the Middle East,' said Karayılan.

> Everybody is curious about what we will do when we have peace. Let peace come; we will have business to do. We do not have any personal demands. We have promised to dedicate our lives to this cause. After the armed struggle finishes, we will continue to serve in whatever way is suitable.[14]

Another KCK leader, Sabri Ok, had a similar point of view, telling the International Crisis Group,

Now is not the time to talk about returns. They will happen when the Kurdish problem is resolved, not the other way around. When the PKK decides that we are at a point of no return in the peace process, then it will go back to Turkey. No one will go down from the mountain before then. It's not just about going home. We see our struggle as permanent. Our primary goal is to solve the Kurdish problem, not to go home.[15]

On the other hand, KCK leader Cemil Bayık signalled a desire to return home and get involved in politics: 'Only if there is absolute peace would I return to Turkey. Turkey is beautiful. What would I do here? I would go into politics, since one cannot retire from the PKK.'[16]

The Turkish government's position on giving amnesty to PKK guerrillas was ambivalent. Even though the matter was not sidelined outright in the debate, technicalities such as conditions for homecoming were never discussed.

More crucial than the PKK leaders' fate was the fate of Öcalan. Although winning freedom for Öcalan was one of the main goals, the Kurdish side did not push for it at the beginning. But the PKK wanted to communicate with him in any way possible, by phone or videoconference. The last time Karayılan had spoken to Öcalan was in 1992, when he was in Russia. They had talked on the phone constantly at that time until Öcalan's arrest. Karayılan had not used a phone since 2006 because the PKK had received a tip-off from a reliable sources that an assassination plan was being hatched for him over phone signals. He abandoned phones the very same day. This was why they were not allowed in interviews. 'At first, of course, I had a lot of difficulty,' Karayılan explained, 'because when I had phones I was able to talk to Europe, Russia and Rojava [West Kurdistan, northern Syria] whenever I wanted; it is not possible now.' The PKK usually communicates with exiled leaders in Europe through a network of couriers, but with guerrilla forces they use a shortwave wireless system. 'Naturally, the Turkish government eavesdrops on all of these radio conversations,' said Karayılan with a smile. 'Sometimes I even address them: "Guys, OK, you are listening, we know, you may even be recording us, but you are also interfering. At least do not interfere."' A sense of humour was obviously a way of surviving on Qandil Mountain.

The Gezi uprising and the Kurds

The Turkish government did not legislate for the PKK's withdrawal, but declared that the governors and the military were commanded not to take action if they encountered guerrillas during the pull-out. A senior Turkish security official was quoted as saying,

> The PKK has to complete withdrawal first to show the Turkish public that they are not a threat any more. They have to convey a sense of trust so that politicians can act. We can't just push laws through parliament: the people have to accept them.[17]

The PKK had proceeded with the withdrawal without a formal agreement, a timeline or a monitoring body. But in their eyes it was a huge concession. Certain groups in the PKK and the Kurdish movement were fiercely critical of Öcalan and the KCK leadership who had complied with Öcalan's call for withdrawal.

The withdrawal started on 8 May 2013. Photos of the guerrillas walking with their AK-47s on their shoulders and their hiking sticks in their hands were published in the papers to show that the PKK was leaving Turkish soil. However, something unexpected happened at the end of that same month: the Gezi uprising began in Istanbul and swept the whole country in a few days, including the Kurdish region.

The Gezi incident started out as a small protest against Erdoğan's insistence on turning Gezi Park and Taksim Square into what he called the 'Historic Topçu Barracks'. He had up his sleeve an urban-development plan involving a new mosque and a mall for Istanbul's heart, Taksim. The initial response to the plan came from a group of environmentalists who opposed the felling of the trees and demolishing Gezi Park, the only public place in Taksim where people could enjoy a peaceful moment. Erdoğan's arrogant promotion of the urban plan fuelled protest among people all over the country, mainly secular leftists and young people who for years had been accused of being apolitical and apathetic.

Erdoğan called the protesters vandals, 'just a few looters',[18] puppets of foreign powers and Israel lobbyists, and insisted on building the barracks and a mosque in Taksim Square. He later mobilized the crowd at a rally to boo the mother of an Alawite boy, Berkin Elvan, who had been killed while going to buy bread for breakfast at the height of the clashes.[19]

The Gezi uprising was an independent and genuine protest against a government that was constantly dictating how people should lead their lives and curbing individual freedoms in accordance with its idea of a 'proper citizen', saying that they wanted to 'bring up a religious generation'.[20] Among other things, the uprising was perhaps a manifestation of young people reclaiming their personal dignity.

The Kurdish movement was not sure what position to take in the very early days of Gezi. Sırrı Süreyya Önder, an HDP MP and a member of the HDP delegation that had visited Öcalan in İmralı, was actually the first political figure to support the movement. He had gone to Gezi Park and stood in front of the designated construction site, symbolically stopping the crane that would pull out the trees and flatten the park. It was, however, a tricky situation for the Kurdish politicians, since they were in the middle of a negotiation process with the AKP government, whose leader, Erdoğan, was denouncing the uprising as a coup and everyone supporting it as a traitor.

Another HDP MP and a member of the HDP delegation to İmralı, İdris Baluken, stated, 'Slogans and images to reinforce the status quo have become the dominant subjects of these protests. As the HDP, we cannot stand alongside these racist, nationalist, sexist, monist, militarist circles under any circumstances whatsoever.'[21] Baluken was referring to many Turkish youths who showed up at the Gezi protests with Turkish flags or posters of Atatürk. A couple of months later we learned from Ahmet Türk, who had spoken to me, that Öcalan had at the time criticized the HDP for 'not comprehending what Gezi was about'.[22]

Gezi was far removed from what Baluken had described. Kurds and the HDP's constituency in particular were in Taksim Square protesting shoulder to shoulder with secular people, leftists and 'White Turks'.[23] Admittedly, once or twice Kurds had had some verbal clash with the representatives of the Labour Party, but that was all.

One evening during Gezi, I received a message on my phone, with a video attached. It came from Izmir, a city described as a Kemalist White Turk fortress, and read, 'Ezgi, at this moment, secular old ladies are dancing the *halay* with Kurds. Has the dream come true?' Five metres away from a lady wearing an Atatürk bandana on her forehead sat youngsters holding an Apo flag. Sometimes one could hear slogans like '*Türkiye laiktir, laik kalacak*' ('Turkey is secular and will remain secular'); at others, '*Biji serok Apo*' ('Long live Apo'). That young person might not have supported that woman's devotion to Atatürk and she in turn might have been disgusted by his love of Apo, yet there was a cascade of tolerance.

The Gezi uprising was an unfortunate opportunity for the secular Kemalists to experience state brutality at first hand. Their sons and daughters on the streets were accused by the government of being terrorists, and rally police mercilessly fired gas bombs at them. This practice was very common in the Kurdish region whenever people took to the streets or even tried to celebrate Newroz, but if you had been following those incidents on mainstream Turkish media, you would think those people were indeed terrorists and the rally police were just doing their job. Gezi helped many to see the discrepancy between truth and what was being portrayed in the media, which had always been a mouthpiece of the state when it came to the Kurdish issue.

Recognition of this reality gap was voiced on social media. One protester, frustrated by the media's coverage of Gezi, tweeted, 'Friends, apologies to you all. We have been following the Kurdish problem through the media for years. We were idiots to do so. Sorry.' Another wrote,

In these last four or five days, I have felt ashamed of what I have done up till now. The people who did this to us – I can't imagine what they must have done to my Kurdish brothers. We woke up to the truth too late.[24]

What the Gezi protests had managed to achieve was a magical enlightenment, which made people realize that if violation of human rights had become part of the modus operandi of the government state, no one was safe. A woman could not be safe where a homosexual was in danger. Wherever a Kurd felt he was suffocating under pressure, no one could go about his or her daily life safely. At any time, anyone could be the target of the kind of slander that had been directed at the Alawites, Armenians or Jews of Turkey for decades. It was this wondrous enlightenment that drew people together on the most fundamental and vital common ground of humanity.

However, like all magical things, it did not last for long. The spirit of Gezi never turned its human capital into a viable political alternative. Why? First, because the majority of Gezi protesters were acting independently as members of generation Y. They did not know or embrace the usual political organizational tools. Second, the protests had erupted spontaneously without a long-term goal, plan or leader. Third, the state's response was so brutal that it managed to destroy the unanimity of the protest. Eight people lost their lives, while 8,000 were injured, 104 of them sustaining serious head injuries.

Incomplete withdrawal and the faltering peace process

In the summer of 2013, following the Gezi protests and developments in Syria, the PKK saw a need to reorganize its leadership. Murat Karayılan, the former chair of the KCK, was moved to head the military wing, the HPG. Cemil Bayık and Besê Hozat replaced Karayılan and became co-chairs of the KCK. Bayık is one of the founders of the PKK and is seen as more hawkish than Karayılan. Therefore, the reshuffle sent a message to the PKK's constituency that it was not soft and would not make any concessions to the Turkish state.

The harsh response to the Gezi protesters also illustrated the mindset of the government. What happened during the protests – all the police violence, all Erdoğan's intolerant statements about the protesters, all the young lives that were lost – caused the peace process to falter and eventually brought the withdrawal to an end.

The KCK Council announced on 9 September 2013 that they were 'stopping the guerrillas':

> Even though the Kurdish Freedom Movement had met its share of the responsibilities, the government neither appreciated any of our efforts nor advanced the process. During the nine-month ceasefire, improvements were made to the military that could not have been done during a time of war. They did not even amend the anti-terror law. They behaved as if there were no talks in İmralı, no negotiation. They acted as if we had not made our demands clear. Therefore, we are ending the withdrawal but the ceasefire will continue.[25]

It is uncertain how many guerrillas had left Turkey during the withdrawal. According to the government, the number was around 15 per cent of the total, while the PKK claimed the figure was nearer 60 per cent. Also, the PKK kept a strong presence in several areas while vacating others. Rather than going to northern Iraq, some militants – particularly those recruited locally – appeared to have simply merged into the civilian population.[26]

✳

The peace process began to falter but somehow continued, in typical Turkish fashion. The Turkish state wanted to inhibit the Kurdish movement and preferred to pursue the process through Öcalan, who was under its control. As a result, the state meddled with the composition of the HDP delegation that visited him in İmralı prison during the process.[27]

Gultan Kısanak, former co-chair of the HDP and the acting co-mayor of Diyarbakır, never had the chance to be in the delegation, even though her party insisted that her involvement would be crucial. The reason for not including her was video footage in which Kısanak's envoy had been stopped by PKK guerrillas and she had taken the opportunity to talk to them and give them a hug.

Ahmet Türk, the then co-mayor of Mardin, was also removed from the delegation because he had criticized the government for not abiding by the ceasefire and sending jets to Qandil.

Altan Tan, an HDP MP who mostly represents pious Kurds, had been dismissed because of what he had said in the first meeting with Öcalan. The minutes of that first meeting had been leaked to the press, causing controversy on several fronts, especially Öcalan's remark about supporting Erdoğan's long-time ambition to become president.[28]

After Altan Tan's dismissal, Sırrı Süreyya Önder was also vetoed by the AKP because of his support of the Gezi uprising. He had been sidelined for months.

The last victim of this 'veto mechanism' was the co-chair of the HDP, Selahattin Demirtaş. After he had failed to approve a democratic package set before the public, he was expelled from the delegation and never returned.

Expelling HDP officials from the delegation served a certain purpose for the government. It was a means of showing both the public and the Kurdish movement that everything was orchestrated by the will of the government, not by the Kurds. The government had also decided when the delegation could travel to İmralı Island and cancelled certain trips when it took issue with statements by the HDP and/or Qandil officials, saying 'the boat [that would take the delegation to İmralı] is broken.' The phrase 'koster bozuldu' – 'The boat is broken' – had become shorthand for the government's arbitrary position.[29]

Pervin Buldan, an HDP MP and a standing member of the İmralı delegation, gave me details of the İmralı visits:

> Öcalan attends the meeting carrying a hefty dossier, but he never opens it. Actually, he did once open it to take out the letters he had written to Qandil, the BDP [HDP] and Europe. It is always the same agent from the MIT who accompanies us during the meetings. The meetings start at noon and end before dawn. Last

time, it lasted for four hours but this time it lasted only two and a half hours because the boat was out of service, so we had to start late for the island. When time is up, the official accompanying us alerts us. Mr Öcalan always lets us have the last word so that we can ask if there is anything we'd like clarified. The weather is crucial, because we return to Istanbul by boat, while the MIT official goes by helicopter. So they don't want us delayed until sunset.[30]

Structurally, the process was designed in such a way as to turn the HDP into a postman whose main job was to do the dirty work of dealing with the terrorists in Qandil. This was a shrewd strategy on the part of the government, and one which had three important consequences. First, it caused the HDP to be squeezed between Qandil, Ankara and Imralı and inhibited it from becoming a powerful actor in the process. Second, it gave the impression that there was an unethical bargaining process going on between the Kurdish movement and the government. Third, and most importantly, it blocked Qandil from becoming an active participant.

It was apparent that, other than Abdullah Öcalan and Tayyip Erdoğan, everyone involved in the process could at some point become disposable and irrelevant. However, it had been crucial for PKK officials in Qandil to speak to Öcalan directly. Advanced technology could have helped to get over the limitations of legality and security. However, although the government had been asked several times to agree to high-ranking PKK officials having video or phone conferencing with Öcalan,[31] the request had been declined.

Not including the PKK as a third party in the process also had its problems in terms of conflict resolution. Jonathan Powell, who had played a small part in the Kurdish peace process after the Oslo talks, also drew attention in Diyarbakır to the downside of this issue:

Negotiation means that you need to have a three-legged table. But here I see only two legs. The government and Öcalan. Whereas talking directly to the people who actually hold a gun in their hands is crucial for a strong negotiating table. In a peace process, you cannot rely on just two leaders.[32]

Unfortunately, this was precisely the situation. The peace process lacked credibility and lay in the hands of two leaders, one of them jailed for life. Relying on a jailed leader had exacerbated the distrust among the guerrillas, who thought Öcalan had been pushed by the government to make concessions. As a result, it had become harder for the top leadership of the PKK to manage the rank and file of the organization.

'Some people [the HDP delegation] are going and meeting [Öcalan]. They are not our representatives. They are not PKK,' explained Duran Kalkan, one of the key players in Qandil:

> They are not guerrillas. Everybody should know this. The HDP is not the same as the PKK; everybody has their own agenda and within that agenda everybody is pursuing their own battle. We are not going to believe anything unless we contact [Öcalan] directly. The guerrillas will not listen to anybody without getting in touch with Öcalan.[33]

Many in the Kurdish movement acknowledged that they trusted neither Erdoğan nor the government but that they trusted Öcalan and believed in him.[34] However, this should not imply that the Kurds did not expect anything from the government. They wanted to see solid steps taken, and taken fast. On the other hand, in terms of long-term goals, the Turkish government had neither a long list nor a foreseeable endgame. The only thing that could have been concluded from its discourse was the disarmament of the PKK. How and when that should be realized was not apparent. The AKP officials demanded a permanent ceasefire, followed by withdrawal of the PKK forces from Turkey, order in the Kurdish region, an end to 'taxation of Kurdish businesses and shop owners by the PKK' and, finally, disarmament.

The Kurdish movement insisted that certain commissions in and out of parliament should be formed. A truth and reconciliation commission would help mend the old wounds suffered in the 40-year war on both the Turkish and Kurdish sides. NGOs with expertise in conflict resolution advised that such a commission should be independent, rather than a parliamentary one, since 'such commissions [in parliament, under the rules of procedure of the Turkish parliament] are generally obliged to produce a report and dissolve after four months, which is too short, since truth commissions typically take years to finish their work'.[35]

Unsurprisingly, no commissions were formed, but a 'wise persons' committee was established. It consisted of academics, journalists, actors and singers, mainly pro-government. The HDP was allowed to decide on a very small number of the members. The main task of the committee was to listen to the concerns of the public and persuade people that a peace process was what Turkey needed. It was, in fact, a PR job. Several of the intellectuals resigned from the committee after seeing the government's response to the Gezi uprising and others stepped down on realizing that 'the committee is another stalling tactic on the part of the government'.[36] Therefore, committee members who had not been embraced by the Kurdish movement in the first place failed to serve their purpose.

So, what concrete contribution did the government make to the peace process, other than forming this futile committee, allowing private education in the mother tongue and lifting the morning pledge of allegiance? Nothing much. In March 2014, thousands of Kurdish activists charged with being members of the PKK/KCK were released because of a law that shortened the pre-verdict detention time from ten years to five.

In July of the same year, a law was passed in the Turkish parliament that gave the government authority to resolve the Kurdish issue, as well as legal protection for all public officials involved. Although this law was hailed as a legal basis for the process, its true purpose was to protect MIT, whose boss had been targeted by the Gülen movement. Close scrutiny of this law shows that it was enacted especially for MIT, giving it the authority to establish direct contacts with all individuals, entities, organizations and institutions and conduct talks with prisoners. It also puts a responsibility on prosecutors to first contact MIT in respect of all denunciations and complaints related to it, and drop investigations if the actions fall within the scope of MIT's work; and it rules out calling the head of MIT to testify in court without the prime minister's permission. This law was intended neither to improve Kurdish rights nor to give the peace process a legal structure. Therefore, it was perceived only as an attempt by the government to keep the ceasefire going until the election of 2015.

The Turkish government was treating the peace process as a Turkish issue without appreciating that it was going to be a definitive component in world politics in the very short term. The Syrian civil war had turned into a quagmire that begat such evils as ISIS. The political branch of the Syrian Kurds, the PYD, was an organization influenced by Öcalan and the PKK, and the PYD and its armed militia, the YPG, proved the most effective fighting force to defeat ISIS and other jihadist groups. Therefore, they have become a proxy force for the US in its war against ISIS, which has changed the whole equation in the Middle East, as well as in Turkey. A successful peace process with the PKK at home would not only contribute to a future stable Syria but also guarantee security and power for Turkey in the Middle East.

FIVE

Syria and the Kurdish Peace

We have brothers in Syria

S ipping his coffee, 30-year-old Zilan[1] looked at me and nonchalantly let drop that he was leaving for Raqqa tomorrow, as if it was the most natural thing to do.

'Al-Raqqa?' I asked. 'Where ISIS is in control? Where they slaughter Kurds and journalists if they find any?' He nodded, with a smile. It was the summer of 2016.

Zilan is a Kurdish journalist from south-eastern Turkey who works as an editor in one of the Kurdish news outlets. He does not remember his father, who died soon after being released from prison. He was ten years old when he first met a PKK guerrilla. In the 1990s it was routine practice for guerrillas to pay visits to communities for propaganda purposes. At that time, not supporting the PKK made people in the Kurdish region subject to neighbourhood pressure. The daughter of one of his relatives joined the PKK and was killed by a Turkish bombardment of the camp where they were training. The whole village went to collect her dead body, along with 13 others. Because Zilan was only 11, they hid him in the back of a truck, which actually saved his life. The village convoy was met by a Turkish military troop, whose soldiers opened fire at them.

'My brother was saved because he was covered by the dead and wounded bodies that fell on him,' he remembered:

They seized the young girls and asked them to bare their chests. They were trying to bring us down psychologically, too. Imagine:

we went there to pick up 14 dead bodies and 13 more people got killed. Most of my relatives did not go back home that day; they joined the PKK. The very same day!

He and his peers were voracious readers during their teenage and adolescent years. They used to attend funerals during the day and come home to read books in the evening. They thought they needed to develop themselves politically in order to take on the state. 'If the state wages war, we have to wage war too. Whatever the state knows, we have to know too.' That was the dominant understanding.

Zilan used to deliver magazines and organize street protests in Diyarbakır. There was a saying going around then: 'Who will stay in the city if everyone goes up to the mountains?' They did not allow the weak and the disabled to go to the mountains anyway, and Zilan walked with a limp. 'One is a guerrilla, another distributes magazines,' Zilan said. 'Another keeps the culture alive through folk dancing.' Everyone felt they had a duty of some kind to fulfil. Even folklore was more than a hobby to them: it was their mission. Everything became a tool for resistance and an expression of patriotism.

One day when he was in his twenties, Zilan joined a demonstration to protest against the arrest of Öcalan. He was arrested and tortured continuously for eight days. His closest friend fell during a protest and was dragged along by a tank for three kilometres. His body was never returned home. His family applied to the European Court of Human Rights and received compensation for the violation of the right to live. 'But we still don't know where the corpse is,' said Zilan. 'Now, tell me what I am supposed to do with all these memories.'[2] Once he was free, he fled abroad and never came back.

His story was typical of those of many Kurdish people who were children during the 1990s.

'Why are you going to Raqqa?' I asked Zilan.

'Because I want to witness history changing,' he replied.

I remembered I had heard that expression several times before from different Kurdish people. One of them was the co-chair of the HDP, Selahattin Demirtaş. 'I can tell you that the ill fortune that the

Kurds have suffered for a hundred years is turning around,' he told me in August 2012 when the Syrian civil war broke out and Syrian Kurds began gaining autonomy in the northern part of the country.[3] They called it the Rojava revolution, a Kurdish term meaning 'Western Kurdistan'.

'Kurds fight against ISIS, and they gain status in Syria; they add value for everyone. Rojava is a source of pride for all Kurds,' explained Zilan. 'The Middle East is a swamp, and Kurds bring not only other Kurds but also Turkmens, Arabs and Christians into the middle of this swamp and create a model that inspires hope.'

A new century was beginning: or at least that was what 30 million stateless Kurds thought. They believed that, with the chaos in Syria, they had a critical moment to regain control over Kurdistan, which had been divided into four parts after World War I. To achieve this goal, Kurds scattered throughout the Middle East needed to think beyond their immediate local issues. The power vacuum in Syria opened an opportunity for the formation of a track along which a Kurdish train could move with some momentum. The PKK, the HDP, the PYD, the KRG, Peshmerga, Barzani, Talabani, Öcalan – would all be the carriages of that Kurdish train. Although these carriages had expressed their differences about political direction over the decades, there was no way they could stop the train once it had started rolling. This time, they believed, the Kurdish train would keep moving and changing the course of history.

An autonomous Kurdish region in Syria does indeed represent a model for Turkey's Kurds. Of course there are serious differences between the political environment in Turkey and in Syria. The power gap that allows the establishment of an autonomous region in Syria does not exist in Turkey. The PKK is aware of that but, for Kurds, Syria serves as a signal to them that they may achieve their goal if they are properly organized, however tough the circumstances are.

Sure enough, the developments in Syria had played a major role in the second year of the Kurdish peace process in Turkey. Many Kurds living on the Turkish side of the border had cousins, uncles and neighbours on the Syrian side fighting against ISIS.

The co-mayor of Mardin back then, Ahmet Türk, explained to me what that means:

> Turkey's Syrian policy is making things harder. And you cannot rationalize this policy by just saying, 'We are against the PYD, not the Syrian Kurds.' I will be very blunt here: if you continue to treat Syrian Kurds in this way, you will lose Turkey's Kurds too. Kurdish people in the region are having a hard time tolerating this because they all have a family member in Syria. Many of the Kurdish tribes are split down the middle on the border, half in Turkey, half in Syria. People in Syria are suffering all kinds of cruelty and they want a safe autonomous region so that they can defend and protect themselves. This is not a threat to Turkey but an advantage.[4]

Rojava and dicing with Turkey

A 'Western Kurdistan' was gaining autonomy in July 2012. Turkey had three options. One was to sit at the table with the PKK, which had more influence over the Syrian Kurds than Iraqi Kurdistan's Masoud Barzani. More than 10,000 people from Syria had joined the PKK over the years. Around 5,000 of the PKK's guerrilla losses were Syrians. Öcalan stated many times that 'they owe so much to the Syrian people for their huge support'. Moreover, the PKK had already spent 20 years training in Syrian camps. All in all, it is hard not to see the impact of the PKK on Syrian Kurds. Therefore, if a meaningful negotiation in Syria was to be entered into, involving the PKK was critical for Turkey.

The second option was to give Kurds in Turkey their rights, so that the 100-year-old Kurdish issue would be resolved before it became entangled with the Syrian war spillover. But Turkey did not play its cards like that and chose instead to pursue a third option, which was to find ways to prevent an autonomous Kurdish entity in Syria – a policy that had a negative impact on the peace process and caused a furore among the Syrian Kurds.

I first met Salih Müslim, the Syrian Kurd leader, co-chair of the People's Democratic Union (PYD), in the spring of 2013. He comes from a family of peasants in a village called Seyran near Kobane. After receiving his education in Syria, he attended the prestigious Istanbul Technical University. He spent time in London and Saudi Arabia before establishing his engineering office in Aleppo.[5] He became acquainted with the Kurdish movement and the PKK during his undergraduate years in Istanbul. But before that, like many Syrian Kurds in the PYD, he sympathized with Mustafa Barzani's ideas. He calls himself a sympathizer of both Barzani and Öcalan, although he admits that after meeting Öcalan several times in Damascus, his affinity with the PKK deepened.[6]

Müslim was one of the founders of the PYD in September 2003. He defines his party as devoted to Syrian Kurds and rejects a direct affiliation to the PKK. On the other hand, it is no secret that the PYD is a part of the umbrella organization KCK and that the PKK has assisted the PYD in its war against the Assad regime and ISIS in terms of manpower and strategy.

Müslim was a regular in Ankara during the first two years of the Kurdish peace process. There have been elements of occasional, unspoken collaboration between Turkey and PYD forces, but nothing further. The Turkish government urged Müslim to fight under the Syrian opposition, give up any desire for autonomy and distance the PYD from the PKK, whereas Müslim asked the Turkish government not to obstruct aid reaching the Kurdish region in order to avoid undermining the fight against ISIS.

The meetings between Ankara and Müslim did not yield any meaningful solution, which was not surprising, since both parties played a blame game, even when there was a dialogue. According to Ankara, the PYD was working with Assad behind the scenes with a view to creating an autonomous region. Müslim and other PYD officials tolerated being portrayed as an extension of the PKK, but the accusation that they were siding with Assad enraged them.

'The Turkish state fails to grasp the idea that Kurds will act according to their own free will when it comes to struggling for their rights,' Müslim told me:

The Turkish regime got on well with the Assad regime from the 2000s onwards, right? We were still against Assad back then, and we still are, because he has always tormented us. And when Turkey had good relations with Assad, he turned out to be our executioner. They signed the Adana Agreement, for instance.[7] Based on that, Syrian leader Bashar al-Assad returned 200 PKK members to Turkey. We were tortured. I can give you a list of the names of Kurds who were killed then, with the exact dates of the killings. That is why it is out of the question for us to side with Assad. On the other hand, we did not play the role that Turkey asked us to play either.[8]

It is worth mentioning that the now bitter adversaries Erdoğan and Assad were once close friends. Erdoğan even used to call Assad 'my brother' and the two had gone on holiday together along with their families. Even though the animosity between the two countries went as far back as the demise of the Ottoman Empire and the birth of Turkey and Syria as separate countries, ties were mended during the initial years of the AKP era as part of then foreign minister Ahmet Davutoğlu's 'zero problems with neighbours' policy. Erdoğan even lobbied for Assad's international image and eventually helped Syria to break the international boycott. But by the beginning of 2011, Davutoğlu's policy had almost completely tanked. So had the familial warmth between Erdoğan and Assad. Thus, PYD leader Salih Müslim was spot on. When it came to building discursive relationships with Bashar al-Assad, Erdoğan had the upper hand over the Syrian Kurds.

The PYD did not stand by the Assad regime, but neither did it join the opposing Free Syrian Army (FSA) when the war broke out, because 'they had memories dating back to Ottoman times'. This created a third option for the Syrian Kurds, which was leading their own revolution. Kurds have never forgotten how they were left empty-handed after fighting with the Turks during World War I. This bitter memory, seared into their consciousness, precluded the PYD from adopting any stance dictated by Turkey. They were against the Baathists, but they would not become a part of Muslim Brotherhood ideology through the FSA either.

Salih Müslim was not a vindictive man. He often smiled while speaking in fluent Turkish and occasionally cracked jokes – dark ones of the kind that I've become familiar with during countless meetings with Kurdish people. But he resented Turkey's Syrian policy so much that he spilled out a list of hurtful things Turkey had done before I could even shoot a question at him:

> Since its inception, the Turkish state put barriers in the way of anything that would benefit the Kurds. It played a role in the disintegration of Kurdistan in 1929, in the execution of Kadi Muhammad [of Mahabad] in 1949 and in the culmination of the Barzani revolution in 1975. They bear a share of the responsibility for our inability to come to terms with the Syrian opposition. Look, it is we, the Kurds, who need democracy most. We asked the opposition to act together. The Syrian National Assembly and the National Coalition for the Syrian Opposition said 'no'. Turkey is behind this attitude that the Syrian opposition has towards us. They provide all kinds of material and military support.[9]

However, Müslim also acknowledged that, since the peace process had commenced in Turkey, communication between Syrian Kurds and the Syrian opposition had improved. Nevertheless, the peace process with the PKK and Turkey's Syrian policy were intricately intertwined; the well-being and coherence of one affected the other, moment by moment.

The Syrian war and a new image for the PKK

The PKK and Turkey's Kurdish movement had invested politically and militarily in the Syrian cause, on the grounds of solidarity of kinship but also for other reasons: the PKK's actions in Syria would function as a way of legitimizing the organization internationally;

its base in Turkey had started to concern itself with Kurdish issues across the border and the PKK had to be a main actor in order to stay relevant; and investment in Syria had the potential to yield a long-yearned-for goal, an internationally acknowledged Kurdistan. Succeeding in these goals required perseverance and a meticulous global strategy.

The peace process afforded the PKK the chance to be a political force in the Middle East. With the eruption of the Syrian war, Turkey was no longer the only issue they considered to be most urgent. The theatre had just grown bigger.

'Minutes before meeting you, I received information that there was a clash in Serêkaniyê [Ras al-Ayn] between the YPG [the Democratic Union Party's (PYD) armed wing] and the Free Syrian Army,' said PKK commander Murat Karayılan:

> The situation is both tense and complicated. Forces have become entangled with each other – the YPG and the Free Army. But this is what has been accepted in Syria now: the Syrian government knows that if Kurds unite in opposition, then its job will become very difficult; for instance, they will lose Aleppo and Hasakah. Kurds are a third force there, independent of the state and the opposition. And this equilibrium must be protected for the sake of democracy.[10]

Even back in 2013, the PKK stood firmly against the Free Syrian Army because it believed that it was not seeking democracy but power, Karayılan explained. He continued,

> Maybe not everybody here defines us as such, but we see ourselves as a movement for freedom and democracy. Our advance along this axis may, we think, open a new door in the region. Yes, your analyses are correct; the Kurdish issue in Turkey is only one of the issues we are interested in. We see the Middle East as a whole; it has been like this almost since the beginning of the movement. It has just come nearer to the surface now.[11]

Leading the PYD through its fight first against radical Islamist groups in Syria, then against ISIS, and underlining its secular, feminist and environmentalist rhetoric in interviews given to Western media helped the PKK build a new image. While the rise of ISIS has exposed the vulnerabilities of the Iraqi KRG's Peshmerga forces, it has given the PKK the opportunity to shine in Iraq and Syria as a transnational player.[12]

The editorial board of the prestigious *Bloomberg* wrote, in an opinion piece, that 'Kurdish fighters aren't terrorists' and

> although the group is cultlike and stuck in a Marxist time warp, its members are also secular and largely pro-Western Sunni Muslims. Its combat troops, many of whom are women, were instrumental in saving Yazidi refugees from slaughter by Islamic State fighters. And the PKK's cause is primarily national, not religious or ideological, so it can be negotiated with – given the right incentives.[13]

While the BBC had been publishing stories about how successful PYD–PKK was in Syria[14] and, for that matter, that it was 'as deserving of international support as is KRG', *Marie Claire*, the women's fashion and style magazine, hosted YPJ fighters' stories in its glossy pages:

> They are the YPJ [...] or the Women's Protection Unit, an all-women, all-volunteer Kurdish military faction in Syria that formed in 2012 to defend the Kurdish population against the deadly attacks led by Syrian President, Bashar al-Assad, the al-Nusra Front (an al-Qaeda affiliate), and ISIS.[15]

News stories such as these that appeared in the Western media were misleading, as they embraced the PKK as if it had emerged yesterday solely to fight ISIS. When ISIS and other radical Islamist groups in Syria were put on one side of the scales and PKK and its Öcalan-inspired Syrian affiliate PYD on the other, the latter seemed like the lesser of two evils. But this should not obscure the fact that the PKK has instigated many violent attacks in Turkey over the last 40 years.

Although these news stories caused a stir in the AKP camp and among the columnists of pro-government newspapers, the government was looking the other way, because it was willing, to a certain extent, to help the peace process along. This implicit attitude persisted until semi-autonomous Kurdish cantons were formed in the Syrian town of Kobani and then in Afrin and Jazira. From that moment, both the AKP government and its media returned to their language demonizing the PKK and the PYD.

Immediately after the PYD had managed to wrest control of the Syrian town Til Abyad from the hands of ISIS, the pro-government media embarked on a propaganda campaign of equating the PYD with ISIS. *Sabah*, a mouthpiece of the AKP, had run headlines screaming that 'PYD is more dangerous than ISIS'[16] and 'PYD's chaos plan was prevented at the last minute',[17] and other pro-government dailies such as *Akşam*,[18] *Yeni Şafak*[19] and *Star*[20] had all lined up in the same order. The vilification of the PYD seriously damaged the Kurdish peace process and the honeymoon enjoyed by the Turkish press and the PKK ended abruptly, even though the YPG – the PYD's armed militia – continued to be portrayed as an ally in the fight against ISIS in the Western media and in Western politicians' rhetoric.

Kobane is 'not' about to fall

According to the Kurdish movement, two significant events contributed to the collapse of the peace process in Turkey and the deepening of the crisis in Syria: the YPG's operations to take first Kobane and then Til Abyad from ISIS. The Kurds' argument runs that ISIS had gained control in Til Abyad with help from across the Turkish border. Til Abyad lies right in the middle of Rojava. Turkey aided ISIS in Til Abyad so that it could have control over Rojava and obstruct any Kurdish attempt to merge two Kurdish cantons, Kobane and Jazira. But it was not until ISIS besieged Kobane and Turkey prevented aid from reaching the canton that the Kurds of Turkey reacted fiercely to this Syrian policy.

In September 2014, ISIS mounted its offensive against Kobane, and by the end of the month it had surrounded YPG fighters. In the minds of the Kurds, Turkey's fingerprints were all over this assault. On the third day of the Kobane offensive, ISIS released 46 Turkish people who had been taken hostage from Turkey's Mosul consulate on 11 June 2014. The Kurds saw this as a sign of collaboration: Turkey had allowed ISIS to seize Kobane in return for the consulate hostages. KCK co-chair Cemil Bayık went so far as to claim that 'a train on the Syrian–Turkish border had stopped in an Arab village close to Til Abyad and delivered boxes of ammunition four days prior to ISIS's Kobane attack'.[21]

Kobane was a make-or-break point. If it failed, so would the peace process, as PKK officials asserted several times. They had not started the peace process 'so that Turkey could move the war to Rojava by supporting the al-Nusra Front, Islamic State […] and al Qaeda affiliated groups'.[22]

The world was following developments in Kobane closely. It was an enticing story to watch unfold: a group of Kurds, who claimed to be secular environmentalists with socialist ideals, were resisting leaving their land to a bunch of barbaric jihadists. Many in the West had not heard of either the PYD or its armed militia, the YPG, but for them the Kobane incident epitomized a climax in the 'clash of civilizations'. While daily reports coming from Kobane perceived the issue as the eternal battle between good and evil, between secular and Islamist, the Turkish government was not just indifferent but also failed to grasp the significance of Kobane for Turkey's Kurds.

During the siege, it was one line uttered by President Erdoğan that caused a backlash among the Kurds. 'Kobane is on the brink of falling,'[23] he said. It was a seemingly simple statement, but his demeanour gave the impression that Erdoğan was happy about it.

On the same day, HDP co-chair Selahattin Demirtaş and the KCK presidency called on Kurds everywhere to rise up in Kobane's defence, which triggered a violent, two-day incident in the south-east of Turkey, mainly between two Kurdish groups. The PKK's youth wing, YDG-H, clashed with sympathizers of Hüda Par (Free Cause Party), a politico-legal wing of Turkish Hizbullah, which had fought with the PKK in the 1990s. Many religious Kurds who, for example, wore Islamic clothes or long beards were targeted as if they belonged to ISIS, along with officers of Hüda Par. The death toll after 48 hours was 51.

These protests were a fierce manifestation of the Kurds' emotional breakdown, the main cause of which was Turkey's apathy towards ISIS's merciless assault on the Kobane Kurds. Kurds, witnessing the aid sent to al-Nusra and the FSA but detecting no clear action against ISIS, were enraged that their brothers and sisters in Kobane had been abandoned to their own devices. They had been seething for some time about Syrian policy as a whole and the lack of any tangible step to help them during the peace process, and it was this sentiment that erupted into the protests.

The clashes between the two groups of Kurdish youths ended with a call from Öcalan. Shortly afterwards, the US airdropped ammunition to the YPG and stepped up air strikes. Acting under international pressure, Ankara allowed Barzani's Peshmerga to enter Kobane via the Turkish border. Kobane was saved. But the same could not be said for the peace process in Turkey. The YPG's conquest of Kobane meant a political defeat for Erdoğan, since now there would be a Kurdish hurdle to his ultimate plan to have a buffer zone on the Turkish–Syrian border. On the other hand, the main purpose of the buffer zone was in any case to prevent the establishment of an autonomous Kurdish enclave.

Therefore, the ever-changing map of Syria had become a challenge for the Turkish government. The first apparent shipment of arms to the YPG in Kobane also marked the beginning of a bumpy road in US–Turkey relations.

The events in Kobane indicated two other things. First, Ankara was neither empathetic towards nor aware of Turkish Kurds' sentiments regarding Syria. Second, it did not have a comprehensive Kurdish policy spanning from home to Syria to Iraq. In the absence of a macro standpoint, Turkey thought that out-of-date micromanagement tactics would work and that it was possible to pursue a negotiation process with Turkey's Kurds while sidelining or cornering Syrian Kurds.

Let us not forget that Turkey had tried and failed to thwart an autonomous Kurdish enclave in northern Iraq following the first Gulf

War in 1991. This mistaken policy had caused many years of hostility in the region and also wasted huge amounts of time in terms of forming the political and economic alliances that have now developed between northern Iraq and Turkey. But the misreading of Syria would have a greater price tag than simply being a waste of time. The peace process was to be the first invaluable opportunity lost.

It was during this time that the HDP delegation met with Abdullah Öcalan for another round of talks in İmralı prison. MP Sırrı Süreyya Önder passed on a message from Erdoğan, which said that 'he would come to an agreement with Apo. But there is only one red line, and that is Syria. He said he would not allow a Kurdish entity to be established like the one in northern Iraq.' Öcalan stopped him short and replied, 'You tell him that we will not allow Kurds to remain in a centralized Syria, and that is our red line.'[24] With Rojava emerged a common Kurdish consciousness, which meant that developments in one part of Kurdistan would have serious ramifications for the others.[25]

The Justice and Development Party (AKP) had initiated the last peace process, not because it was a strikingly just and democratic party but because the developments in the Middle East had had a tremendous impact on internal politics, thus forcing its hands. But now it was the Middle East that was shaking the ground under the negotiation process. Why? Because of what many call a Kurdish phobia. The fear of a 'Rojava' in Syria that would give rise to another in south-east Turkey not only caused a hopeful peace process to stumble but also hindered the fight against ISIS.

Was Ankara really helping ISIS?

If you put this question to someone from the Kurdish movement, you will most likely get a straight 'yes' for an answer. However, Turkey's attitude towards ISIS is rather ambivalent.

Since the beginning of the Syrian war, there have been numerous reports that Turkey was sending not only food and medical supplies to the opposition groups but also weapons. In 2012, Robert Fisk became the first Western journalist to be granted access to Assad's military prison in Damascus. He met a Turkish prisoner who said that he had come from Gaziantep, a city in south-eastern Turkey, to be a jihadist and a Salafi, and who claimed to have been radicalized in a Turkish refugee camp.[26]

When I talked to Fisk, he revealed to me something he had not written in his article in the *Independent*. The Syrian army had shown Fisk a cluster of weapons they found in Aleppo. According to Fisk, the weapons were made in Sweden and had found their way to Aleppo from Turkey.[27]

In the following years, other reports, usually in Kurdish and/or pro-Assad news outlets, claimed Turkey was supplying arms to Syria.

None of these claims in the media was enough to prove a direct link to an arms deal between Turkey and Syrian opposition groups or ISIS – that is, until four trucks full of ammunition were stopped by the Turkish gendarmerie, one in Hatay on 1 January 2014 and three in Adana in 19 January 2014. First reports from the scenes suggested that there were MIT officers in the truck and they had clashed with the gendarmerie, who had tried to confiscate the truck's contents and arrest the officers. Hatay's governor intervened and demanded the release of the officers, 'since they were subject to Law Number 2937 [MIT law], under which the personnel have a special status and work in direct subordination to the prime minister's office, [and] their undue detention would result in criminal consequences'. But the trucks were searched and videoed, despite the efforts of MIT officers to obstruct this.

When the news broke, the then interior minister, Efkan Ala, and prime minister Tayyip Erdoğan claimed that the trucks were carrying humanitarian aid to Turkmen and accused the prosecutors who had ordered the search of being members of the Gülen movement and belonging to the parallel state structure.[28]

A broadcast ban was immediately imposed on the case. All relevant online content was deleted by a court order, and even commenting on the subject was prohibited. The prosecutors and gendarmerie officers who conducted the investigation were arrested on suspicion of espionage. However, despite all the attempts at a cover-up, the trucks' search documents and testimonies of the gendarmerie included in the charges were leaked.

At the time of the incident, Turkey's Syrian borders near Hatay and Adana were controlled by the jihadist Ahrar al-Sham group.[29] There was therefore a possibility that the trucks were bound for them, but the gendarme who wrote the documents claimed that 'the trucks were carrying weapons and supplies to the al-Qaeda terror organization'.[30] The ammunition on the trucks was stacked in six metallic containers which had 25–30 missiles, 20–25 crates of mortar ammunition and Douchka anti-aircraft.[31] According to the driver's testimony, 'he had twice carried the same shipment and delivered it to a field around 200 meters beyond a military outpost in Reyhanli, a stone's throw from Syria.'[32]

The so-called 'MIT trucks' came to be a painful thorn in the side of the Turkish government's image and policy vis-à-vis Syria and accordingly it swore to silence anyone who brought up the subject for further investigation.

Cumhuriyet, the oldest newspaper in Turkey, published the documents and the video footage of the MIT truck search in May 2015. An infuriated Erdoğan said that its editor-in-chief, Can Dündar, would not get away with this and would pay a heavy price. Shortly afterwards, two journalists, Dündar and Cumhuriyet's Ankara bureau chief Erdem Gül, were charged with revealing state secrets, espionage and aiding a terrorist organization, namely the Gülen movement, since the government believed that the interception of the trucks was masterminded by Fethullah Gülen operating through the prosecutors and the gendarmerie.

Although Cumhuriyet and Dündar have received several prestigious press awards for their reporting, they have been put through hell ever since the incident. After Dündar and Gül were arrested, they served several months' imprisonment before being released on probation, acquitted of the charge of aiding a terrorist organization, but were then sentenced to five years for revealing state secrets, before surviving an assassination attempt in front of the courthouse. While he was awaiting trial on other charges, Dündar left Turkey in the summer of 2016. His wife's passport was summarily confiscated while she was going to meet him.

After Russia became an active partner of the Assad regime in Syria and Turkey downed a Russian jet in November 2015, diplomatic relations between the two countries tumbled into crisis. Russia now claimed that Turkey was sending weapons to ISIS disguised as humanitarian aid.[33] Russia also revealed drone footage of trucks moving between ISIS-controlled areas of Syria and Turkey, allegedly smuggling oil.[34] Turkey denied this accusation outright.

Sending military aid and supporting the Islamist opposition in Syria are one thing; tacitly condoning the presence of ISIS on the Turkey–Syria border is another. Turkey paid heavily for the latter.

Since the end of 2013, Turkey's Syrian border had almost been a line in the sand that anyone could cross. This 'open-border policy' had created a great opportunity for ISIS recruits from Turkey and around the world to move freely. The influx of people trying to cross the border either from Turkey to Syria or vice versa even created 'lively' businesses. The *Kilis Postası* (*Kilis Post*), a local newspaper in Kilis Elbeyli, a town neighbouring the ISIS-controlled area over the border, gave its readers 'happy news' in November 2014:

> It can be observed that there is an increase in the taxi ranks in Kilis, not only in the centre of the city but scattered all around. The number of taxis near the bus station has also risen tremendously. It should also be noted that these taxis are used for transport to the border. The overall impact of this development on our economy is positive.[35]

The impact was, however, not positive, since it was those taxis that many ISIS recruits had been using. Mahmut Gazi Tatar, who was captured and questioned by Kurdish YPG forces in Til Abyad, was an ISIS member from Istanbul. His route from Istanbul's poverty-stricken Güngören district to Syria involved taxis in Kilis:

> I took a bus to Antep, then to Kilis. My contact in ISIS had told me that taxi drivers in Kilis would help me to cross the border. So they did. A cab driver called a Syrian, who took me to a place where there were 17 others.[36]

A 29-year-old ISIS member, known as C. A., who was arrested while trying to cross the border from Syria to Kilis, was from Ankara. He had spent nine months in ISIS's heartland, Raqqa. According to his account, he 'took a bus from Ankara to Antep. At the Antep bus station, a taxi came and took [me] to the border. Another car was there waiting for [me] on the other side.'[37]

The open-border policy continued until Kurdish forces took control of Til Abyad in June 2015, which cut the main supply line of ISIS to its 'capital', Raqqa. Furious, ISIS started attacking Kurdish targets in Turkey. The Syrian PYD in Rojava had warned the Kurdish party, the HDP, that 'an ISIS assault team of 100 had crossed the border in July and would target Kurdish officials'.[38] As stated in the warning, HDP co-chair Selahattin Demirtaş would be the first target. Officials of the party brought up this issue in parliament in August 2015 and asked the government if they too had such intelligence. They received neither a response nor extra police protection. Unfortunately, the tip-off that came from Rojava was right.

Turkey suffered major ISIS attacks from the summer of 2015, most of which could have been prevented. *Radikal* newspaper, of which I was editor, followed the ISIS cells in Turkey closely. In September 2013, we published a series of interviews with parents in Adıyaman, a city in south-eastern Turkey, who lamented that their sons had gone to Syria to become jihadists. They had reported this to the authorities, but nothing had been done.[39]

A year later, the fight between the Kurds and ISIS in Syria spilled over into Turkey. At the end of May 2015, two bombs exploded simultaneously in HDP's Mersin and Adana headquarters. Demirtaş was on his way to the building in Mersin when the bomb exploded. He escaped by minutes.

It did not end there. Another bomb hit the HDP's rally in Diyarbakır and killed five people, a week before the June 2015 general elections. The bomber, Orhan Gönder, happened to be a young man from Adıyaman whose parents *Radikal* had interviewed.

In the newsroom, we pulled out our reports from back then and tried to construct a map of an ISIS cell in Adıyaman. At the heart of the Adıyaman cell lay a teahouse called Islam Çayevi. The Diyarbakır bomber Orhan was handpicked from there, his parents had told us. So a week later I wrote an article saying, 'Young people from Adıyaman in eastern Turkey are crossing to Syria to become jihadist fighters. We have reported on them numerous times. We even know their names. Doesn't the government know what we know?'

Despite the fact that Orhan Gönder was on a list of 'missing persons linked to terror', he had been able to plant a bomb at the HDP rally. He would not be the last ISIS recruit from Adıyaman to cause bloodshed. A month later, in July 2015, Turkey lost 34 young people in a suicide bombing in Suruç, a district near the Syrian border. The perpetrator was 20-year-old Şeyh Abdurrahman Alagöz from Adıyaman. He had been reported missing six months before, just like the other jihadists whose stories we had published. His mother did not know where he went; she assumed he was working with his brother in Gaziantep, also in south-eastern Turkey. Although the father was a truck driver and away from home for long periods of time, he was the one to realize something was up. He had gone to the police station and told officers, 'My sons have gone to Syria to become jihadists.' Just as Orhan Gönder's parents had.

The Adıyaman police department had been handling the phenomenon of young people joining ISIS for two years. It looked into the incident and included Şeyh Abdurrahman Alagöz and his older brother Yunus Emre Alagöz on the list of 'missing persons linked to terror', based on the information provided by their father.

In other words, the perpetrator who staged the Suruç massacre was among the persons believed to be at risk of committing an act of terrorism, according to the police. And yet no one had been able to prevent him from committing this atrocity.

Following the Suruç attack, my column in *Radikal* ended with this paragraph:

Orhan Gönder, who committed the Diyarbakır attack, and Şeyh Abdurrahman Alagöz, who carried out the Suruç attack, were friends. Their friendship and their ties to ISIS developed at the

Islam Çayevi [Islam Teahouse] in Adıyaman. The manager of the teahouse was Yunus Emre Alagöz, the older brother of Şeyh Abdurrahman Alagöz, the Suruç bomber. It is highly likely that he is in Syria or planning another attack. In other words, a new bomb attack may be closer than we expect. If Turkey's intelligence agency cannot find its way despite so many road signs, then it should be considered responsible for all kinds of similar disasters that will happen to us from now on.[40]

Two and a half months later, on 10 October 2015, Turkey suffered its deadliest terror attack since the founding of the republic. Thousands had gathered for a peace rally at the heart of the capital, Ankara, when twin bombs exploded, killing 107 and injuring more than 500. One of the suicide bombers was a young man from Adıyaman: Yunus Emre Alagöz. The manager of the Islam Teahouse. The older brother of the Suruç bomber. The missing person whom I had mentioned in my column on 23 July 2015.

I have never felt so bad to be proven right.

Later, a police report published in *Hürriyet* revealed that the mastermind behind the massacres in Diyarbakır, Suruç and Ankara was a Turkish ISIS member called İlhami Balı, known as Abu Bekir, ISIS's Turkey Amir. He was also managing the traffic of recruits on the Syria–Turkey border. Balı had been under Turkish police surveillance since 2002 and served three years on charges of being a member of al-Qaeda. When he was released, he went to Syria and joined al-Nusra and then in 2013 become an ISIS member. Interestingly, the trail went cold on Balı right after the Kobane incident in 2014, and it was during that time that he orchestrated the deadliest ever terrorist attacks on Turkish soil, mainly targeting Kurdish people.

These ISIS attacks not only cost precious lives but also jeopardized, if not practically ended, the Kurdish peace process. Since the Kurdish movement thought that the government was complicit in ISIS attacks on Kurdish targets in Turkey, the PKK retaliated. Following the Suruç massacre, two policemen were executed in their beds. Although the PKK leadership claimed that they had not ordered these assassinations, they did not deny the possibility of a link between the organization and the perpetrators. Turkey responded with an aerial campaign against PKK bases in Qandil, leading the insurgency in south-eastern Turkey to explode.

Just as those dreadful attacks by ISIS could have been averted, so could the collapse of a most optimistic peace process. Why had war rather than peace once again become Turkey's fate?

Because of epic miscalculations and ghastly personal ambitions.

Because of an abominable political gamble that had been taken in January 2015.

SIX

No Presidency, No Peace

Discontent among the Kurds

While raising the hopes of many Kurds scattered around the world, the prospect of an autonomous Kurdish region in Syria also begged the question of who would have the principal say over that piece of land. A power struggle among the Kurdish leaders regarding Rojava reared its head. Masoud Barzani, having managed to secure a land for Iraqi Kurds to rule, considers himself to be the guardian of the Kurds in the Middle East and the most accomplished of their leaders. On the other hand, according to Öcalan and Öcalan-influenced organizations such as the PKK and the PYD, 'Barzani always collaborated with international and regional powers to energize himself and advance his position,' which blocked any possibility of Kurds uniting in the Middle East.[1] After the formation of Rojava, there were talks of a Barzani plan to employ a military power of 100,000 Peshmerga in western Syria.[2]

The basic rift between Barzani and the PKK regarding Rojava's future actually stemmed from a difference in ideologies. While the PKK/PYD wanted to pursue Öcalan's democratic confederalism idea by starting to form an autonomous democracy, Barzani and the KDP aspired to a traditional federal structure resembling the one in northern Iraq. Barzani, in general, represents a more conservative and traditionalist brand of Kurdish politics. Parties opposed to Barzani's KDP, such as the YNK and Gorran, were committed from early on to Rojava's becoming an autonomous region.

Another aspect that challenged the equilibrium of Kurdish forces in the Middle East was Turkey's strategic backing of Barzani. Turkey saw Barzani's Kurdish Regional Government (KRG) as a proxy force in Rojava. It was contemplating using the KRG to acquire control over Rojava and to thwart any attempts at autonomy. However, the KRG had its own limitations in that respect. The first was that this plan would require fighting with other Kurds outside its own borders. The second was that Kurds in Rojava were supported by the PKK and Barzani's attempt would mean a direct clash with the PKK, which he wanted to avoid. Therefore, it would be very difficult for the KRG to accomplish the task that Turkey had assigned to it. Nevertheless, PKK leaders in Qandil did not welcome Barzani's alliance with the AKP government.[3] It was obvious that Barzani was taking the AKP's side in the peace process, accusing the PKK of being selfish and undoing the good deeds of the Turkish government.

When the peace process started, Öcalan had demanded that a Kurdish National Congress (KNC) be convened, at which Kurdish parties from all around the Middle East would come together. He hoped thereby to win support from other parts of Kurdistan for the peace negotiations and also to create an inclusive platform to discuss the future of the Kurds.

However, the KNC failed to materialize in its proposed form, amid fears on the part of other Kurdish entities that such a congress would elevate Öcalan to the top of the leadership in the Kurdish region. That was something neither Erdoğan nor Barzani would approve of. The content and plan for the congress changed, drifting away from its original goal.

Kurdish leaders started agitating for more seats for their delegates at the congress. The main question was whether the only criterion for determining the number of seats allocated to each Kurdish party was the amount of Kurdish people each party represented or the political influence each party held. Of 600 places, the PKK was assigned 230 seats, while the KRG would have 150, Iran's Kurdish party, the PUK, 90 and Syria's PYD 130 seats. But this composition meant that the PKK and its Syrian brother, the PYD, would have the majority influence over any decision taken at the congress. This was not acceptable to the Turkey-backed KRG.

During the heated negotiations about the KNC, Barzani also hinted at his wish to have a military force of his own in Rojava, which the PYD immediately rebuffed.[4] This was an indication of irreconcilable differences. Unifying the Kurds of the region had to wait for another attempt.

There were signs of discontent within Turkey's Kurdish movement too. In 2014, while the Kurds fought for influence over Rojava, the representatives of the Kurdish movement – the political wing HDP, the military wing PKK and the imprisoned leader Öcalan – began to engage in their own tussle for authority. This was a golden opportunity for the AKP government, since their thinking was that a fragmented Kurdish movement would pave the way for the government to have the upper hand at the negotiating table.

✳

The AKP pursued a simple strategy that would and did foment the differences in the Kurdish movement: the government officials who were responsible for managing the peace process curried favour with one group while lambasting the other two in order to pit them against each other. AKP cadres started voicing their discontent with certain statements by Qandil and the HDP, and claimed that these two did not abide by Öcalan's rulings.

They expected to be able to portray the Kurdish movement as having unstable leadership. According to the government, at the time of the peace process, the Kurdish movement had at its head good cops and bad cops. The good cop was, ironically, Öcalan, whom the Turkish government had for decades mobilized every means at its disposal to demonize. The bad cops were either the PKK leaders in Qandil or the HDP's MPs, depending on the particular point of criticism.

This tactic, which was rooted in the basic Ottoman 'divide and rule' discourse according to the Kurds, bore its own dangers. It put the government in the position of not having a real counterpart at the negotiating table, which diminished the legitimacy of the process in the eyes of the public. However, the government chose to carry on along this line.

Erdoğan's then chief adviser, Yalçın Akdoğan, was the main implementer, making constant public appearances. 'We care about the HDP but their messages are provocative,' he once said in an interview. 'That makes the HDP pointless and will undermine Öcalan. The HDP should realize their responsibilities. We see that Öcalan is reading the process more accurately.'[5]

The government spokesperson and deputy prime minister at the time, Bülent Arınç, also targeted the HDP over its alleged disconnect with Öcalan: 'You do not realize,' he said, addressing them, 'that you are sidelining Öcalan. Whose representatives are you that you are trying to cast Öcalan in a bad light?'[6] The suggestion that Qandil and the HDP were following a different agenda from Öcalan had attracted increasing numbers of supporters during the course of the process. Abdülkadir Selvi, a pro-government columnist based in Ankara, claimed, 'Öcalan wanted the PKK to declare that it had ceased its armed struggle within Turkey but Qandil resisted this message and dragged its feet.'[7]

A government appointee from the Wise Persons' Committee also believed that Qandil was acting against Öcalan's will. 'When there is no regular contact with Öcalan, hardline PKK leaders like Cemil Bayık and Duran Kalkan can speak more freely,' he explained. 'They can stir up the militants in the mountains.'[8]

Abdullah Öcalan's brother, Osman, whom he regards as a traitor to the movement,[9] had also put his own construction on the public conversation between the HDP, the KCK and İmralı:

> I think there are two PKKs. One is the PKK of İmralı and the other is the PKK of Qandil. The PKK of Qandil will say yes to Apo but then implement what is on its own agenda. They do everything the way they reckon it should be but they act as if they are complying with Apo.[10]

When the road became bumpier, the rhetoric of government officials became harsher. '[HDP and Qandil] are looking for ways to disable

Öcalan, to become principals, to blow the wind in a different direction. If you are not listening to what Öcalan says, then why are you going to İmralı? For a picnic?' said Yalçın Akdoğan.[11] After the process collapsed and the clashes reignited, Akdoğan adapted the discourse to indulge in some finger-pointing: 'Both the PKK and the HDP betrayed the process. The HDP has come under the influence of Qandil. They buried Öcalan alive in İmralı prison.'[12]

These views were not those of Akdoğan alone but were also shared by President Erdoğan, as demonstrated by some of his statements, such as 'It is obvious that there is a serious rupture between İmralı and Qandil. There is also a division in the political party [HDP]. One says one thing, the other says a completely different thing.'[13]

Although the government had a different motive for falling in with the AKP's good cop, bad cop strategy, there were elements of truth in what it had been saying. There did indeed seem to be some pluralism in the Kurdish movement. The International Crisis Group, which had conducted interviews with PKK leaders, also came to the same conclusion: 'While no PKK organs or officials are able to bypass Öcalan, the exiled insurgent leadership has some influence over him.'[14] The split had become more apparent when the question of disarmament was discussed.

The Kurdish party HDP, shuttling between Ankara and İmralı, had taken up the idea of putting disarmament on the agenda as a major issue for public debate at the end of 2014. This caused a backlash in Qandil. The KCK co-chair, Cemil Bayık, berated the HDP's co-chair for calling on the PKK to disarm: 'The HDP cannot make a declaration [about disarmament]. Neither can the leader, Apo, who is living as a prisoner in İmralı.'[15] The KCK co-chair, Besê Hozat, responding to the HDP's statement that 'Öcalan is the authority to declare disarmament', wrote in her column in the daily paper Özgür Gündem, 'It is a huge mistake for certain people from the HDP to rise to the bait of the AKP and to identify Apo as the fountainhead of disarmament.'[16]

While the public had witnessed overt strife between the HDP and Qandil over Öcalan's functionality, Öcalan in İmralı had not been happy with some of Qandil's behaviour and had felt somewhat challenged.

The dialogues between Öcalan and the HDP delegation that visited him bore traces of that sentiment:

7 DECEMBER 2013

HDP MP Pervin Buldan: We met with [Turkey's national intelligence chief] Hakan Fidan. He wanted to meet us. He said that some annoyance is felt about Salih Müslim's and Qandil's statements.

HDP MP Sırrı Süreyya Önder: Fidan said that Qandil is using a language that can only be used by the leadership [Öcalan] and this is causing debate in the government about which party is responsible.

Öcalan: Mr Hakan knows these issues very well. Cemil [KCK co-chair Bayık] should pay attention. Only I can deliver statements like 'Negotiations start, negotiations finish.' Neither Duran [Kalkan] nor Cemil [Bayık] should use that kind of language. Their rhetoric should be kept within their limits.

26 APRIL 2014

Öcalan: Qandil should not have decided on HDP's election candidate. Qandil should not interfere in these things. Qandil make out that they are devoted to me but when it comes to the reality they do not act that way. Do you think Qandil is turning against me? What is your observation?

HDP MPs Pervin Buldan and İdris Baluken: No, on the contrary, they are very devoted to you. That is what we have observed.[17]

The dialogues between Öcalan and HDP envoys, the KCK leaders' anger towards the HDP and the covert disagreements with Öcalan can be interpreted as a rupture in the Kurdish movement. The flip side of the coin is that there can be no serious split nor any significant challenge to Öcalan in the Kurdish movement, only disagreements. There are several reasons why that is so. First, members of the Kurdish movement are known to have a tradition, rooted in their Marxist legacy, of harshly criticizing one another in their periodic meetings and congresses – that is, having differences of opinion is an everyday thing for the movement. Second, Öcalan's dialogues with the HDP delegation in İmralı prison, in which he rages against Qandil, have been published in book form. If there were truly a rift, Öcalan would not have requested that the book be published, Qandil would not have approved it and the PKK officials in Europe would not have gone ahead with publication. Another dialogue in the book shows that the Turkish government, which promulgated the idea that the Kurdish movement was crumbling, was opposed to the publication of the book.

26 JUNE 2014

Öcalan: How many pages of notes do you have?

HDP MP Buldan: For each meeting it adds up to 25–30 pages of notes.

Öcalan: How many pages of notes does the Qandil have?

HDP MP Buldan: I believe around 400–600 pages.

Öcalan: Is Qandil considering making these notes into a book?

HDP MP Buldan: We will forward that proposal to them.

9 JANUARY 2015

Undersecretary of State for Public Security and Order: We hear rumours that the notes of these meetings will be turned into a book in Europe. This is not something we approve of.

Öcalan [to the HDP delegation]: Tell our friends to be careful.[18]

It is fair to conclude that if there were signs of a division or a dispute between Qandil and Öcalan they would not have disclosed it at a time when Öcalan's leadership was still undisputed among Kurdish people. When asked about a split, the PKK leadership usually explained it by saying that Öcalan has one role and they have another. 'We cannot assume Leader Apo's role, nor can he assume ours,' they say:

> Leader Apo is the leader of a people and he is the chief negotiator. Our position is different. The two should not be confused. It is just as wrong to equate one with the other as it is to cast them as opponents. Perhaps some people are intentionally pitting them against each other. There is no question of any conflict, nor can there be.[19]

Ruşen Çakır, a prominent journalist who has been following the Kurdish issue for decades, believes that there cannot be a major difference between Qandil and İmralı, 'because these leaders have been acting together since the mid-1970s. They know one another very well. Even if they are not in direct contact, they know how the other would act in any given situation.'[20] Öcalan, Çakır says, would not resort to weakening the organization in order to strengthen his own position, nor would the administrators of the organization resort to weakening Öcalan's position, knowing that this would lead to a serious crisis within the movement and even cause it to fall apart.

Pervin Buldan, an HDP MP and the only constant member of the HDP delegation to İmralı prison, also refers to 'a different level of communication' between Qandil and Öcalan:

> Judging from the meetings that we had in İmralı and Qandil, I have not witnessed any break-up. We are talking about people who have been acting together for 40 years. Sometimes [Qandil] may extract a sentence with tweezers from the notes we took [in İmralı]. Neither we nor the government would understand what that sentence actually refers to, but it may have the potential to change the course of the process for them.[21]

We will not make you president

One of the critical events that put the Kurdish movement and the then prime minister Erdoğan on a collision course was the presidential election that was to be held on 10 August 2014. It was the first time in the history of the republic that the Turkish president would be elected by popular vote. For Erdoğan, this election meant that he would be one step closer to the presidential system he desired and a step further away from the parliamentary system. Before 2014, presidents in Turkey were appointed by the parliament and the post of the president was more symbolic than executive. However, since a referendum in 2007 in which the vote was 68 per cent in favour of a constitutional amendment, presidents are elected by popular vote every five years.

In 2014, whereas the main opposition parties, the CHP and the MHP, had nominated former Secretary General of the Organization of Islamic Cooperation (OIC) Ekmeleddin İhsanoğlu, the AKP's candidate, unsurprisingly, was Recep Tayyip Erdoğan. What intrigued many people was who would be nominated by the Kurdish party, the HDP. The rumour was that the HDP would opt for a low-profile candidate and tacitly mobilize its electorate to vote for Erdoğan for the sake of the continuation of the peace process, as angering him might provoke him to end negotiations. However, this turned out not to be the case. The HDP nominated as their candidate the party's co-chair, the most popular Kurdish politician apart from Öcalan, namely Selahattin Demirtaş.

İhsanoğlu, the joint candidate of the CHP and the MHP, was a long-time diplomat who had had little experience of the harsh nature of politics in Turkey. He certainly was not good at delivering effective speeches, and his conservative background meant he was not embraced by the CHP's secular electorate. His weaknesses left the campaign arena free for Demirtaş and Erdoğan to go head to head. Both were brilliant orators and power brokers in the eyes of their followers.

Demirtaş's candidacy served as a statement to sceptics that the Kurdish movement was not being brought to heel by the AKP just because it was in the middle of a negotiation process. On the other hand, Demirtaş's popularity came with its own risks. There were reports in the pro-government media that his nomination ran counter to Öcalan's will. Some implied that Öcalan was jealous of Demirtaş, while others claimed he feared for the assurance of the peace process. Öcalan denied these claims, telling the HDP delegation that visited him in İmralı prison that 'whoever said Apo does not want Selahattin is lying' and that he had put in huge efforts to 'improve' Demirtaş.[22]

Demirtaş's witty, inclusive and social media-friendly campaign helped change the image of Kurdish politicians, not only in western Turkey but also abroad. British and US media outlets quoted him, nicknaming him 'the Kurdish Obama'.[23]

The result of the presidential election on 10 August 2014 was no surprise to anyone. Erdoğan emerged victorious, with 51 per cent of the votes, while opposition candidate İhsanoğlu won 38 per cent and Demirtaş 9.7 per cent. Compared with his rivals, Demirtaş's share of the vote may seem modest, but what he actually achieved was huge. He had expanded his party's electoral potential by almost 4 per cent, making it more likely to cross the 10 per cent threshold at the next elections. It was actually Demirtaş's success that allowed the HDP, a year later, to participate as a party in the general elections, rather than fielding independent candidates as Kurdish parties had previously been in the habit of doing.

'The press is writing, "A new star is born, but Apo will put the skids on this historic development – he will stonewall it." Now give me a break!' Öcalan said a week after the presidential elections, trying once again to make his position regarding Demirtaş clear. 'Could such nonsense ever be possible? I love and respect Selahattin. The HDP is now at a very critical juncture. You have to let it flourish.'[24]

And flourish it would.

✳

Within a month, foreign minister Ahmet Davutoğlu had replaced Erdoğan as the new chairman of the AKP and prime minister. He seemed determined to pursue the Kurdish peace process at a time when it looked as if it was on the brink of collapse.

An unexpected episode occurred on 28 February 2015. The violent two-day protests in south-eastern Turkey during the Kobane siege by ISIS in October 2014 had caused resentment on both sides. The AKP was accusing HDP co-chair Selahattin Demirtaş of inciting people to take to the streets. He was later sentenced to 24 years in prison for 'provoking an armed insurgency of a group of people against another and causing unrest'.[25] On the other hand, both the HDP and Qandil were claiming that the AKP government was the source of ISIS attacks in Turkey. While the bitterness was at its peak, a historic meeting took place.

It was the first time that HDP's İmralı delegation and AKP's peace process envoy had jointly presented their understanding of the situation, which they did in the form of a declaration at the nineteenth-century Dolmabahçe Palace, where administrative work had once been performed by Ottoman sultans and where Atatürk had spent his last days. The palace was turned into an office for Tayyip Erdoğan during his time as prime minister.

The contents of the declaration and the person who had penned it made the meeting even more historic. The AKP, represented at that time by Yalçın Akdoğan, head adviser to the prime minister, minister of the interior Efkan Ala and AKP deputy chairman Mahir Ünal, sat across from the HDP's İmralı delegation, comprising Pervin Buldan, İdris Baluken and Sırrı Süreyya Önder. The meeting was broadcast through every news channel in Turkey. On live TV, the AKP government announced for the first time that it was officially taking over the process from the MIT and in a way promising to pursue it as a political policy of the party. It also meant a great deal for any official of the Turkish government to be present at a meeting when a letter from the PKK leader Öcalan was being read. Öcalan was an enemy of the state and yet there was the state to all intents and purposes approving his words.

The letter was not an ordinary demonstration of goodwill. It involved a road map of how the negotiations should proceed and reach their ultimate destination. Read live on TV by HDP MP Sırrı Süreyya Önder, it consisted of a call to the PKK and ten articles. The articles looked more like chapter headings of a larger paper and did not clearly define the future steps of the process. They read as follows:

1. Definition of democratic politics and content.

2. Definition of national and local dimensions of democratic resolution.

3. Legal and democratic safeguards for free citizenship.

4. Headings for relationships between democratic politics and the state and society and for its institutionalization.

5. The socio-economic dimensions of the process of resolution.

6. Addressing the relationship between democracy and security in the process of resolution in a manner that will protect public order and freedoms.

7. Safeguards for women and solutions for their legal, cultural and ecological problems.

8. The development of a pluralist democratic understanding recognizing the concept of identity and its definition.

9. The democratic definition of a democratic republic, joint homeland and people, and the introduction of legal and constitutional safeguards within a pluralist, democratic system.

10. A new constitution that aims to embed all these democratic transformations.[26]

It was later announced that these articles were actually a summary of a 70-page report Öcalan had prepared.[27] The most compelling part of the letter was not the ten articles but the following appeal:

> I invite the PKK to convene an extraordinary congress in the spring to make a strategic and historic decision in the interests of ending the armed struggle on the basis of minimum agreed principles. This invitation is a historic declaration of intent for politics to replace armed struggle.[28]

The meeting and the call to end armed struggle raised the public's mood and expectations. The EU issued a statement the following weekend, welcoming the joint declaration by the government and the HDP, describing it as yet another positive step towards solving the Kurdish problem. The preparation had begun for a monitoring committee agreed by both parties.

However, things did not go as planned. There were unexpected setbacks and sharp turns from President Erdoğan with regard to the Dolmabahçe meeting. At this point, it is crucial to follow the chronology meticulously.

On the day of the meeting, when President Erdoğan was asked about his views, he said:

> The call to lay down arms was very important for us. This is a call that indicates an end to the armed struggle alongside the solution process. These appeals are good, but we have to see how they are implemented.[29]

Although this reply was cautious, the president did not seem to disapprove of the Dolmabahçe meeting as a whole. His attitude would change drastically in the following weeks.

On 20 March 2015, three weeks after the meeting, Mr Erdoğan's views revealed a completely different tone:

> [With regard to the monitoring committee] I am reading this from the papers. I did not know anything about it and I don't approve of it. During my time as prime minister, when I was asked if I approved the proposal to send a group from the Wise Persons' Committee to İmralı [prison, to meet Öcalan], I said I did not approve. This is not right. From the start, the intelligence agency is the body that should manage these things and that is the way it should stay.[30]

After Erdoğan's statement, something startling happened. The government spokesperson and long-time political comrade of Erdoğan Bülent Arınç issued a challenge to him:

It would be impolite for me to comment on Mr President's words. But the formation of a monitoring committee is an outcome of the negotiation talks. Our government sees this as appropriate. There is a road map outlining who will act in what role and how. Our government is in charge of leading the country and it is the government's responsibility. It is also impossible for our president not to be informed.[31]

A day after Arınç's challenge, on 22 March 2015, President Erdoğan made another statement totally denouncing the whole Dolmabahçe meeting:

I don't approve of [it]. Because I personally don't approve of a government representative being in the same frame with [the HDP] in front of the media. And as for the 10-article declaration, I don't see any call for democracy [in it]. How can I approve of such a text in the name of democracy?[32]

These statements signalled not only a division in the government but also an end to the negotiation process. The HDP delegation had last visited Öcalan in İmralı on 5 April 2015, after which all communication had been cut off. Erdoğan's words on 2 May were the last nail in the coffin:

They [the HDP] say that we will demolish the Religious Affairs Directorate because it doesn't have anything to do with religion. They go as far to say that Jerusalem belongs to the Jews. In their camps on the mountain they teach Zoroastrianism. They have a Kurdish TV channel. They have Kurdish lessons at university. In our country, there is no Kurdish problem, but our Kurdish people have some problems.[33]

Things went spiralling downwards from this moment on.

The HDP delegation went to Qandil to meet the KCK leadership. Following a six-hour meeting, the HDP announced that the PKK was halting its preparations for a congress where the disarmament decision would be approved. The PKK was not to convene a congress, as demanded by Öcalan's letter that had been read at Dolmabahçe, because 'President Erdoğan [had] made his declarations that dealt a serious blow to peace'.[34]

Was it only Erdoğan who disapproved of the Dolmabahçe meeting, or was it the AKP government as a whole that had an abrupt change of heart?

According to the notes of İmralı meetings with Öcalan, two months before Dolmabahçe, the HDP delegation, Öcalan and the Undersecretary of State for Public Security and Order, Muhammed Dervişoğlu, had gathered around a table at the prison.[35] They first had lunch and then got on with the agenda. Undersecretary Dervişoğlu was the first to speak: 'This may look like a humble table but this gathering is historic. And upstairs people are working on a bigger table and [on providing] a meeting room for a larger delegation to come here.'[36] His opening remarks indicated that the state had been planning to have a monitoring committee in İmralı consisting of 15 to 20 people. This was one of the demands Öcalan had posed 'in order to undertake a strategic role in the peace process'. The government's agreement to open İmralı to a wider group of people would signal the start of another stage in the negotiations.

There were other signs that the then prime minister Ahmet Davutoğlu and his envoy were ready and keen to drive the process further. In that same meeting in İmralı, Öcalan asked the HDP delegation if they had sensed a determination on the part of the government to move in that direction. When HDP MP Sırrı Süreyya Önder hinted that there was no common and clear course of action, Undersecretary Dervişoğlu cut in, 'Did the Prime Minister not show determination in that meeting? Did he not say that there is no impediment to advancing the process?' 'Yes,' Önder had to acknowledge, 'the prime minister did say that we can move on to the negotiations.'[37]

Not long after he was appointed prime minister, Davutoğlu called the HDP İmralı delegation for a meeting.[38] During that meeting, on 10 September 2014, Davutoğlu guaranteed to advance the process on condition that the PKK cease its illegal activities of setting up its own trials, roadside checkpoints and harassment of travellers until 15 October.[39]

The pro-government media later claimed that neither the HDP nor the PKK had abided by this condition. It was during this time that Turkey's parliament voted to authorize military action against ISIS. Kurds assumed that the government would misuse the bill to also attack the PKK and the PYD. The bill had two separate mandates that would enable Turkish troops to be deployed along the Iraqi and Syrian borders to defend Turkey against both Assad's forces and the PKK. This provoked unalleviated distrust of the government among the Kurds. The Kurdish movement believed that the Turkish state had a history of acting both ways.

An influential figure in the movement once illustrated this sentiment for me:

> I went to a guerrilla funeral last week. Do you know what the mood was like? It was one of not expecting anything, of disappointment, of weariness. They were saying that the government is talking to Öcalan on one side and killing our sons on the other. So what is the use of these meetings? This way of thinking legitimizes war in the layperson's mind.[40]

The Kobane unrest on 6–7 October 2014 had been the embodiment of cumulative resentment against the government's way of handling the war in Syria and the peace process at home. However, neither that infamous event nor the HDP's broken promises were the real cause of the process ending. We now have retrospective information that, a couple of months after the Kobane events, a big meeting room was constructed in İmralı prison, which would have signalled an upgrade for the process and greatly boosted trust in it among the Kurdish audience.

If the HDP and the PKK had not kept their promises, as the pro-government media liked to insist, and if the Kobane events were an improvisation of an uprising, as they were portrayed in the

pro-government media, then why had the government pushed forward
the move towards peace and carried on with the Dolmabahçe meeting?

What happened during and after Dolmabahçe provides invaluable
clues as to why the Kurdish peace process had fallen apart. It was
President Erdoğan who decided that the process was not going in the
direction that he wanted. But why? Why would he throw a spanner
in the works when the undisputed leader was calling on the PKK to
disarm? Why would he choose to waste an opportunity that the country
had been awaiting for 40 years?

There are several theories. In June 2015 general elections were to be
held in Turkey, and President Erdoğan had never hidden his ambition
to change from a parliamentary system to an executive presidency; he
wanted to have a presidential regime in place. Transforming the political system required a constitutional change, but the opposition parties
were not willing to accept that. Erdoğan once stated that the day he
became the first president to be elected by popular vote, in August 2014,
the Turkish parliamentary system collapsed and a de facto presidential
system replaced it. Using this argument, he backed the AKP's election
campaign, even though, as president, the constitution required him
to be impartial. During the rallies and his many TV appearances, he
exhorted people to vote in such a way that just one party, namely the
AKP, would get 400 MPs. 'We tried to create a new constitution but the
opposition parties did everything they could to block it,' he said. 'Now
there is a reality: 400 (lawmakers) should be given. Give 400 deputies
and let's have a new constitution easily. I am at equal distance from
all parties, but give 400 deputies to whoever you want.'[41] His agenda
was that the 400 MPs who would deliver him the executive presidency
should be from the AKP.

The HDP's decision to enter the general elections as a party was a
setback to Erdoğan's calculation. Before 2015, Kurdish parties, including the HDP, went into the elections with independent candidates to
bypass the 10 per cent threshold. It was because the Turkish constitution
imposes a threshold of 10 per cent of votes for any political party to be
represented in parliament. However, independent candidates are not
subject to the same threshold. HDP took the risk. If their votes had

remained below 10 per cent, the Kurdish movement would have no presence in parliament. But if they passed the threshold, the rewards would be great. The party could almost double the number of its MPs. Due to electoral laws, many votes were going to waste when they ran as independents, while running as a party could change the situation.

The meeting at Dolmabahçe had been planned to mark a new stage in the peace process. However, Erdoğan's attitude ensured that the attempt failed. In retrospect, it is possible to see exactly when President Erdoğan did an about-turn and blew the initiative out of the water.

For the first time, a Kurdish party had vowed to pass the threshold. A lively election campaign followed the HDP's risky but rather bold decision. And it was one man who infuriated Erdoğan more than any other.

Selahattin Demirtaş as a game changer

Particular incidents always mobilize Kurds to enter the political arena. For Selahattin Demirtaş, the HDP co-chair and former presidential nominee, this was the funeral of Vedat Aydın, a Kurdish human rights activist and politician. He was found dead, with his head smashed in, on a road near Malatya on 7 July 1991. Aydın's murder was the first in a spree of assassinations in the 1990s whose perpetrators were believed to be part of an extrajudicial intelligence and counterterrorism unit inside the gendarmerie, known as JİTEM. Hundreds of thousands of people gathered for his funeral in Diyarbakır. The clashes between the police and protesters at the funeral left three dead and hundreds wounded. For Demirtaş, then 18, witnessing these events changed his path in life.

Demirtaş was the middle child of seven siblings. His parents were from a peasant family from Elazığ. They moved to Diyarbakır in their 20s and led a modest life. His father was a plumber by trade, who managed to earn enough to educate all his children to university degree level. Politics was never a live issue in the household. A cousin who had served time in jail during the 1980 coup was the only one in the family who was politically active. Nevertheless, he was a member of the Turkish Communist Party (TKP), which meant that he was not part of the Kurdish movement but of the Turkish left. Demirtaş encountered the Kurdish movement when he went to İzmir as an undergraduate.

Many of his friends from Kurdish villages were fluent in their mother tongue, while Demirtaş could neither understand nor speak a word. 'It was a matter of shame for me,' he confessed:

> My parents had raised us not like Turks but in Turkish. They never spoke to us in Kurdish because they were scared that it would bring us harm. They were not educated people but their judgement was that if we acted like Turks and didn't flaunt our Kurdishness, we wouldn't get into any trouble with the government.[42]

It was only after meeting other Kurdish friends at the university that he admitted to being a Kurd himself. He had never denied it, but neither had he proclaimed it.

Demirtaş's older brother Nurettin was arrested at the end of his first year at university and served 14 years in prison. Upset and resentful at this development, Selahattin Demirtaş decided to 'go to the mountains' and join the PKK when he was in his early twenties. At that time, you needed to find a courier, write your wish and background on a piece of paper and then, if the leadership approved, the courier would come and take you to the PKK camp. Demirtaş had gone through with the process, but the courier who was supposed to take him to the mountains was arrested on his way to pick him up. Another courier and date were assigned, but again they could not meet. He remembers:

> Then I had time to think and realized that this was not my way to go. I was not afraid of the mountains. I was not afraid of dying. I was afraid of killing. I imagined myself holding a gun and saw that this was not in my nature.[43]

He took the university entrance exam once more and managed to get into Ankara University Faculty of Law, one of the most prestigious schools in Turkey. His cousins and siblings followed him, leaving their undergraduate studies at medical and engineering school and deciding to study law. 'It was necessary for Kurds back then to study law. When my brother was arrested we could not find a single lawyer to defend him. It was shaming,' he explains.

Having qualified as a lawyer, he started to do *pro bono* work for the Diyarbakır branch of the Human Rights Foundation and also served as its chairman until he became an MP in the Kurdish party in 2007.

While he was doing his mandatory military service, he was chastised and threatened by a general in the military. 'We know who you are,' the general had said. 'Now you see the power of the Turkish army. From now on, act accordingly in Diyarbakır, or...' Demirtaş stood to attention as he listened, but then he broke in. 'In a week's time,' he said boldly, 'my service will be over and I will be a civilian, a lawyer again. But you will still be a soldier. Remember my name. We will meet again.'[44] In saying this, he was thinking of the possibility of meeting that general in a court of law. Neither the general nor he could know then that he would be the most popular Kurdish politician in Turkey in a decade's time.

Demirtaş's good work at the Human Rights Foundation was praised by the Kurdish movement and attracted the attention of prominent figures, who pressed him hard to run for parliament. 'I never liked politics,' Demirtaş confided. 'I got involved because many people thought I should. I still believe I could be just as useful as a human rights lawyer for the people.'[45]

His popularity started rising with his presidential candidacy in 2014. He mastered social media and the language of young people so skilfully that no other politician could even come close. He was brilliant in debates, although of course he was rarely invited to participate. The real reason for his prominence was that he knew how to empathize, as he pointed out:

During my undergraduate years, I was in İzmir and Ankara. I had time to interact with the secular Western Turks and realized that they sincerely held the state in some affection, but as Kurds we kept saying that the state is brutal, the state has killed our family and friends, the state is merciless. When you put it that way, they don't want to listen to you. So I decided not to burden the Turkish people by constantly labelling the government atrocious. I said, 'Let's work together to change this government, so that each and every one of us is happy.'[46]

Kurds and a considerable number of secular Turks embraced him for that reason. Moreover, he was a great public orator, well capable of challenging Tayyip Erdoğan.

On 17 March 2015, the HDP gathered at the parliament for their weekly group meeting. Selahattin Demirtaş went up to the podium and delivered his shortest speech: 'Mr Recep Erdoğan,' he began, 'as long we are here, as long as the HDP is present, we will not make you president.' Then he repeated, 'We will not make you president,' and then for a third time, 'We will not make you president.' The standing ovation he received ended the HDP meeting and triggered the failure of the peace process.

Demirtaş's extremely short speech swept social media and became a favourite election slogan for many people, including the Kemalist CHP electorate. Only three days later, an irritated Erdoğan publicly made his first dismissive comment on the Dolmabahçe meeting. Many of the AKP MPs did not know whether to take President Erdoğan's side or to support their party, which only a month ago had been prepared to go ahead with the meeting. Erdoğan's unexpected U-turn thrust even the most fervent government mouthpieces into a state of ambivalence.

The HDP thought there were election polls behind the U-turn. During the time between his initial stance and the 'I do not approve' statement, Erdoğan had received the results of several polls, which showed an increase in HDP votes, while support for the AKP was static. 'We learned about it from inside the AKP,' claimed Selahattin Demirtaş:

The president asked his aides, 'Why are we engaged in this if there is no benefit in it for us?' And growls started to be heard inside the

AKP. It was not reflected much in public, but our delegations were in contact with each other.[47]

The agreed outcome of the Dolmabahçe meeting was that a monitoring committee would first be formed and that the PKK would then hold a convention on laying down arms. However, many in the AKP thought that the sequence should be the other way round, meaning an immediate PKK convention and announcement of disarmament. Hence there was disappointment.

Still, none of this should have been a surprise for President Erdoğan, since he had been informed every step of the way. The minutes of the İmralı meetings used to be handed to him within hours. According to Demirtaş, President Erdoğan was so involved in Dolmabahçe that he actually decided who sat where in front of the cameras that day.[48] Therefore, Erdoğan was not telling the truth when he said that he was not informed about the meeting, implying that, if he had known before, he would not have let it happen.

On 7 June 2015, the HDP received 13 per cent of the votes and became the first Kurdish party to enter parliament in Turkey. With this victory, the HDP would become the second-largest opposition party, relegating the Turkish ultra-nationalist MHP to third place. While support for the secular Kemalist CHP held firm, the AKP received 41 per cent of the votes, down from 50 per cent during the general election of 2011. Thus, the AKP's 12-year one-party rule was over. The 7 June election results also indicated an end to Erdoğan's dream of an executive presidency.

The ultra-nationalist MHP said that it would not be part of any talks if the Kurdish HDP were present, which immediately dashed any hope of a coalition. While the AKP and the CHP started negotiating, President Erdoğan threatened a snap election. After several weeks of meetings, the AKP and the CHP declared that, even though they had reached a consensus on a number of issues, they had failed to resolve their differences on some principal points, including foreign policy, education and the president's role.[49]

Everything was falling apart at the same time. A snap election was ahead, and the peace process had collapsed, ending a two-and-a-half-year ceasefire. Following the killing of two police officers, Turkey said it would start air strikes on PKK and ISIS targets in northern Iraq and Syria. The campaign was perceived as a cover for reducing the Kurdish presence in Syria, since these air strikes targeted Kurds more than ISIS zones. Not only had the Turkish government brought the bulk of its security apparatus to bear on the PKK, but it had also sought to use the international campaign against ISIS to further its conflict with the PKK.[50]

The PKK responded to Turkey's offensive first with its usual tactics, such as attacking the security forces, but then it switched to waging urban warfare, carrying the clashes into the cities. The YDG-H, the PKK's youth wing, dug trenches and built barricades in the middle of the streets in Cizre, Nusaybin and Sur, districts in south-eastern Turkey. Curfews were imposed, lasting in some cases for 100 days. The country was dragged deeper into chaos every day, with ISIS and PKK attacks in towns and cities.[51] The instability fanned the flames of the nationalistic rhetoric of Erdoğan and his AKP, which aimed to attract the nationalist constituency of the MHP.

Erdoğan always addresses his own constituency and does not care if to others he sounds outrageous or ominous. When asked about the clashes and the unrest in the Kurdish region and his '400 MPs' request prior to the elections, Erdoğan said, 'If a party had received enough votes to get 400 MPs, the situation [in Turkey] would be very different.'[52] What he meant was a warning signal for the upcoming elections: if you do not vote for the party I identify, the chaos and the misery will continue.

The electorate heard him and got the message. In the autumn of 2015, his agenda was to recoup the AKP's electoral losses and make it the single ruling party again. So many things were at stake for him, possibly even his freedom. Following the leaked corruption tapes of December 2013, several opposition members were agitating for him to stand trial at the Supreme Court. There was a good chance of him being formally charged, but only if he lost his grip on power. And hence he did everything he could to consolidate his position.

On 1 November 2015, the AKP not only regained the proportion of votes it had lost but also saw its greatest ever success in a general election, enabling it to reclaim its one-party dominance. The AKP had won, and so had Erdoğan. But Turkey had lost an invaluable opportunity: the chance to end a 40-year-old war, and therefore the chance of sustained peace.

From then on he would throw off the shackles of the country's constitutional and social norms. He would also break ties with his long-time comrades. From the outset, Prime Minister Ahmet Davutoğlu was obedient to the president's demands. However, that was not good enough for Erdoğan. Davutoğlu had gone beyond his remit and asked MIT chief Hakan Fidan to be his foreign minister, and the latter had resigned his post to take up the offer, only to return to his position in the MIT after Erdoğan vetoed the appointment. Erdoğan was also not comfortable with Davutoğlu's foreign policy ventures. He had been breaking deals with the EU on the Syrian refugee crisis and securing a one-on-one with US president Barack Obama. But it was mostly the steps taken during and after the Dolmabahçe accord with the Kurdish movement that enraged Erdoğan.

Almost everyone from the AKP who had been associated one way or another with the process was disposed of, along with Prime Minister Davutoğlu. Bülent Arınç, Yalçın Akdoğan and Efkan Ala had taken their place in the list of unwanted AKP members, which was already crowded with old allies, good friends such as former president Abdullah Gül, former chair of the parliament Cemil Çiçek, and also Beşir Atalay and Sadullah Ergin, who had once framed the AKP's standpoint on the Kurdish issue, including the peace process. Once they were out of the way, a different kind of club, whose members did not come from an Islamist background but had proved themselves to be extremely loyal to power, had aligned itself next to Erdoğan. They were mostly crude nationalists, conspiracy theorists and toadies who said whatever Reis – a macho nickname for Erdoğan, meaning 'chief' but with paternalistic connotations – wanted to hear.

The new line-up was an indicator of Erdoğan breaking ties not only with the possibility of a new Kurdish peace process but also with the AKP as we had known it.

Of course, no one had realized back then that a startling and gruesome event was to unfold, whose outcome would be another moment of truth for Turkey under Erdoğan.

SEVEN

What Do Kurds Want?

The PKK's young recruits and urban warfare

In the spring of 2016, one piece of horrible news followed another. In Cizre, a town in south-eastern Turkey, a dozen Kurdish people were trapped in a basement by clashes between Turkish soldiers and militants of the PKK. They were shot and killed when the building was burnt down. Two days later, seven Turkish officers were killed and 27 others wounded in a car-bomb attack carried out by the PKK in Diyarbakır.

This was a bloody war. A war that had been reignited after hopeful peace negotiations had collapsed in July 2015. A bloody war in which 100 days of curfews were imposed by the government. A war that forced almost 1.5 million Kurds to relocate and caused the deaths of thousands on both sides. A bloody war that broke out just when the people of Turkey thought peace was possible and within touching distance.

✳

Was it only Erdoğan's war? He could have prevented it, yes. He chose to go to war so as to be able to stay in charge for a few more years, yes. However, the PKK was also responsible for the resumption of the clashes.

According to the common narrative in government circles, the peace process had collapsed because 'the warlords in Qandil had exploited the process and used it to reorganize and augment their military capability'.

In fact, the peace process collapsed for three main reasons. First, the Turkish government's fear of a Rojava, an autonomous Kurdish region being forcibly inserted into Turkish territory. Second, Erdoğan's ambition to hold an executive presidency. Third, the PKK's gullibility in falling for Erdoğan's game and their anticipation of turning the Kurdish region of Turkey into a Rojava.

The PKK had miscalculated. It thought that the HDP's election victory on 7 June 2015 could be interpreted as support for the PKK. On the contrary, its unprecedented success at the ballot box meant support for the peace process, for a ceasefire and for the HDP's rhetoric on democracy and equality, not for the PKK. According to a PKK source quoted in *Al-Monitor*, the organization had received reports insisting that the people were ready for a popular uprising, and the PKK had believed it. The same source said many prominent names in Kurdish politics had tried to dissuade the PKK, but to no avail.[1]

The PKK anticipated that the legitimacy and the backing it had received in Syria for fighting ISIS would continue for the urban warfare they had started in Turkey. It believed that the Turkish government would not – and could not – use its full force to retaliate, for fear of civilian casualties. The PKK leaders were wrong. The party's youth wing, the YDG-H, started a trench war in places where the HDP received its highest numbers of votes in the June elections. In Diyarbakır's Sur district, the HDP received 79 per cent of the votes, in Şırnak 91 per cent, in Silopi 89 per cent and in Nusaybin 90 per cent. Those were the places where the violence had peaked.

Demirtaş, whose party was the main political victim of the clashes, observed,

> To me, the PKK is made up of honourable people who stood up against the state to protest at the persecution of the Kurds. I never endorsed their method of resistance but I always tried to understand why they chose violent means. After the 7 June elections, when we had created a wide-open window for politics to enter the field, I do not understand why they continued with violence. I know it is hard for them to disarm when there are threats like

ISIS in the Middle East, but they should not have used violence against Turkey.[2]

When the PKK realized that it was not receiving any social support from its constituency and that Western powers preferred a stable Turkey to bolstering their proxy force, the PKK/YPG, in Syria, they tried to rationalize their decision to go to war.

The leaders in Qandil claimed that the Turkish state was determined to sink the peace process because of the developments in Rojava and that this had been agreed on by Turkey's National Security Council in October 2014. What the PKK implied was that no action by the PKK would change the course of events, since the government would pursue its offensive against the PKK regardless.

The urban warfare that manifested itself in appalling clashes between the Turkish security forces and the YDG-H lasted almost a year, ending in May 2016. The damage was severe. Reports by the Human Rights Association, the Human Rights Foundation and Diyarbakır Bar Association showed unarmed civilians, including women and children, being deliberately shot by snipers or from tanks. The reports also '[quoted] witnesses and relatives in Cizre which suggest that more than 100 people were burned to death as they sheltered in three different basements that had been surrounded by security forces'.[3] The apartment buildings where those three basements were located were on Bostancı Street, Narin Street and Akdeniz Street, three once lively and vibrant places. When the fighting ended, neither those apartment blocks, which were almost totally burned down, nor the rest of Cizre were recognizable to the town's inhabitants.

Residences and many community buildings and parts of the infrastructure were massively destroyed. Cities where clashes occurred were sealed off and no proper communication maintained. No journalists were allowed at the scenes. During the ensuing blackout of the region, which lasted several weeks, all forms of ill-treatment and arbitrary 'security' measures became commonplace.

According to the Ministry of Internal Affairs, half of the population in four districts – Nusaybin, Cizre, Sur and Silopi – had been affected by the fighting to some extent, among them 100,000 people who'd had to flee their homes.[4] While other representatives of the AKP government estimated a much larger figure, 355,000 people,[5] human rights groups put the number of displaced at 1.3 million. The death toll was 285, 38 of whom were children.[6]

Fifteen-year-old Ibrahim was shot in his garden by a sniper while he was seeing his brother-in-law off in December 2015. 'I called the ambulance nearly 20 times. Nobody came until the morning,' said his father, adding,

> After he was pronounced dead at the hospital, they called us to come and collect his body but we could not go, because there was heavy gunfire around our house in Sur. We could not leave the house for 28 days. The government buried our son.[7]

Hediye Şen, a 32-year-old mother of three, was shot eight times as she was walking towards the outdoor toilet. 'We were about to eat our supper when I heard the gunshots. It was a sniper,' her husband explained. 'It is impossible for the security forces not to have known we were civilians. They killed my wife. The *sarma* she cooked is still in the fridge.'[8]

How does a nation get over such trauma? It does not. How could Hediye's children, Ibrahim's siblings and many others go on with their lives without feeling anger and resentment? They could not. How could they not curse their bad luck for being born in the wrong part of the country? Would they (inevitably?) hold a grudge against the government? Or would they resent the PKK's actions? No one knows.

✻

This is a vicious circle. The Republic of Turkey's history is full of these painful stories that build up one on top of another. The Kurdish youngsters of the YDG-H who slung on a rifle, dug trenches and built barricades were the sons, daughters, brothers and sisters of those killed in the south-eastern region during the fighting of the 1990s. They had witnessed the worst, most obscene kinds of brutality. Children of the region in those years had seen their friends blown to pieces because they stepped on a mine.[9] They had to live with the bodies of their dead relatives for days because of continuous gunfire. Those were the children who cannot forget that smell. The smell of death, the smell of mercilessness, the smell of being trapped.

'No kid who lived in the region in the 1990s could say they lived well. You wake up one morning, the police raid your house, kick your father, harass your mother,' says Ayhan from Hakkâri, adding,

> Curfews were imposed as part of a state of emergency that lasted for years. My little brother was a few minutes late coming home because the police had beaten him badly. He was 12 years old. The following morning, he left the house and never came back. He joined the guerrilla forces.[10]

Vehbi from Diyarbakır remembers coming home from school one day in 1993 and seeing his house being burned down by soldiers:

> 'We are very poor: please don't burn our house down,' I begged the soldier, but he did not listen. I cried when the house went up in flames. It was not only our house; my childhood was being destroyed there. I never cried again in my life. Never.[11]

Here is another poignant story of how youths lost hope and defected from the system they were once happily a part of: the Turkish media had met Uğurcan, a sweet chubby boy, in 2009, when he was a 13-year-old high-school student. He had been among a crowd waiting for Turkey's then president, Abdullah Gül, to pass by in Dersim, a mainly Kurdish and Alawite city in eastern Turkey.

When the president drew near, he shouted a line his parents had taught him, 'We don't want dams in Munzur Valley!'[12] President Gül turned towards the voice and asked the boy to come forward. After kissing the boy's hands, he listened to his worry.

Five years later, Uğurcan signed up for his compulsory military service in Turkey's army. A peace process between the PKK and the

Turkish government had already begun. For all Kurds and democrats in the country, the process lit a spark of hope. An unconventional but bloody 40-year-old war could soon be over. Kurds like Uğurcan would be granted their birthrights, such as education in their mother tongue. The prohibition on free speech and the suppression of human rights through anti-terror laws could cease. Uğurcan believed in this promise, as did many Kurdish young people.

When the peace process collapsed in the summer of 2015, the chubby boy whose hands had been kissed by the president thought there was only one thing for Kurdish young people left to do. He went up to the mountains and joined the PKK. A year later, in October 2016, Uğurcan was one of 13 PKK members killed in the rocky terrain of Dersim province.

What was it that led a boy from the affectionate greeting of the president to the harsh ambience of the mountains? How would a high-school graduate, who was once so eager to be conscripted that he falsified his legal age, end up fighting the Turkish army three years later?

This was a narrative of how one is radicalized. This was a radicalization process that even the PKK was struggling to put a stop to.

In the 1990s, the PKK had a strong top-down hierarchy. The top leaders used to control and claim responsibility for every act of violence by the PKK, but the post-peace process indicated a shift of strategy – not only in terms of transferring the battle from rural to urban places, but also of using a looser chain of command. Accordingly, the PKK leaders gave smaller units on the ground the sole authority to instigate violent attacks. The YDG-H militants on the street said that they were 'self-organized PKK sympathizers' and since 'they knew that the government would drop the peace talks, they grew and organized themselves in the meantime'.[13]

The Turkish government accused the PKK of exploiting the peace process and arming young people in Kurdish cities. Whether the PKK would have carried on with urban warfare even if the peace process had gone well, or armed young people as a back-up plan if the process had failed, is unknown.

When I put this as a written question to Karayılan, he denied sending any arms to the cities while the peace process was going on, saying, '[T]hose weapons were already there, before the process. We also asked the YDG-H twice to refrain from violence, but these young people could not stand the attitude of the police in the region.'

He also admitted that, although the main goal was to 'announce self-rule in certain districts', 'using arms as a tool for that purpose was not a good idea'.[14] Other PKK leaders followed Karayılan's lead in regretting the urban warfare. 'The balance sheet has recorded some heavy numbers,' claimed Duran Kalkan. 'We didn't expect such a response from the government. We made a mistake. We thought our enemies were human beings.'[15]

What is certain is that the PKK relied on the anger of those young people who unfortunately were born into a war zone in the 1990s and misinterpreted the victories of the Syrian Kurds. The PKK thought it could declare certain districts in Diyarbakır, Hakkâri and Şırnak autonomous, as the PYD/YPG had done in northern Syria. This did not work, and the PKK returned to its earlier strategy of attacking security targets with vehicle-borne explosive devices (VBEDs).

Although the PKK reverted to its original violent methods, a Pandora's box had been opened. Furious young Kurds, whom the elders of the Kurdish movement used to call the Storm Youth, had been armed in the cities. Öcalan had described the YDG-H as 'a disordered structure'[16] and expressed his displeasure to the HDP envoy who visited him in February 2015. He might have been the only one to have an influence over those youngsters, since they 'considered the Turkish state as the enemy, the Kurdish people in jail as hostages and the Kurdish political party very lightweight, not forceful enough'.[17]

That was the case at the beginning of the clashes. In July 2015, prominent members of the Kurdish movement went to Cizre to try to subdue the masked militants of the YDG-H, but they were unsuccessful. Even Qandil reportedly had difficulty convincing and controlling them at times, ever since the first decade of the 2000s.[18]

The reason for this was very simple. The grandparents of those young militants, although aware of the implications of the state's Kurdish policy, led their lives alongside Turks, with whom they had social and commercial relationships as well as familial and emotional ties. But their grandchildren have grown up with war, watching their parents' suffering. To them, a Turk means the gendarmerie, the police and the prosecutors – people who make life difficult for them. They are an outraged generation, embittered and wrathful.

The 'Saturday Mothers', who lost their loved ones during the horrible period of the 1990s, are also called Peace Mothers, because whenever they gathered together, they stressed that they sought not revenge but peace. They held their hands out to Turkish soldiers' mothers, saying, 'We lost our children, and we wish that no Turkish mother should lose hers.' The same feeling does not prevail among their grandchildren. Kurdish youth now have a different philosophy: 'If they won't leave us alone, if we cannot live a humane life here, then everybody may as well be tormented and suffer.'[19] They are angry at the state, at their party, at their parents. They are angry with anyone who tries to mitigate their anger. They are just angry. Their fervent bitterness will not be assuaged until their people, the Kurds, get what they want.

'You Kurds have everything!'

Several years ago I visited a shanty *kahvehane*[20] in Tarlabaşı, Taksim. Provoked by my questions, two elderly men playing backgammon started talking politics in a bantering sort of way, joking and teasing each other. 'You Kurds, you have everything,' one of them bellowed. 'What don't you have that I have as a Turk? This country has given you everything. You can do business as Turks do. You can earn money the way Turks do. You can be an MP or even prime minister. Don't be ungrateful.' These two men had been neighbours for 15 years and were very close friends. 'What is this language you are speaking, huh?' responded the Kurdish man. 'This is your mother's language. I don't speak my mother's language. I don't know how. My children and my grandchildren are the same. Yes, yes, we are equals, but only when we lead a Turkish life. Am I ungrateful? No, the government is ungrateful to us.' They went on rolling dice as if nothing had been said, and agreed to watch the football match together at the *kahvehane* after supper.

In Turkey, *kahvehane*s, like cabs, are regarded as the real social media of the people, barometers of social tension and revealing vignettes from the national discourse about power and control. This dialogue about the Kurdish issue superbly illustrates this function. Saying things like 'What more do Kurds want? We have given them everything' cleverly allows the speaker to get away with sounding scrupulous and patronizing at the same time. State indoctrination keeps Turkish minds in a comfort zone. They do not feel the need to follow the phrase 'We have given you everything' with any of the obvious questions. Why would you be in a position to 'give' a certain individual his birthrights? Why would you bestow on your next-door neighbour, your fellow citizen, the opportunities that you enjoy just because of the accident of being born Turkish? If Kurds feel they have equality when they act as Kurds, why have they been fighting for the last four decades? Would someone, anyone, fight just because they are ungrateful? These questions do not enter into the average person's thinking. This may be a good thing in the sense that obliviousness to the issue creates the space for people to roll the dice and get on with their day. For the younger generation, with their keen awareness, however, the rules of the game have changed over the years.

When the peace process began in 2013, the demands of the Kurdish movement could be summarized as follows: equal access to education in their mother tongue; the release of sick prisoners convicted of being members of the PKK and/or KCK; amendments to the anti-terror law that limited freedom of speech and the right to organize; an amnesty (with certain exceptions) for PKK fighters post-conflict; dismantling of the 50,000-strong, pro-government Kurdish village guard militia in the south-east region; improvement of the prison conditions of Abdullah Öcalan; a change to the definition of citizenship in the constitution; and, above all, devolution of power in the state structure. What looked like a few legislative reforms that could be delivered in the space of a month by a government determined to make these concessions had proven to be almost impossible. The most challenging of the Kurdish demands were related to Öcalan's conditions of imprisonment and the devolution of power.

One of the main reasons why the Kurdish conflict in Turkey has remained unresolved for decades is 'separation phobia' on the part of the government and the Turkish public. Even mention of the word 'Kurdistan' fuels that phobia and is found offensive by many Turks.[21] On the other hand, the Kurdish movement has never ceased to declare that what it is looking for is not 'an independent Kurdish state' but a solution within Turkey's borders. However, from the narratives of Kurdish politicians, it is not easy to obtain a clear picture of how this solution within Turkey would be realized.

'For me, İmralı prison has become a battleground of realities in terms of the Kurdish issue,' wrote Abdullah Öcalan in his book *Kürdistan – Devrim Manifestosu (Kurdistan – Revolutionary Manifesto)*,

> especially overcoming the concept of the nation state. I thought this concept was a Marxist–Stalinist–Leninist principle for a long time. It was an irreplaceable dogma for me. We never thought a different kind of nationalism could be possible. If there is a nation, then there must be a state too. If Kurds were a nation, then there must be a Kurdish state. That was our thinking. But when I focused on social facts, I realized that the nation state is a cage for societies and that freedom and society are more valuable concepts. From that moment, I knew I was a victim of capitalist modernity.[22]

As Öcalan observed, the Kurds did not – at least not in the short term – demand independence, but only a serious devolution of central authority to regional assemblies in the Kurdish region.

Twice in the last decade, the Democratic Society Congress (DTK) declared 'autonomy', which was intended as an irritant, rather than a statement of fact, and which did not alter the status quo. These declarations stayed on paper and had no effect. The first was in the summer of 2011 and coincided with the terrible news of a clash between the

PKK and the Turkish army, which led to the deaths of 13 soldiers in an ambush. Unsurprisingly, the negative reaction to the declaration of autonomy doubled. Like much of the rhetoric coming out of the Kurdish movement regarding autonomy, this did not involve any specifics, only general principles. The declaration expressed the aspiration not only to build between 20 and 25 autonomous regions within Turkey but also to reshape the Middle East with Öcalan's decentralized paradigm that involves village communes and city assemblies.[23]

Tarık Ziya Ekinci, one of the first Kurdish politicians to demand rights for the Kurds, poured scorn on the declaration:

> Declaring autonomy has no meaning. There are two things: one is essence, the other is form. When you look at their declaration, you find a nice form with references to international agreements, but look more closely and you'll wonder what it has as its essence. What the DTK has done has no practical consequence.[24]

The 2011 declaration of autonomy comprised eight dimensions, namely Political, Social, Cultural, Economic, Ecological, Diplomatic, Legal and Self-Defence,[25] and is summarized below:

POLITICAL DIMENSION: Starting from the grassroots, village communes, town, district and neighbourhood councils and city councils will organize themselves in the form of a confederate organization that will have democratic representation in the body politic. The Democratic Congress of the Autonomous Kurdistan Community will send its representatives to the parliament of the Democratic Republic of Turkey and take part in the politics of the common homeland. Democratic Autonomous Kurdistan will have its own original flags and symbols that represent them. In addition, different communities in the democratic autonomous region will use their own symbols. Decision-making authority in each democratic autonomy primarily belongs to the delegates of village, neighbourhood, district and city councils. Through the people's assemblies, each community will express, discuss and make decisions. It is based on participant, pluralistic and direct popular democracy.

LEGAL DIMENSION: We see Turkey and Kurdistan as a common homeland. The law of democratic autonomy should be recognized as part of the new Constitution of the Republic of Turkey and EU law and secured through mutual agreements.

SELF-DEFENCE DIMENSION: With the acceptance of democratic autonomy, under the supervision of the democratic organs, self-defence can be established not as a military monopoly but for the external and internal needs of the society.

CULTURAL DIMENSION: All barriers to the use of the Kurdish language in public should be removed and the Kurdish language should become the language of education from kindergarten to university. The constitution and laws should provide legal protection to all languages and their dialects spoken in our geographical region (Assyrian–Syriac, Arabic, Armenian, etc.), used in education and developed alongside the Kurdish and Turkish languages, which are the official languages of Democratic Autonomous Kurdistan. The language for social services should be Kurdish and the original names of the settlements will be reinstated.

SOCIAL DIMENSION: The re-establishment of society in Democratic Autonomous Kurdistan will be realized with the free organization of labour, education, health, solidarity and similar social elements, under the leadership of women and youth in particular. The social dimension of Democratic Autonomous Kurdistan has the potential to discuss, take decisions, restructure and put a plan into operation, and for that reason will be the basis for other dimensions to be implemented. The leading forces of democratic confederate organization in Democratic Autonomous Kurdistan are women and young people. Therefore, the role of women is essential in communal life and in all areas.

ECONOMIC DIMENSION: Democratic autonomy should establish its own economic model in order to permanently institutionalize the system of free and democratic life for the Kurdish people. It is an undeniable reality that the deepest crisis facing society is caused by capitalism. Expressing this reality, the leader of the Kurdish people has stated that 'capitalism is not an economy but is against the economy'. The economy requires socialization and democracy.

ECOLOGICAL DIMENSION: The ecological destruction perpetrated for militaristic, political and economic reasons has done serious damage to the geography of Kurdistan and its social structure. Many villages and forests have been burned and residential areas demolished as a result of dam projects, and other development plans jeopardize historic cultural monuments. Some pastures have been flooded, while others have been left with no water and have turned into desert. Thousands of square metres of farmland have been sown with mines, making farming impossible. It is necessary to oppose urbanization that is damaging the ecological balance, dam structures that change the flora of an area and the flooding of historic sites that wipe out the Kurdish people's history.

DIPLOMATIC DIMENSION: Diplomacy in Democratic Autonomous Kurdistan should play a role in developing peace and brotherhood for our region; it should encourage economic development and increase wealth. Diplomacy with stateless nations, peoples, groups and societies struggling for democracy and freedom will be conducted in mutual solidarity and trust.[26]

The second declaration of democratic autonomy by the DTK came shortly after the peace process collapsed in 2015. The declaration, which was announced with opening remarks by HDP co-chairs Selahattin Demirtaş and Figen Yüksekdağ, had 14 points:

1. Based on geographic, cultural and economic proximity, one or two cities will be declared autonomous regions.

2. All these regions will be governed by autonomous bodies, which will be appointed from the democratically elected assemblies. These bodies will also be represented equally in the Turkish General Assembly (TBMM).

3. The authority to depose elected people will be removed from central government in order to destroy its ascendancy.

4. Councils of the town or village, women and young people will be directly involved in the decision-making process.

5. Women will be represented equally in the decision-making process and in the cadres of the autonomous system of governance. No decision that deals in any way with women's issues will be implemented without the approval of the women's councils.

6. Young people will be represented equally in the autonomous bodies.

7. Education policies at every level will be decided in the autonomous bodies. All mother tongues will be [accepted as] the language of education alongside Turkish. Local languages will be considered as official alongside Turkish.

8. Religious bodies will be decentralized and organized independently.

9. All levels of healthcare will be the responsibility of the autonomous regions.

10. The judicial system will be re-established according to the autonomous regions.

11. Land, water and energy resources of each region will be managed by the relevant autonomous assembly.

12. Transport services will be managed and monitored by the relevant autonomous body.

13. A fair amount of revenue from taxpayers will be given to the relevant autonomous body.

14. Local security forces will be formed that will operate under the provisions of the autonomous state. They will act in coordination with the central security and defence bodies.[27]

Since the collapse of the peace process, the Turkish government's discourse concerning the Kurdish demands has reverted to expressing the original separation phobia, coinciding with the developments in Syria. President Erdoğan, addressing the cabinet in his presidential palace, said, 'Turkey is at the crossroads and she will either expand or shrink in this new status quo in the Middle East.'[28] The idea of the National Pact (Misak-ı Millî) was resurrected to justify Turkey's military presence in Syria and to prevent the Kurdish cantons, which are not contiguous, from appropriating land in order to link up with one another. On the other hand, the establishment of Rojava meant that Turkey's Kurds will not be satisfied with anything less than an autonomous state of their own. 'A decentralized Turkish government will not suffice at this stage, because it is not a full solution but only a partial one. The Kurdish region demands an autonomous council elected by the people.'[29]

The PKK and its constituency place great emphasis on Rojava, making symbolic references to its own birth. It was in 1979 that Öcalan and a handful of his comrades crossed the border from Urfa, Suruç, to Kobane after agreeing to form the PKK. Thus, it was crucial not only to fight to take control of Rojava from the regime forces but also to establish a system of democratic confederalism, which was the brainchild of Öcalan.

In the last 15 years, Öcalan (and thus the PKK) has developed three integrated projects: a democratic republic, democratic autonomy and democratic confederalism.[30] The democratic republic proposes a citizenship rights-based democracy within the framework of a reform that will enable a transformation from a 'nation state' to a 'citizen state' in the Turkish political system. Democratic autonomy signifies people describing and celebrating their own cultural features in the new citizen state, whereas confederalism means the right to self-organize, from the bottom up.

Based on this formula, 'democratic republic' represents a project for reforming the state, whereas 'democratic autonomy' and 'democratic confederalism' represent an idea of politics beyond and without the state. One of the main goals of the PKK is to realize the democratic confederalism project and establish the Kurdistan Democratic Society. This means that independence is possible through a real democratic confederalism, rather than the classic state-building process that establishes an all-inclusive governing structure. In this model, 'capitalism, the nation state, and industrialism' are replaced with a 'democratic nation, communal economy, and ecological industry'.[31]

Why is Rojava so important to Kurds?

In the spring of 2016, two scholars, one from an Ivy League university and one from Oxbridge, met in a room at the House of Commons to talk about the Kurdish issue. When the topic eventually turned to what was happening in Rojava, the two scholars succumbed to the utopian ideal that had been generated by this piece of land in Syria. Rojava had become a spark of hope for others, too, an ideology that represented an alternative to statism and already failing democratic institutions. But how might it work, and – more importantly – how sustainable would it be?

After a deadly attack on Bashar al-Assad's key figures on 18 July 2012, the opposition had taken control of Jerablus and Munbic. The Syrian regime had come to a crossroads. In order to control the country's main lifelines, it needed to transfer more military force to Damascus, Hama, Dera and Homs, which meant that it could not afford a front line in the northern parts of the country where Kurdish rebels led by the PYD were holed up. Pulling out of Rojava (northern Syria) signalled a tacit connivance with a Kurdish entity, which actually served Assad's purpose for three reasons. First, Kurdish rebels were not collaborating with the Free Syrian Army, which was composed of international proxy fighters. Second, Assad calculated that, after the war ended, he would be able to negotiate with the Kurds more easily. Third, creating a window for an autonomous Kurdistan near the Turkish border would act as an irritant to the Turkish government, whose leadership, according to Assad, was pursuing a neo-Ottoman dream of expanding Turkish influence over Syria.[32]

It was not the first time that the Syrian regime had employed such a strategy. While persecuting the Syrian Kurds in the 1980s, it had allowed the PKK to flourish on its soil. According to Öcalan, it was a tactical alliance between Hafız Assad and the PKK leadership and each was using the other as a bargaining chip against Turkey.[33] More than three decades later, Hafız Assad's son was playing the same game in a different setting with a slightly different cast.

A day after regime troops withdrew from Rojava, on 19 June 2012, the PYD took control of Kobane, Afrin and Amude. The Movement for a Democratic Society (TEV-DEM), formed as an umbrella organization of left-wing Kurdish entities including the PYD, rose to the occasion and began to establish an autonomous region. The framework relied on Öcalan's democratic confederalism idea. Öcalan had adopted American social theorist Murray Bookchin's interpretation of socialism known as libertarian municipalism[34] and construed it as democratic confederalism.

The democratic confederalism idea also bore many similarities to the Zapatista movement in southern Mexico, such as 'the pursuit of creating an autonomous government, the rise of popular assemblies, the emphasis on gender equality and empowering women on every level of social and political life, the anti-imperialist and anti-authoritarian ideology, the stress on ecological preservation'.[35] It is also impossible to ignore the resemblance of its communal scheme to the Paris Commune.

In January 2014, the Rojava administration declared a 'Charter of the Autonomous Regions of Afrin, Jazira, and Kobane'. The main focuses were decentralization, free education in the mother tongue, healthcare, housing and an end to child labour and any discrimination against women. The charter also claimed not to recognize the concept of a nation state based on military power, religion and centralism. The 'Social Contract of Rojava Cantons in Syria' read:

> We, the people of the Democratic Autonomous Regions of Afrin, Jazira and Kobane, a confederation of Kurds, Arabs, Syrics, Arameans, Turkmen, Armenians and Chechens [...] unite in the spirit of reconciliation, pluralism and democratic participation so that all may express themselves freely in public life. In building a

society free from authoritarianism, militarism, centralism and the intervention of religious authority in public affairs, the Charter recognizes Syria's territorial integrity and aspires to maintain domestic and international peace. [...] In pursuit of freedom, justice, dignity and democracy and led by principles of equality and environmental sustainability, the Charter proclaims a new social contract, based upon mutual and peaceful coexistence and understanding between all strands of society. It protects fundamental human rights and liberties and reaffirms the peoples' right to self-determination.[36]

Under the terms of this contract, the PYD's armed militia, the YPG, was designated as the sole military force of Rojava, which comprised three cantons. For the policing, an Asayish (Kurdish for 'security') force was formed, and improvised local councils, self-defence committees, Kurdish language schools, courts and banks were set up.

Although Rojava was built on fertile land rich in important oil resources, it was solidarity from Kurds abroad that helped Syrian Kurds to meet their basic needs at the beginning, since both Turkey and the KRG had imposed an embargo on Rojava.[37] In fact, 40 per cent of Syria's wheat supply came from the processing plants in Cizre and Kobane. Before the civil war erupted, the Syrian regime had obtained 60 per cent of its oil from the resources in Rojava. Nonetheless, owing to the embargo and not being acknowledged by international organizations as a legitimate entity, the Rojava administration could export neither oil nor wheat. According to the Academy of Social Economy in Rojava, 'their communal economy relies on a network of cooperatives that allows private ownership but blocks monopoly'.[38]

The three cantons in Rojava are composed of approximately 300 communes, each of which has two co-chairs, one man and one woman, like all political entities influenced by Öcalan, including those in Turkey. The communes form committees of three to five people, according to the needs of their village or district. In 2014, this system inspired the governance of several villages in Hakkâri, a city in south-eastern Turkey.[39]

The 735 inhabitants of the village of Üzümcü decided to found communal assemblies to resolve their local problems. According to the co-chair of the commune, they managed, through communal effort, to build roads and fountains in common spaces, with clean drinking water.[40] Although this kind of practice, called *imece*, used to be very common during the early days of the Republic and was a crucial part of Atatürk's developmental strategy, it would never be seen as such in the eyes of the current Turkish government.

The Turkish government did not realize that it was not that Rojava was influencing Turkey's Kurdish movement but the other way around. The umbrella organization KCK – which includes the PKK and PYD, along with many other Kurdish political organizations in the Middle East – and the DTK of Turkey, which consists of representatives from more than 500 civil society organizations, labour unions and political parties, were part of the PKK and Öcalan's plan for democratic confederalism. The provisions for democratic autonomy that the DTK had proposed in 2011 and 2015 were actually a blueprint for what was being established in Rojava.

The government structure in Rojava was socialist, whereas the government in northern Iraq, which likes to boast of being the first Kurdish autonomous region, is nationalist conservative. Rojava served as the laboratory for developing a system of governance that was an alternative not only to capitalism but also to the existing model of socialism.[41] It was also an experiment to test if the PKK's proposal for democratic autonomy could work on the ground. This was precisely why so much importance was attributed to Rojava by the Kurdish movement in Turkey and Syria. On the other hand, it was also the main reason why the Turkish government was so disturbed by the developments in Rojava and redesigned its Syrian policy solely to put a spoke in Rojava's wheel.

Ironically, the same reasoning applies to ISIS's special hostility towards Rojava. According to a 2015 report by Diyarbakır-based research company SAMER (Siyasal ve Sosyal Araştırmalar Merkezi), ISIS sees the Rojava model as a threat to its raison d'être, not to mention to its ideology. 'IS thinks that unless neutralized, this model could be preferred all over the Middle East, even by its base supporters.'[42] Hence, it is crucial for ISIS to obstruct any influence coming from Rojava and to prevent the PKK from gaining a stronghold in the Middle East.

Undoubtedly, questions were raised regarding Rojava's inclusiveness of all ethnicities and the sustainability of the system. The portrayal of Rojava as a utopian dream by the Kurdish movement and Western socialist, libertarian, leftist circles may not be the whole picture. Although there are almost a dozen opposing political organizations in Rojava, such as KDP-backed nationalists, they are not allowed to have their own defence units and can only function under the YPG umbrella.

Within the existing system, one of the main obstacles is connecting the PYD, the administration and all laws and institutions to a highly ideological social project (a social revolution and the development of 'democratic autonomy', as theorized by Öcalan). The political party that wants to participate in Rojava's political arena should first recognize the PYD-led administrative system and social contract. Otherwise it will not be represented within the system. On top of that, it has been reported that those parties that did not recognize the PYD as the administrative power experienced arrest and detention of activists and leaders, and that offices were raided and media outlets closed.

At a council meeting in Irbil in 2011, Iraqi Kurdistan's Masoud Barzani sponsored the foundation of a Kurdish National Council (KNC/ENKS in Kurdish), which consisted of more than a dozen Syrian Kurdish parties. Because the KNC as a whole does not recognize the PYD-led administration, the political parties within the KNC have taken to actively opposing the Rojava administration. Harriet Allsopp, author of the book *The Kurds of Syria: Political Parties and Identity in the Middle East*, who is also working on a field report regarding the situation in Rojava, says,

Even within local communes, respondents to my research in Syria report their domination by Havals [friends of the PYD]. And whilst the process of direct democracy is implemented in many local societal issues, there is a clear gap between democratic processes relating to policy and to local society and a bias towards supporters of the PYD/administration.[43]

Even though the PYD-led administration has processes for self-criticism, evaluation and reflection at all levels, 'the non-participation of KNC parties and of much of the population suggests that ideological and political fault lines will remain obstacles to the revolution and to achieving democratic representation for all the Kurds there.'[44]

An Amnesty International mission that visited northern Syria in October 2015 revealed that there has been a wave of forced displacement and home demolitions of Arabs and Turkmen, amounting to war crimes, often 'in retaliation for people's perceived sympathies with, or family ties to, suspected members of IS or other armed groups'.[45] A former US ambassador to Damascus, speaking at a Senate panel on Syria, claimed that 'even though YPG is indispensable for the coalition against ISIS', it is 'driving people into the arms of Isil [ISIS], executing prisoners and killing hundreds of people in recent inter-factional fighting'.[46]

Not surprisingly, the Rojava administration denied these allegations outright, saying the witnesses Amnesty had talked to were fake.[47] Nevertheless, it should be noted that civilians had become collateral damage in numerous attacks by the YPG's default patron, the PKK, in Turkey. Although the PKK leadership has occasionally apologized for such incidents over the years, this has not prevented it from waging offensives in places where civilian casualties were highly likely.

According to the officers of Rojava, '80% of the people in Rojava support the revolution, with a significant percentage of the [other] 20% feeling reluctant, primarily because of fears that Assad's army would return and seek reprisal'.[48] However, Arabs and Chechens have serious reservations about supporting and adhering to the Rojava promise because of a belief that the project is doomed to fail. According to the secretary general of the Kurdish Democratic Progressive Party (KDPP),

Arabs and Assyrians say that the administration in Rojava does not mean anything to them, while Kurds feel that there is nothing special for the Kurds in Rojava. Hence, they are worried that Rojava will not pose an answer to the Kurdish issue in the Middle East.[49]

Cizre canton's legislative council chair, Ekrem Huso, on the other hand, shoots holes in the ideal of the so-called 'Rojava Revolution' in terms that are reminiscent of George Orwell's *Animal Farm*, where a proclamation of 'all animals are equal but some are more equal than others' was made. 'Here all components of a democratic nation are equal,' said Huso. 'But Rojava is Kurdi. We hope that when our troubles are resolved in Syria, Rojava will become a Kurdistani region.'[50]

Surmounting the nationalist ideals of the people living in Rojava therefore looks like a bigger challenge than penning an idealistic charter.

The overwhelming reverence for Öcalan as almost a spiritual being, who cannot be criticized or challenged in any way in the Kurdish movement, is sharply at odds with Rojava's non-hierarchical structure and 'people's governance'. As the experience in Turkey shows, the PKK leadership have a tendency to be condescending and to assert their mastery over the legal political parties. There are, for example, recorded incidents of PKK leaders deciding who should stand as a candidate for the political party HDP in the general elections in Turkey.[51] It cannot be assumed that the PKK/Öcalan-influenced YPG would not act in the same fashion at times of disagreement.

Whether people in Rojava would find ways to overcome challenges such as these, which threaten the much-vaunted principles of democratic confederalism or fall into the trap of nationalism, is not yet known. But it is certain that the administration in Rojava is unquestionably the most progressive secular Muslim entity in the Middle East, in a region where sectarianism and fundamentalism, blood and tears have long been the norm. Rojava has also evidently passed a threshold for the Kurdish movement in Turkey by showing that, under certain circumstances, the people have the ability and organizational skill to build a self-ruling structure. They will no longer settle for anything less. And now they also have a model to point to when they are asked the ultimate question – what do Kurds actually want? The answer is already there: something like Rojava.

EIGHT

The Coup Attempt that Shook Turkey

What really happened that night?

S ome people would be astonished to learn how many academic articles and news stories made confident statements such as 'it is highly unlikely that there will be a coup in Turkey at this stage'. And yet it happened. Again. On 15 July 2016, Turkey experienced its fifth attempt at a *coup d'état*. The first one, on 27 May 1960, had led to the then president, prime minister and others being tried for treason and hanged. The military took over on 12 March 1971 to 'restore order'.

The worst and most brutal coup took place on 12 September 1980, after clashes between right- and left-wing groups erupted into palpable unrest all over the country. Half a million people were detained, hundreds of thousands were arrested and tortured, while dozens were executed following the coup. The fourth, on 28 February 1997, is characterized as a post-modern coup, since there was no actual military takeover; instead, due to pressure from the army, the Islamic-based Welfare Party's leader, Necmettin Erbakan, founder of the National Vision movement from which the AKP and Recep Tayyip Erdoğan had emerged, was forced to step down.

The majority of ordinary people and the intelligentsia in Turkey did not expect another coup, not because Turkey had already had its fair share in the past, but simply because of the misperception that Erdoğan and his AKP, in collaboration with the Gülen movement, had tamed the army and intimidated any probable junta clique with trials like Ergenekon and Sledgehammer.

Many also took the army at its word; two months before the botched coup, it had publicly announced that 'several allegations that a coup is being planned' were completely 'unfounded'.[1] In hindsight, not only the Turkish public but also the higher echelons of the military were caught off guard on 15 July.

It was 9 p.m. on a Friday, a time when Istanbulites are usually stuck in traffic over the bridge or are strolling along the shoreline to enjoy the evening with friends and family. If you live in a country like Turkey where there is a 40-year-old violent conflict and a quagmire called the Middle East on your doorstep, you learn to put it to one side and get on with life. You go out with friends on a Friday, even though ISIS attacked your city's biggest international airport just a few weeks ago.[2] You like to believe that shrugging your shoulders and saying 'C'est la vie' makes you brave rather than uncaring, because you do not surrender to the tactics of terrorists. You keep on going. No doubt it is just a basic human defence mechanism, but this is the attitude that kept Turkish people sane through the attacks of ISIS and the collapse of the peace process.

But just when you, the ordinary Turkish person, thought that it could not get any worse, it did. Several squadrons barricaded one of Istanbul's best-known landmarks, the Bosphorus Bridge. Perhaps, you thought, intelligence had been received, warning of another disastrous ISIS attack, and the soldiers were there to protect people from a terrorist threat. A frenetic hour later, it was clear that the soldiers were not there to protect the people but to attack them. It was a coup attempt. But what kind of a coup was it? It did not bear any of the hallmarks of previous military coups, so people were left confused, caught between *A coup is happening* and *Coups don't happen like this*.

Military takeovers, as the Turkish public knows well, happen before dawn, not during the Friday rush hour, with jets flying low in Ankara and the gendarmerie closing down the Bosphorus Bridge in Istanbul. In Turkey, people sometimes talk of 'waking up to the noise of an army tank', referring to a midnight military takeover. This coup had not been planned thoroughly from the start, since communication was still flowing freely through social media and TV stations. While the coup plotters went to the state TV headquarters and forced the staff there to broadcast their manifesto, the ministers of the ruling Justice and Development Party (AKP), the former prime minister and the president made statements via FaceTime on privately owned TV channels.

Following the call from President Erdoğan through social media, which he once described as a menace to society, people went out onto the streets. Almost 250 people died during clashes with the soldiers. People's resistance contributed to the failure of the coup attempt, but it was the army itself that fought against the plotters in its midst.

Condemnation of the attempt came unanimously from all sections of society and political parties. On the night of 15 July, MPs from opposition parties gathered at the parliament, along with AKP MPs, to show solidarity. The stance of the main opposition party, the CHP (Republican People's Party), was crucial, because the CHP represents the centre-left Kemalists and secularists, an influential component of Turkish society.

Secularists, despite their strong opposition to the AKP's policies, opposed the coup because they knew all too well that what is worse than an authoritarian regime that consistently aims to crush a robust civil society is a military takeover – particularly in this case, when the military takeover was thought to have been orchestrated by Gülenists.

After the coup failed, an illusionary spring bubbled up in society, which seemed to indicate that the stark polarization created by AKP followers and secularists was reducing. An adviser to the former prime minister even said, 'If it weren't for the people, the media and the secular political parties, either the government would have collapsed or a civil war would have erupted.'[3]

A week after the coup attempt, a rally was organized by the AKP in Istanbul, which aimed to show the world that Turkey was united and stronger than ever. It attracted almost two million people. All opposition leaders – except the Kurdish leader, who was not invited – attended the rally, where, in addition to the president and the leaders of all the main political parties, the chief of the armed forces, who was taken hostage during the coup attempt, gave a speech.

There was an unprecedented consensus among AKP voters, Kemalists, nationalists and Kurds that the Gülen movement was very dangerous, that it had deeply penetrated the structures of the state and that its leader was the mastermind of the coup attempt. In a nationwide poll conducted only four days after the coup, 65.7 per cent of respondents claimed that they had taken to the streets that night and 64 per cent believed the Fethullah Gülen movement was behind the coup.[4] What remained unexplained was why a distinct majority accepted that an Islamic cleric living in Pennsylvania was able and willing to orchestrate a coup in Turkey. This was something many Western politicians and journalists could not fathom at first, since the Gülen they had come to know was a peaceful moderate imam of Islam. Joshua Hendrick of Loyola University, who has been researching the Gülen movement since 2005, acknowledged that fact in the best possible way in a post-coup article:

> If Gülen helped orchestrate the coup, tens of thousands of affiliates and sympathizers, as well as those of us who have tried to more objectively study this man and his movement, will need to come to terms with one of the most fantastic frauds in modern history.[5]

Was Fethullah Gülen behind the coup?

'Where were you at the height of the coup?' was the question that elbowed its way into many conversations in Turkey. President Erdoğan was at a hotel in Marmaris. Later, when asked how he learned about the coup, the president said that his brother-in-law, rather than the MIT or any of the army officers, had informed him that night. The former chief of the armed forces, İlker Başbuğ, was watching a TV series when a lawyer friend phoned and urged him to change channel.

Anecdotally, there were also elderly Kemalists who were at first relieved on hearing news of a coup but then shattered to learn that the plotters were not secular groups but the Gülenists. Owing to the Kemalist army's portraying itself as the bastion of secularism and its egregious record of coups, the 15 July event was first thought to have been the work of the Kemalists.

In fact, even several months later, there were still considerable numbers of people in Western circles who believed the attempt had originated with Kemalists, their rationale being that if there was a coup in Turkey to topple Erdoğan, it must have come from the secular Kemalists. This was not the case, but Erdoğan's image as an authoritarian leader had become so tarnished that many couldn't conceive of a different reason for the coup attempt. It was the culmination of a rivalry for control of the state, the capstone of an enmity between two state structures, one led by Erdoğan and the other by Gülen disciples.

There had just been one coup attempt, but there were dozens of theories surrounding it. One suggested it was a 'false flag' event staged by President Erdoğan to gain more power, but common sense dictates that the event went too far for this to be the case. The Kurdish movement embraced the idea that Kemalists in the army had tricked the Gülenists into staging a coup. They knew it would fail and that it would lead to a long-awaited cleansing of Gülenists from the military. The history of previous coups in Turkey suggests that there has always been more than one junta clique in the army.

The former chief of the armed forces, İlker Başbuğ, who was in office during the Ergenekon case – which was later revealed to have been masterminded by Gülenist police chiefs and prosecutors – had his ear to the Kurdish movement and its theoretical impetus. 'There were three layers among the coup plotters,' he explained.

> The main operation was conducted by the Gülen movement. The second layer consisted of non-Gülenists, who later changed their mind and did not pursue the original plan. The third layer were a group of soldiers who were not Gülenists but thought that they could take advantage of a coup.[6]

Deputy prime minister Tuğrul Türkeş, whose father Alparslan Türkeş was the founder of the ultra-nationalist movement in Turkey, speculated along similar lines: 'I want to underline the fact that, even though the Gülen movement masterminded the operation, it might have been done in collaboration with other groups in the army.'[7]

For sceptics, neither of these theories was enough to explain the sloppiness of the coup attempt. At the height of the event, the American news channel NBC had incorrectly reported, in a number of later deleted tweets, that President Erdoğan had fled Turkey and was seeking asylum in Germany. According to one expert speaking on a live NBC show that night, 'If you are planning a coup, the first target should be to take the leader of the country.' Like him, many who believed it was a false flag pointed to the fact that Erdoğan had not been captured as 'proof' of this. The real story was that Erdoğan had been targeted. But the pilots who were given orders to snatch him from his holiday residence in Marmaris later reported a broken chain of command and a few pilots refusing to play along, which had given Erdoğan the chance to slip away and land in Istanbul.

It later emerged that the AKP government had been planning to arrest Gülen-supporting army officials on 16 July in order to cleanse Gülen from the army.[8] The police force and a few AKP MPs claimed that, when the coup plotters learned about this campaign of arrests, they initiated the coup earlier than planned. Seen in that light, the failed coup, which looked like a kamikaze raid rather than a thoroughly planned military takeover, may instead have been an attempt to head off those arrests in a pre-emptive strike.

A pro-government journalist who has close ties to the National Intelligence Organization had written two articles three months before the coup attempt, the first on 2 April and the second on the 24th. In those articles, he claimed that Gülenists were afraid that their links to the movement would be revealed, and for that reason they might attempt a coup on the orders of Gülen himself. The most intriguing section in these articles was the journalist's warning to the Gülenist soldiers that the state was using all its units to watch them – the intelligence service, the army, politicians and NGOs. 'The state was waiting for them to commit a crime, and then it would get them all.'[9] Putting this information together, one might conclude that the very top people in the government had prior knowledge of the coup but had chosen not to prevent it, in order to blow the Gülenists' cover and reveal them in their true colours. This theory does make sense, considering that

Erdoğan did not remove either MIT chief Hakan Fidan or his army chief of staff General Akar from their posts following the July attempt, whereas failing to detect a planned coup would normally cost top officials their jobs.

The attempted coup was portrayed in several pro-government newspapers as a small affair. It was not: 8,651 soldiers took part, the equivalent of 3 per cent of the Turkish military, and 274 armoured vehicles, 35 planes, 37 helicopters, three ships and 3,992 weapons were used.[10] Some of the plotters denied any connection to the Gülen movement; however, there were signs that linked the upper echelons of the junta to the movement. The strongest of these was the testimony of the chief of the armed forces, Hulusi Akar, who had been taken hostage on the night of the coup. He claimed that one of those in the junta had told him he could put him in touch with their 'opinion leader Fethullah Gülen', so that he could be persuaded to lead the coup. The general summarily dismissed the offer.[11]

General Akar's aide-de-camp, Levent Türkkan, was one of those who admitted that he was affiliated with the organization and that he had been acting according to orders from his 'brothers' in the Gülen movement.[12] He had grown up in a poor neighbourhood, the son of a farmer, and encountered the Gülen movement during his middle-school years. He was a bright student and always dreamed of being a soldier. In 1989, he took the military academy's entrance exam. Although he was confident that he would pass the test, 'his brothers in the movement [to make sure of it] still brought him the questions at midnight before the day of the exam at one of the movement's houses in central Bursa.'[13] Türkkan's story exemplifies the way the Gülen movement operates in the state structure and how its disciples are more loyal to the movement than to the institution they work for. 'After I was promoted to the aide-de-camp position in the general staff, I started to execute orders given on behalf of the movement,' he said, adding,

We used to listen to [former chief of staff General] Necdet Özel Pasha with a bug all the time. A 'brother' working at Turk Telekom [the biggest and oldest telecoms company of Turkey] provided the device. Once in a week [*sic*] I was taking the bugs to the 'brother' [in the movement].[14]

Türkkan was no doubt a valuable member of Gülen's so-called Golden Generation, a generation that was to reconquer state bureaucracy. Raising this generation required bright students, as well as devout and bright teachers who were also deeply spiritual and close to God.[15] Thus, every member was subject to a rigorous selection for the Gülen schools, by entrance exams that at times have been 'held in stadiums in Central Asia because of the high number of applicants'.[16]

Even though Fethullah Gülen's Golden Generation was destined to bring about a perfect Muslim society, the schools' curricula involve no Islamic preaching. They conform completely to the national education systems of the countries in which they operate. This is part of Gülen's approach, summed up as 'Do not fight the system, but work with it and then incrementally change it.' However, this does not mean that Gülen's way of Islam is not imposed. Students at Gülen schools also live in the Gülen dorms, where they get their first initiation and are linked to a 'brother' or 'sister' who 'with strict discipline teaches them the message of the movement'.[17]

The students who come from poor households stay loyal to the movement for the rest of their lives, not only because they are indoctrinated by this system but also because they are grateful for the opportunities they receive. Knowing that the education system lies at the heart of the Gülenists' larger strategy, and following on from his disagreement with Gülen himself, Erdogan took the initial step in 2014 of closing down the movement's university prep schools in Turkey.

At the funeral of one of the people who was killed on the night of the coup, the imam's sermon contained the line 'Dear God, protect us from the evil of the educated.' Erdoğan nodded his endorsement. This was not just a sign of the anti-intellectualism of the AKP era, but also a sly message to the Gülen movement's education business.

✳

The top ranks of the 15 July junta revealed another story, which evidenced that the Sledgehammer case was actually one of the factors that had precipitated the coup. In that case, staff colonels in the naval forces – those who were the most successful holders of their offices, who held postgraduate degrees, who had served abroad and who were expecting to be promoted to the position of admiral – were arrested on fabricated evidence, in order for admirals who had taken part in the coup to secure their own promotions and positions. These admirals had all been promoted to their current positions between 2010 and 2016, 2010 being the year the Sledgehammer case commenced.[18]

It was not only the portrayal of the naval forces or the testimonies of top general Hulusi Akar and his aide-de-camp that pointed to a link between the Gülen movement and the junta. Ahmet Zeki Üçok, a military prosecutor, had carried out a comprehensive investigation into the Gülenists in the armed forces in 2009. He had discovered a large secret network within the army and identified many members of this unlawful organization by name.[19] However, he could not complete his investigation, as he was detained on the grounds that he had tortured certain witnesses by 'hypnotizing' them and also as part of the Sledgehammer case. He spent almost five years in prison. Immediately after the botched coup, he declared that its leaders corresponded perfectly with the list that he had. Referring to the F-16s that bombed the Turkish parliament, he recalled the words of now-retired colonel Selçuk Başyiğit in the court records: 'We are now very strong. We have F-16s, F-4s, that can take off at a single order from Fethullah Gülen.' Üçok's findings are corroborated by many soldiers who fought against the coup attempt or by soldiers who were the victims of the Sledgehammer case.[20]

It should also be underlined that, even though Fethullah Gülen rejected the allegations that he had masterminded the coup attempt, he could not deny the mass of circumstantial evidence linking his disciples to the plot. Claiming that he did not know 'even 1 per cent of his followers by name', he insisted that if there were any Gülenists among the junta, this should not implicate him or the movement as a whole.[21]

According to the former chief of the armed forces, İlker Başbuğ, the tipping point at which the Gülen movement's presence in the military started to grow was in 1992, when, for the first time in Turkish history, a civilian was designated as chief of MIT. The military's own intelligence branches are responsible for foreign intelligence and the activities of military personnel when they are within the compounds, but the military relies on MIT to report any unusual activities of its personnel beyond these boundaries. 'After 1992, our relationship with MIT was downgraded,' says Başbuğ:

> I became a general in 2002 and left office in 2010. During those eight years, MIT provided us with no intelligence regarding the Gülenists in the army. There were reports of certain officers being related to a Nur tariqa called Mehmet Kurdoğlu, which is a rival to the Gülen movement, but nothing about Gülenist infiltration. Therefore, between 2002 and 2010, none of those who were sacked from the military were Gülenists.[22]

Başbuğ and several other retired generals hold MIT accountable for failing to see the Gülenist infiltration in the army:

> There are several intelligence units in the Turkish military, called S2-G2 and J, but they all receive information regarding individuals from MIT. On the other hand, when the military asks MIT about individuals, instead of working systematically, they gather information from village headmen or local police officers.[23]

The military itself was shocked by the revelation that the Gülen movement's presence in the army had culminated in staging a coup.[24]

Ironically, the former head of the Turkish military, İlker Başbuğ, and his default arch-enemy, Abdullah Öcalan, were unknowingly of the same mind in their understanding of Gülen's goals and targets in the state structure. According to Öcalan, 'The underlying reason for the battle between Gülen and Erdoğan was that the Gülen movement wanted the Kurdistan offices of the National Intelligence Agency (MIT).'[25] Speaking to the HDP envoy on 7 December 2013, he claimed that he had said this a long time before, but the state authorities did not believe him.

The notes of the meetings in İmralı during the peace process show that the Gülen movement and its probable intentions occupied a great deal of Öcalan's mental energy. These notes also indicate the ironic fact that Öcalan was actually the first person to call the Gülen movement a 'parallel state', a term that was first used publicly by President Erdoğan – although Öcalan may have inspired him, since the president had received the minutes of each İmralı meeting hours after it ended.

'This parallel state is off its leash,' Öcalan had said. 'They plan to terminate the peace process.' He had warned emphatically of possible strikes on the peace process that might come from the Gülen movement.

The most interesting thing is that Öcalan, who had been in jail since 1999, had predicted that a *coup d'état* organized by Fethullah Gülen was on the cards. During the meeting in İmralı prison with the HDP delegate on 9 March 2014, he said the following:

> Despite all my efforts, I could not entice Mr Tayyip [Erdoğan, then prime minister] away from the Cemaat [Gülen movement]. I said, 'There is a coup dynamic here, a major performance is being staged.' It is this [negotiating] table, the peace process, that is preventing that coup. The Gülen movement completely tied Prime Minister Erdoğan's hands. They wanted total control of the state. Had they succeeded, and had Hoca [Fethullah Gülen] gone to Ankara the way Khomeini did, an extreme fascism like that in Iran would hold sway, putting an end to all opposition.[26]

As explained in earlier chapters, Gülen constantly told his followers that they should keep out of sight until the very last moment, when they would have accumulated enough power. In hindsight, this was what the Gülenist soldiers had done since 2010 in the military, the institution that boasted of being the stronghold of secularism and Kemalism. However, it should certainly be noted that it was the AKP government that condoned or sometimes empowered the Gülen movement's presence in the army. One of the alleged masterminds of the coup, General Akın Öztürk, the highest-ranking officer among the plotters, is a good example. The four-star air force general was appointed by the AKP after his predecessor was sacked during the Sledgehammer trial.

The coup attempt not only showed a very dark side of an Islamic network but also revealed the fragility of the draconian state the AKP had built. President Erdoğan's government did not replace the previous elite with sound constitutional changes and democratic reforms; it simply transferred power from the Kemalists to others who they thought were their close allies. The process pursued was 'conquering rather than democratizing'.[27] This is why Erdoğan kept saying that 'they were stabbed in the back' by 'those to whom he had given whatever they required'.[28]

The 15 July coup and the Kurdish issue

It may be tempting to think that there was not much of a connection between Turkey's Kurdish problem and the most recent coup attempt. However, a closer look reveals a more nuanced picture. The failure of the peace process, and the resulting high-intensity conflict in its southeast that Turkey had endured for almost a year prior to the coup, may be cited as one of the factors that encouraged the plotters. After all, coups require political instability to justify themselves. The collapse of the peace process and Turkey's entanglement in Syrian issues were among the chief reasons for its ongoing instability.

The fact that the coup was bungled should not obscure the fact that it was attempted in the first place. The mere fact that it *could* be attempted has a significance regarding the state of the political environment and culture in Turkey. According to Samuel E. Finer, in order for a military intervention to take place, there needs to be a motive (disposition to intervene) for the army, and an opportunity.[29] Yaprak Gürsoy, author of the book *Between Military Rule and Democracy: Regime Consolidation in Greece, Turkey, and Beyond*,[30] argues that

> a motive for the Turkish army, which saw itself as the guardian of the secular state, had existed since the AKP, a party rooted in Islam, came to power in 2002. In that sense, the disposition for a coup was stable but the opportunity was lacking.[31]

In other words, the army had felt threatened since the AKP first came to power, but they did not have the so-called 'opportunity' to justify an act to rid themselves of this threat.

So why did the putschists intervene? According to Gürsoy, they were desperate. Reports indicated that an investigation was underway and that they were highly likely to face jail because of their ties to the Gülen movement; thus, they were prepared to take the risk.[32] This theory certainly seems logical. But how did the plotters think that they would be able to justify their act to members of the public?

Analysing this question, Yüksel Taşkın of Marmara University argued that among the main factors were the instability which had emerged due to the secularists feeling they had been persecuted by the AKP government, and the boiling point that the Kurdish issue had reached.[33] In fact, the name that the putschists chose for themselves is significant in this regard: 'The Council of Peace at Home'. The underlying reference here is to a saying of Mustafa Kemal Atatürk: 'Peace at home, peace in the world.' The putschists wanted to give the impression that they were Kemalists, to appeal to the secularists, and they also wanted to convey the message that they could pacify the conflict in the country. It follows that one of the main factors that they wanted to present as justifying their egregious act was the ongoing conflict in the country.

In that respect, one of the most significant events that may have contributed to Finer's 'opportunity' factor was the collapse of the peace process. As explained in the previous chapters, there were numerous attempts by the AKP's predecessors to negotiate with the PKK, but those talks were covert processes through backchannels. The failure of those talks did not therefore lead to the same level of frustration as the latest collapse. In the latter case, because every step of the process was known to the public, hopes were high. So was the disappointment at the end.

Indeed, it is a well-known fact that unsuccessful ceasefires and peace agreements in internal conflicts give way to renewed, and often escalated, violence.[34]

Kurdish young people in particular presumed that there was no longer any point in negotiating with the government, since even the most hopeful process had collapsed: peaceful negotiation would get them nowhere. Any shred of emotional ties to the government and its values had disintegrated. Encouraged by the developments in Syria, the Kurdish insurgency following the failure of the talks rose to an unprecedented level.

The peace talks had also been perhaps the strongest constraint on the government's authoritarian tendencies, forcing the lawmakers, especially President Erdoğan, to take their place at the negotiating table, where a reasonable stance would, Erdoğan believed, win him the Kurds' support for his executive presidency. In other words, the prospect of winning the Kurdish vote was the only incentive left for Erdoğan not to go down the authoritarian route. With the collapse of the process, that incentive was also gone.

There was, therefore, a strong causal link between the collapse of the peace process and the coup attempt. The former created the fertile ground for the latter in the eyes of the plotters. In fact, the connection between the coup and the Kurdish issue intensified following the events of 15 July. The rising tide of authoritarianism in the country further dimmed whatever hope was left for a peaceful solution. Unsurprisingly, once the draconian forces of the state were unleashed, they not only targeted the Gülenists but also the members of the Kurdish movement.

※

There is no doubt that the Kurdish problem may be solved in an environment where individual rights and freedoms are fully respected and enhanced. Accordingly, the post-coup environment further darkened the prospect of a resolution to the dispute.

The consensus in the following days that the Fethullah Gülen movement had perpetrated the coup attempt did not equate to genuine political and social unity. Moreover, events gave Erdoğan a rare opportunity to get rid of his enemies with almost the full support of a great majority of the people. 'It is a gift from God,' he said, a day after the attempt.[35]

Following the declaration of a state of emergency, the government conducted a massive purge of alleged Gülen followers in both the public and private sectors, including the media, the police and the judiciary. Tens of thousands of people were detained.

Initially, secular people and democrats supported the removal of Gülenists from state institutions, although they raised concerns about human rights violations and the erosion of the rule of law. But after a certain point, it was evident that the cleansing operation was targeting not only Gülenists but also leftists, Kurds, Kemalists and Alawites.

In the post-coup environment, it had become much harder to criticize the government. Any criticism was considered as casting aspersions on 'a unified Turkey' and was countered with a campaign of slander. Critics were accused of supporting either the coup or a terrorist organization such as the PKK or the Fethullah Gülen movement, which has been portrayed as a terrorist organization in Turkey since March 2016. Erdoğan did not even pretend to hide his glee over the expansion of his power, which now seemed boundless, even better than the executive presidency he lusted after. 'We now have the power to do things that we weren't able to do under normal circumstances,' he said.[36] Within just three months, 105,000 state employees and 3,465 judges and prosecutors were dismissed, 30,000 people were arrested and 15 universities, 2,100 dorms, 1,254 associations and 180 media outlets were shut down.[37] At the time of writing, these numbers have increased significantly.

Post-coup, the imposition of a state of emergency in Turkey has effectively suspended the rule of law, as well as notions of freedom of speech, freedom of the press and freedom of travel and communications. While all rights and freedoms were downgraded to the status of accessories, Erdoğan started trying to destroy the last pillars of a free press. Since he is well known for regarding journalists as potential enemies, it would be surprising if he had not struck a blow against them.

※

Silencing the critical media and replacing it with chauvinistic and sycophantic voices destroys any chance of solving the Kurdish problem, and merits further attention.

In order to break up the 'old Turkey', as he liked to call it, Erdoğan believed that it was crucial to fragment media ownership. His media takeover and crackdown therefore dates from way before the coup attempt.

When the AKP came to power in 2002, pro-party businesses owned less than 20 per cent of Turkish media outlets. Since then, the AKP has used legal loopholes, amended laws and set up a 'confiscate-and-sell' mechanism to change the media landscape in its favour. Now almost two-thirds of the mainstream outlets are in the hands of AKP supporters.

The Savings Deposit and Insurance Fund (TMSF) is a body attached to the prime minister's office, which recovers debt owed to banks and failed financial institutions. This body has become an effective instrument for gaining control over the media. For example, the Sabah Group, Uzan Group and some TV channels were transferred to the TMSF during the 2001 economic crisis, when interest rates had reached 3,000 per cent. The two media outlets were then put on the market, at which point then prime minister Erdoğan stepped in. Sabah and ATV were purchased by the Çalık Group, whose vice president was Erdoğan's son-in-law, Berat Albayrak. Albayrak was subsequently appointed minister of energy in 2016.

Media corporations Akşam, SHOW TV and Digiturk, part of another big holding, the Çukurova Group, were also handed over to people Erdoğan identified through the same mechanism. Akşam was sold to Ethem Sancak, a wealthy businessman who talked effusively about his deep devotion to Erdoğan.

A US$2.7 billion tax fine had been imposed on the Doğan Group after its main newspaper, *Hürriyet*, had published stories of the Deniz Feneri corruption case in 2008, which had strong ties to the AKP government. The group's subsequent negotiations resulted in the fine being reduced to US$590 million in 2011. However, it was forced to sell its influential newspapers, *Vatan* and *Milliyet*, as well as the very popular Star TV, to business groups run by government cronies. The huge fine also served as a clear – and intimidating – warning to other media owners of the cost of challenging the government.

The slandering and targeting of Doğan Group members and journalists continued apace through pro-government dailies, TV channels and paid social media agents. After a prominent columnist of *Hürriyet* was beaten in front of his house, several columnists from the Doğan Group, including me, were given state protection for three months, since we were similarly accused by the pro-government media of 'conspiring with the terrorists'.

This of course was a very small (and probably milder) version of what many journalists working in the Kurdish provinces go through every day. If a well-established mainstream media outlet had experienced this appalling treatment, it can only be imagined what small, independent outlets and news agencies had to put up with.

The spring of 2016 proved that newspapers belonging to the Doğan Group were not that well established either. The liberal left *Radikal*, the newspaper on which I worked for half my journalism career and of which I was the editor-in-chief, was shut down. With its demise, the last strong voice in the mainstream media with expertise on the Kurdish issue was silenced.

In this day and age, though, turning the conventional media into a monopoly was not enough. The AKP then invented its own methods of meddling with digital and social media – which can be summarized as simply cutting them off. Websites blocked either by court order or by an institution called the Telecommunications Communication Directorate (TIB) numbered approximately 115,000 as of 2016.[38]

A 2014 statute on regulating the internet allowed the TIB to block any website for a day without first seeking a court order. It also obliged internet service providers (ISPs) to store all data on web users' activities for two years and make it available to the authorities upon request. The two social media giants Facebook and Twitter differ in their relationship to the Turkish government. Because Facebook's structure is not built for breaking news, it was Twitter that was slowed down during times of crisis to stop the spread of information.

✳

According to a 2013 report by the *Wall Street Journal*, after the Gezi protests the AKP established a propaganda vehicle on Twitter of around 6,000 paid people, so-called 'AKP trolls'.[39] AKP trolls were intended to act like a lynch mob on Twitter when they got a signal from certain pro-government columnists, advisers to Erdoğan or AKP youth branch members. Many opposition journalists, artists and academics have fallen victim to these trolls. The first such victim after 15 July was a popular singer who declared that she was not going to take part in the post-coup rally, as she thought it was an unnecessary show. Hours after her announcement, she became a trending topic via thousands of libellous tweets. Her concerts were cancelled, and she had to announce that she was taking a break for a while 'from social media and life'.[40]

The Twitter accounts of journalists with perceived links to Kurdish parties were withheld. The same applied to the accounts of Kurdish dailies and the news agencies. Most of these media outlets had already been closed down by decrees issued by the government acting on its state-of-emergency powers, thus making it even harder to receive news from the Kurdish region. The people of Turkey were cast into a chilling blackout.

On 29 October 2016, the Turkish government issued another decree shutting down 15 Kurdish media outlets: 11 newspapers (*Özgür Gündem, Azadiya Welat, Batman Çağdaş, Cizre Postası,* the *Güney Express, İdil Haber, Kızıltepe'nin Sesi, Prestij Haber, Urfanatik* and *Yüksekova Haber*), two news agencies (DİHA – Dicle News Agency and JINHA – Jin News Agency) and three magazines (*Tiroji*, *Özgürlük Dünyası* and arts and culture magazine *Evrensel Kültür*).

Among these newspapers, *Özgür Gündem* and *Azadiya Welat* were the most popular and oldest. With *Azadiya Welat's* closure, the only Kurdish-language daily was removed from the scene. The closure of JINHA was a blow not only to the Kurdish movement but also to the women's rights community. It was the first ever news agency that focused on women's rights and gender issues, and it only employed female journalists.

In 2012, I was at JINHA's office, a small flat on the second floor of an apartment at the centre of Diyarbakır. The reporters, editors, photographers and camerapersons, all of whom were women, were racing to get ready for publication the following day. The two Kurdish journalists Hazal Peker and Hangül Özbey, who had put all their savings into founding this news agency, had told me that their main goal was to overcome the homogeneous masculine rhetoric of the media. 'Like Virginia Woolf once said, we will write without considering what the men would think,' Hangül had told me. 'For the women living on the Aegean side and also for the women in Iraq.'[41]

They cannot write for anyone now, solely because they had tried hard to report on what was happening in the south-east after the collapse of the peace process. The feminist JINHA has fallen victim to an operation of silencing the last remnants of Kurdish voices in Turkey.

✻

Already dominated by a battery of pro-government news outlets, Turkey's mainstream press was also subject to another crackdown on 31 October 2016, two days after the closures of Kurdish outlets. The houses of *Cumhuriyet's* columnists, editors and board members were raided. Police arrested the paper's chief editor, Murat Sabuncu, its leading cartoonist, its chairman of the board and more than a dozen columnists, among them the International Press Institute's (IPI) Turkey chief, Kadri Gürsel. An arrest warrant was also issued for the paper's former editor, Can Dündar, who had already served time for publishing articles on MIT trucks loaded with weaponry bound for Syria. However, Dündar had already fled the country.

Only days after the *Cumhuriyet* raid, on 4 November 2016 at around 1 a.m., the last nail was hammered into the coffin of democratic Kurdish politics. A slew of arrests took place concurrently in Diyarbakır, Ankara and Mardin, targeting prominent Kurdish politicians along with HDP co-chairs Selahattin Demirtaş and Figen Yüksekdağ, and a dozen MPs. Subsequently, Ahmet Türk, the mayor of Mardin and the wise man of the Kurdish movement, was also sent to jail. Like in the case of Demirtaş, Türk's arrest was very symbolic. He had been previously jailed in the aftermath of the 1980 coup and had dedicated his life to peacefully resolving the Kurdish issue, as was well known. 'What difference does it make if I am in prison or not? But how will this bloodshed end? How will this issue reach a resolution? These are the questions,' Türk said right before his arrest.[42]

During these arrests, the government cut off the internet in some parts of the country and blocked social media, such as Twitter, Facebook and even WhatsApp, for fear of a backlash on the streets. A couple of weeks later, they also issued an arrest warrant for and demanded a red notice from Interpol for Syrian PYD leader Salih Müslim. The peace process was long over, but it was as though the arrests were aiming to completely bury any prospect of it restarting.

From failed peace to the brink of a failed state

While *The Economist* acknowledged the developments in Turkey with an article entitled 'Goodbye, "Republic"',[43] the eminent chair of Türk Ceza Hukuku Derneği (the Turkish Criminal Law Foundation), Professor Duygun Yarsuvat, felt the need to issue a warning: 'If one considers the unlawfulness dominating the country and the spiralling violence, the Republic of Turkey is on the verge of being a failed state.'[44]

The demise of the rule of law certainly has implications not only for politics but also for all other aspects of social life. According to Daron Acemoğlu from Massachusetts Institute of Technology, co-author of *Why Nations Fail*,[45] only inclusive governments can build inclusive economic institutions. His main thesis is that growth is much more likely under inclusive institutions than 'extractive institutions'.[46] With extractive institutions, stagnation is inevitable. If there is a democratic deficit, lack of law and order, and insecurity for property rights, extractive institutions dominate, which then impel a nation to fail. 'If a nation elects a leader with 51 per cent of the popular vote, but then that leader curbs the rule of law or press freedom,' Acemoğlu explained to me, 'we cannot talk about inclusive institutions.'[47] Very much in line with this erudite wisdom, the Turkish economy has been losing its spark as fast as the system becomes authoritarian. Talk of an impending economic crisis – or a stagnation, at the very least – is the dominant discourse at present. This in turn will make it much more difficult for Turkey to solve its Kurdish problem.

If we cannot talk about inclusive institutions, democracy and rule of law, how should we then characterize the present Turkey? What we can talk about is a 'new authoritarianism' formulated by the AKP.[48] Murat Somer, of Istanbul's Koç University, argues that this new model creates a different state–society relationship, in which people believe that the benefits provided to them are linked to a certain individual or a party, not to impersonal state institutions and legal–institutional rights.[49] In the minds of the people, this means that they can only maintain their status by continuing to support that party or leader, namely, Recep Tayyip Erdoğan in the case of Turkey. According to this analysis, what the people were defending against the coup plotters on 15 July was arguably not their democracy but the status quo, which was bound up with their leader, Erdoğan. In that sense it is more than ironic, since Erdoğan and the AKP had emerged at the beginning of the century as a reaction to the status quo at that time.

Erdoğan was confident that his illiberalism would not diminish the support of his constituency, for two reasons. First, he trusted the clientelistic model he had built over the last decade. Second, when jailing Kurdish leaders, he had based his populist rhetoric on ultra-nationalism, which is very hard for opposition parties, especially the CHP, to challenge. On the other hand, his vehemently ultra-nationalistic discourse has enabled him to have a partner, namely the MHP, which propelled him to the presidential system. However, to keep this new partnership intact, Erdoğan had to become increasingly hawkish on the Kurdish issue, which further escalated the crisis in Syria and also took its toll on domestic and international stability.

Nowadays, the mood in Kurdish politics in Turkey is as grim as it has ever been. But now Kurds are not alone in their sentiment of despair. On 10 November 2016, the 78th anniversary of Mustafa Kemal Atatürk's death, a crowd flocked to his mausoleum in Ankara, Anıtkabir, a sanctuary for secularists since the start of the AKP's rule. Secularists tend to visit Anıtkabir to bemoan their bitter fate at the hands of increasingly authoritarian Islamists to Atatürk.

But this time it was different. A 40-year-old liberal friend had phoned me and said it was the first time since primary school that she had cried at a 10 November remembrance, 'because it felt like the end of an era, the end of the Republic of Turkey as we know it'. Ahmet Altan, a famous liberal novelist, and fervent critic of Atatürk, sent a message from his prison cell saying that even he himself missed Atatürk, at the hands of Erdoğan.[50] He had been arrested two months earlier for an alleged link to the Gülen movement and the putschists. The country, many thought, had changed irreversibly, and not in a good way.

Turkey was never a proper democracy. It has not been able to transform its institutions into inclusive ones following the 1980 coup. But what it is experiencing now is also unprecedented. While dismantling the old elite and conquering the establishment, the AKP constructed its own dependent crowd. Before then, Islamists and Kurds felt excluded. In this new political arrangement, secular groups and individuals appear to have become the 'other' and 'unfit'. What has remained stable in Turkey's oscillation between different types of oppressive models of government is the persecution, 'otherization' and exclusion of its Kurds.

Ironically, solving the Kurdish issue is the one thing that can break this vicious cycle and jump-start a democracy. This can be achieved only if the miraculous human capital and spirit that showed its face during the Gezi uprisings in 2013, which brought Kurds and the secular, Westward-looking Turks together, is reactivated. The steps that the political opposition will take determine whether or not this is on the cards.

✴

On 16 April 2017, Turkey voted in a constitutional referendum whose result bore clues as to the direction democracy in the country is taking. People had two options that day: Yes or No. There was no question written on the ballot paper. Even though many find it incomprehensible that millions were compelled to answer a non-existent question, there was a rationale behind the referendum. The constitutional changes, comprised of 18 articles, proposed a new regime that would suspend the separation of powers and give the president extensive control of all parts of the state and society. The real question that was being asked was not written on the ballot paper: *Do you wish Turkey to become a one-man show or not?* Apparently, the winning Yes – despite being voted through by a razor-thin margin – was the last piece of the puzzle in President Erdoğan's new Turkey project.

The Yes camp consisted of the AKP and the ultra-nationalist MHP. The result indicated that the MHP's constituency had not backed the constitutional amendments. It also revealed that the AKP was far from consolidating the right-wing base that is made up of around 65 per cent of voters. The Felicity Party (Saadet Partisi), the party of the traditional Islamist movement from which the AKP had sprung, had repeatedly announced that it was not supporting the Yes camp. The attempted merger of Islamism and ultra-nationalism had not worked, despite the recent military campaigns and hostile rhetoric the AKP had adopted against the Kurds to consolidate the two.

How the referendum campaign played out and the irregularities on election day itself also had consequences for the rule of law and for civil liberties in Turkey. Since its foundation, many adjectives have been used to describe the type of democracy in Turkey, but the perception of free and fair elections has never been contested before, with the exception of its very first multi-party election in 1946. Unfortunately, this referendum in April 2017 seems to have undermined that final pillar of democracy. There is a widespread belief in the No camp (around 24 million people) that the election was rigged way before the election day. As observers from the Organization for Security and Co-operation in Europe (OSCE) reported,

> The referendum took place on an unlevel playing field and the two sides of the campaign did not have equal opportunities. [...] One side's dominance in the coverage and restrictions on the media reduced voters' access to a plurality of views.[51]

Against all the odds, there has been a silver lining to the referendum result: countries on both sides of the Atlantic who are tackling populist strongmen may learn valuable lessons in how not to run a democracy in the long term. Building democracy in Turkey has always been a difficult task; saving whatever democracy is left has become even more difficult at a time when democracy itself has become such an unpopular concept across the globe. Moreover, the fragility of such institutions as the judiciary and free press has made this task all but impossible.

Even though the democratic backslide is very palpable in Turkey at present, the situation is perhaps no more worrying than it was before the referendum. It may even be less so. The referendum result was a huge blow to the MHP's leadership, who had appeared to be unresponsive to the needs and emotions of their constituents. This non-responsiveness is not sustainable, and may lead to the formation of new right-wing parties and/or a change in leadership. Similarly, the outcome may also trigger a rethink at the CHP.

Such change may then create an opportunity for alternative political parties and voices to flourish. The No camp – made up of CHP voters (mostly urban, educated, Westward-looking middle-class Turks), HDP voters (secular Kurds) and the Turkish nationalists who opposed their party's (the MHP's) decision to support the Yes vote – all worked for a common purpose despite their differences, some of which were very great.

An important factor in the rise of illiberal populism around the world is the lack of political alternatives to contest it. In that respect,

1. Frontline Turkey :
   the conflict at the
   heart of the
   Middle East
   Barcode:
   31621214233401
   Due Date: 2019-
   11-21

losing by a small margin may be better than winning by a small one for the No camp if it creates an avenue for new contesters to challenge Turkey's one-man rule. The fact that President Erdoğan's victory speech involved bringing back the death penalty illustrated that dark days await the country. But no one said that saving democracy is an easy undertaking. The world as a whole is being challenged to win the battle between openness and closeness, or cosmopolitanism and parochialism. The main difference between Turkey and the rest of the world, though, is that there is much more at stake in Turkey for those who choose to oppose its leader.

CONCLUSION

The Kurdish Issue Goes Global

Turkey's Kurdish issue is no longer one which is remote from the rest of the world. There was little reason for many in the West to worry about the fate of the Kurds throughout the twentieth and early twenty-first centuries. This is no longer the case. The Eastern and Western fronts have perhaps never been so close, not even during the two world wars. In our current state of global turmoil, the two fronts are very much neighbours, and the Kurds are one of the main actors in this struggle.

In the 1990s, when the fight between the PKK and the Turkish state was as bloodthirsty as it is now, the Western countries were still able to find a way to tackle the issue. Even during and after the first Gulf War, they devised a strategy for keeping the Kurds and Turkey in equilibrium, albeit at two different ends of the spectrum. Sometimes they used the 'Kurdish card' to scare or irritate the Turkish government. At other times, they collaborated with the government to chastise the Kurds. Sometimes, they simply ignored the whole thing.

In the early 1990s, Kurds overran the Turkish consulate in Munich and launched arson attacks on Turkish-owned shops and restaurants across Germany, which led the EU to outlaw the PKK in 1993. Another spillover of Turkey's Kurdish issue into European countries took place when Abdullah Öcalan was captured in 1999.

Now a successful businessman, Seyit[1] told me about a time when he was trying to build a new life in the UK. 'When I heard that Serok Öcalan had been captured in the Greek consulate in Kenya, I gathered my friends from local *kahvehanes* [coffee houses] and raided the Greek embassy in London,' he told me, looking at the enormous wall of

Windsor Castle opposite the café in which we had sat for the interview. He recalled,

> We occupied the place and took one Greek officer hostage. I was answering external calls on the phones. I was saying, 'Hello, this is the Kurdistan embassy. How can I help you?' We meant no harm, but we wanted to make a point regarding the Kurds. We wanted our cause to be heard. But then we found out that the Greek officer with us had diabetes and we panicked. We decided to cook pasta for him. Unfortunately, our comrade in the kitchen made a mess and burned the pasta badly. Smoke was coming out of the windows. Police thought we were burning the building. I could not tell them that it was just pasta because I was embarrassed. We started negotiating. The British police ensured that none of us would be arrested.

On the third day of the protest, they gave themselves up to the police and were detained, to be released a day later. There were similar protests all around Europe in areas where the Kurdish diaspora mostly reside.

Kurdish media outlets operating in the Netherlands, Germany, Belgium and Norway had always been a source of diplomatic strife between Turkey and those countries. Turkey had long been demanding that Kurdish radio and TV stations and websites be shut down on the grounds of their alleged links with the PKK. EU countries disagreed and perceived the issue as a matter of press freedom. This caused distrust between the parties.

For its part, relations between the US and Turkey regarding the Kurdish issue have had their ups and downs over the last two decades. After the tumultuous times of the first Gulf War and its aftermath in the 2000s, the divergence of interests and concerns over the Middle East first became apparent when Turkey's parliament voted against permitting US troops to launch a ground invasion of Iraq from its territory in 2003. This incident led to a deterioration of relations between the two countries. The US initiated a closer alliance with Iraqi Kurds, which proved to be a catalyst in the formation of an autonomous Iraqi

Kurdistan. But, all in all, the Kurdish issue was still considered by the rest of the world to be Turkey's internal affair.

In November 2007, Turkish journalist Fikret Bila interviewed senior generals in the Turkish army and found a widespread belief among them that the US had directly or indirectly supported the PKK. Almost all of them regretted the Turkish parliament's 2003 decision to refuse to let US troops enter Iraq. 'Whenever the US entered Iraq, it helped the PKK and this hurts us. Particularly during the second Gulf War, it enabled the PKK to gain significant strength,' said Hasan Kundakçı, who had served as the commander of gendarmerie in the Kurdish region between 1993 and 1995, during the most violent clashes.[2]

After these interviews, at a time when PKK had reactivated its raids and Turkish public opinion was once again becoming more anti-American, a critical meeting took place between then president George W. Bush and then prime minister Erdoğan, the outcome of which was an agreement for new cooperation between their respective countries. The US agreed to provide 'actionable intelligence' to help the Turkish military fight the PKK, and President Bush declared the PKK an enemy of the US. At this announcement, anti-American sentiment abruptly evaporated from the media. The sharing of the so-called actionable intelligence continued until US troops left Iraq at the end of 2011.[3]

Times have changed. Neither the predicament of the Kurds nor the PKK's 'grand vision' is constrained within Turkey's borders. And the consequences of neglecting this new status quo will be much more severe than debates on Kurdish TV channels or pasta-burning embassy raids.

Why is it different this time? For several reasons. First, the PKK and its sympathizers have grown, in the last four decades, into a socially and politically strong organized movement. Second, owing to the developments in Syria, their demands for autonomy in Syria and in Turkey are beyond recall in the long run. Third, in the eyes of the West, Syrian Kurds led by the PKK are the most effective force to crush the ISIS threat on the ground in Syria, which gives the PKK great international leverage. Fourth, while this is the situation on the Kurdish frontier, Turkey is going through a tumultuous period under the leadership of an unpredictable and erratic strongman who depicts the West as an enemy in order to keep his popular support at home.

How did we all end up here?

The most recent years of the AKP's incumbency and the coup attempt were hugely disappointing for the West, because both Western media and politicians had wanted to believe a different story about the AKP and the Gülen movement. They thought these two represented a trans-formation of political Islam into a moderate understanding that was reconcilable with secular principles. For the West and even for Arab countries such as Egypt and Tunisia, Turkey had become a model for accommodating Islam within the democratic political system.

The capitalist outlook of these neo-Islamists was an important part of their appeal in the world. Money was bringing down age-old barriers between civilizations.[4] The so-called Muslim Calvinists were praised in the press and academia. Unlike the Kemalists, they were Turks who were embracing their Muslim roots but also believed in global economic integration. The AKP's version of Islamism was very pro-business and flexible in terms of interpreting Islamic doctrines; since 2004, the system had therefore been endorsed by global powers such as the US and the EU, up until the start of the Arab Spring in December 2010.

However, with the Gezi uprising, which was at its height in the May and June of 2013, Erdoğan's image as the mighty deliverer of the best possible political Islam was shattered. The niche designed by the West and Turkish liberals had become too small for a leader who daily became more powerful and authoritarian. Erdoğan's personality, ambitions and fears also played a huge role in the failure to establish a real democracy.

After 2013, the tone in the West regarding Turkey shifted. The West's moderate Islamic role model had vanished. Erdoğan had fallen from grace. He reacted harshly to that change of heart. 'The European Union is stalling us,' he once infamously said. 'Let us say *au revoir* to the EU and join the Shanghai Cooperation Organization.'[5]

By that time, Turkey with its human rights violations and its crackdown on the media had already said goodbye to the EU's accession process for a while, until the Syrian refugee crisis emerged and posed a big threat to all European countries. EU leaders who occasionally criticized Erdoğan's oppression decided to negotiate a deal with Turkey. However, owing to the stalemate in Turkey–EU relations, reaching a deal was difficult. Meanwhile, 2.7 million Syrian refugees and other migrants had posed a serious challenge for both parties. While Turkey initially used its own national resources to accommodate such incomers, it needed European assistance.

On the EU's part, there was an increasing sense of panic about how to handle the refugee crisis. The EU countries had international obligations regarding accepting the refugees and granting them refugee status. This was the background against which Turkey and the EU made a deal that envisaged cooperation on border controls to manage irregular migration, assistance to refugees, financial support to Turkey and visa liberalization for Turkish citizens. Syrian refugees had become a political lever for Erdoğan and an opportunity for scaremongering vis-à-vis the EU. On the other hand, the plan was critical to the future of Turkey–EU relations, as well as to Turkey's journey towards democratization.

Unsurprisingly, the post-coup climate did not contribute to the flourishing of this tentative, fragile deal. Erdoğan was furious at the EU, since its leaders were either late or weak in condemning the coup attempt. No EU leader had paid a visit to Turkey to show solidarity in the weeks immediately afterwards, and none had acknowledged the Gülen movement as a probable perpetrator of the coup, except for the UK, whose ambassador in Ankara said, 'I don't have any difficulty in accepting what the government is saying, that Gülenists were involved in this coup.'[6]

Relations between Turkey and the US also entered their most bitter phase ever in the aftermath of the coup. This was first because of the memory of the 1980 coup, of which the then US national security adviser Paul Henze allegedly had said, 'Our boys did it.' Second, many in the ruling AKP elite seriously apportioned a large degree of blame for the coup to the US. Although the tone of this message was lowered after high-level visits from the US, it continued to be fed avidly by pro-government media. The main grounds for this view were Gülen's residence in America and the refusal of the US to extradite him to Turkey, which was construed as evidence that he was supported by his new home country. Another underlying assumption was that an imam from central Anatolia could scarcely have reached the level of global power that he had without the support of a superpower.

However, the major rift in Turkey–US relations had started in 2014 during ISIS's siege of the Syrian Kurdish town Kobane. The US was caught between the devil and the deep blue sea.

'Let me say very respectfully to our allies the Turks that we understand fully the fundamentals of their opposition,' US Foreign Secretary John Kerry said. 'But we have undertaken a coalition effort to degrade and destroy Isil [ISIS], and Isil is presenting itself in major numbers in this place called Kobani [Kobane].' He continued, 'It would be irresponsible of us, as well [as] morally very difficult, to turn your back on a community fighting Isil as hard as it is at this particular moment.'[7] Kobane amply demonstrated the conflicting interests of Turkey and the US regarding the Syria and Kurds.

The US distributed weapons and ammunition to the Kurdish forces in Kobane, to Turkey's annoyance, but the real fanfare came after US envoy Brett McGurk, Obama's Special Presidential Envoy for the Global Coalition to Counter ISIS, visited Kurdish-controlled northern Syria in February 2016. It was the first officially declared trip to Syrian territory, and it was specifically to visit the Kurds.

McGurk posted photos of his visit on his Twitter feed the same day. He had gone to a cemetery and, as he put it, 'paid respects to over 1,000 Kurdish martyrs' from the battle of Kobane waged by the YPG. He also had received a thank-you plaque from YPG commander Polat Can, a move which drove the pro-government press into a frenzy. What the government mouthpieces did not pick up on was the importance of another photo, in which McGurk was standing next to Şahin Cilo, a high-profile PKK leader. Fifty-year-old Cilo had worked closely with

Öcalan during the 1990s and had later played an active role in the establishment of the PKK's European network.

This photo was an indication that dealing with the YPG meant direct contact with the top ranks of the PKK. The US could not have avoided this, even had it contemplated so doing. Not surprisingly, Erdoğan was enraged by this trip: 'How can we trust [you]?' he stormed. 'Is it me who is your partner or the terrorists in Kobane?'[8]

US State Department spokesperson John Kirby's reply indicated that this issue would continue to fracture the bond between the two countries. 'We recognize that the Turks do [label the PYD as terrorists], and I understand that,' he said. 'Kurdish fighters have been some of the most successful in going after ISIS inside Syria. We have provided a measure of support, mostly through the air, and that support will continue.' So it did, both militarily and politically. McGurk paid a second visit to Kurdish-controlled Syria in September 2016.

A *Foreign Policy* article, with the perfectly apt title 'What happens in Turkey doesn't stay in Turkey', argued,

> The bedrock of any US plan should be a durable peace agreement between Turkey and the PKK. Washington must engage with both Ankara and the PKK to try to get them back to the negotiating table and provide diplomatic and financial guarantees for a comprehensive peace plan. [...] If the United States wants a secure and stable ally in a difficult region – one that is capable of making peace with the Kurds and of assisting in the fight against the Islamic State – it must work over the long-term to ensure these institutions develop.[9]

Undoubtedly, Turkey's toxic relations with the West pushed it closer to Russia. Since the collapse of communism in the USSR and Eastern Europe, the relationship between Turkey and Russia has depended on common areas of interest, such as the trade of energy and agricultural products, and tourism.

In the last decade, with Erdoğan and Putin at the helms of their respective countries, a closer relationship has developed between the two like-minded leaders. Their authoritarian rule, chauvinistic rhetoric, pragmatism, crudeness and opaque way of doing business have served each his purpose. Anti-Western discourse and a sense of victimhood at the West's hands have also been used by both men to steer internal politics. The two leaders are the embodiment of an illiberal populist tide in world politics.

The Syrian war had become the main rift between these two pragmatic leaders. At the beginning, President Erdoğan was very confident that it would be a mere matter of months before Assad was ousted. In 2012, he bragged about going to Damascus and praying at the Umayyad Mosque. Things did not go as he planned. Turkey's Syrian policy has proved to be an epic failure which turned Turkey, among other nations, against Russia, after Russia chose Assad as its proxy in Syria.

When Turkey downed a Russian jet near its Syrian border, the decade-long honeymoon between Putin and Erdoğan ended in a bitter fight. It was then that Turkey realized that it not only depends on Russia for trade and energy but also cannot compete with it militarily in Syria. This led to Erdoğan being forced to give Putin what he wanted: a belated public apology and compensation for the Russian pilot. The rapprochement was proudly flaunted to Europe and the US. Immediately, a deal for the construction of a major undersea gas pipeline was signed. Putin and Erdoğan also vowed to seek common ground on the war in Syria. A week later, Alexander Dugin, special representative to Putin (aka Putin's brain), told a Turkish envoy that Russia had warned Turkey about the coup a day before it happened. He also said that the coup had been launched because Turkey had decided to mend ties with Russia. So, according to this rationale, Russia had also been a target of the coup attempt. 'You know,' he added, 'they are not welcoming Turks in Europe. Yet, while Europe's doors are closed to you, Russian ones are open.'[10]

There was one other element in the resumption of the two leaders' relationship: both Turkey and Russia saw the Gülen movement as evil. Russia had in fact been the first country to close down Gülen schools in 2014. This common enmity brought them closer at a time when

Erdoğan believed no country was taking the Gülen threat as seriously as it should. Pro-government media in both countries also claimed that the pilots who had downed the Russian jets were affiliated with the Gülen movement.

The question was how far this relationship with Russia would go. Would Turkey jeopardize its NATO membership? Economically, socially and militarily, Turkey cannot be isolated from Europe; going that far would not serve Erdoğan's pragmatism. But this historic orientation should not diminish the fact that Turkey's relations with the West had been tainted as they had never been before in the last couple of decades.

Neither the disaster that is Syria nor the ISIS threat is likely to be resolved in the near future. The humanitarian crisis of the millions of Syrian refugees is a problem for the world to solve. And then there remains the overarching issue of the Kurds, which has the power to either illuminate or further eclipse the land on which it is being played out.

It did not have to be that way. If only Turkey had chosen to collaborate with the Syrian Kurds, rather than trying to undermine them, not only would Turkey be a safer place but also its relationship with NATO countries, especially the US, would not have reached its present stalemate.

Turkey could indeed have taken another tack, which, as a special operation by Turkish soldiers in Syria showed, can very well work in practice.

Around midnight on a murky night in February 2015, 600 Turkish troops with nine tanks and 57 armoured vehicles crossed into Syria to save from destruction the tomb of Suleyman Shah, the grandfather of the Ottoman Empire's founder, which was located in the Manbij district of Syria. ISIS had threatened to destroy the tomb, surrounding the area and putting 38 Turkish soldiers guarding it in terrible danger. Turkish soldiers therefore entered Syria from Kobane, evacuated the guards and transferred the remains of the tomb to Eshme, a town north of Kobane. No one was hurt and Turkish pride was saved, along with the tomb. The interesting part of that operation was that it was conducted in collaboration with YPG militias, whose vehicles escorted the Turkish tanks to Eshme.[11] The concert that this operation had showed to be possible later coined Öcalan's phrase 'the Eshme Spirit'. This spirit could have been the key to resolving the main conflicts of the Syrian imbroglio. But it was smothered soon after it had emerged.

On the same day that Turkey issued an arrest warrant for him, PYD co-leader Salih Müslim was at the Oxford Union to give a talk on the Rojava revolution. The students' many questions to him following his talk were premised on praising the PYD/YPG and the revolution.
I had a different kind of question for him.

Your party's armed group, the YPG, escorted the Turkish tanks along those dark roads between Manbij and Eshme to rescue Shah's sacred tomb. Yet now there is an arrest warrant out for you. When do you think the rift began?

He shook his head sadly. 'My people and I helped Turkey whenever they got into trouble in Syria,' he said, adding,

You know... I was in Ankara with Turkish officials on the night of the tomb operation, to advise them. But Turkey took all our efforts and good intentions for granted and then turned against us. We were tricked. Turks and their Ottoman tricks!

Kurds are not only stateless but also forgotten. They are used, manipulated and deceived by great powers. They are lynched and hurt by their friends and neighbours. They are discriminated against and forcibly assimilated by various countries. They are massacred. They are killed by many – and they have killed many.
As I write, there is a Kurdish train leaving Syria and Turkey carrying a huge load of baggage: a load of despair, hate, anger and remorse, but also of love and hope for a better and more peaceful Middle East.

This train will stop at every city in the Western world and affect relations between East and West. It will influence immigration and rear its head in the construction of counterterrorism policies and democratic structures around the world. The Kurdish problem has become a global one, and it is here to stay for the foreseeable future.

Notes

Introduction

1 Ezgi Başaran, interview with Kadir Selamet, 13 February 2017, unpublished.
2 Ezgi Başaran, interview with Göksel Ilgın, 13 February 2017, unpublished.
3 Murat Somer, 'Understanding Turkey's democratic breakdown: old vs. new and indigenous vs. global authoritarianism', *Southeast European and Black Sea Studies* 16/4 (2016). Available at http://dx.doi.org/10.1080/14683857.2016.1246548, p. 2.
4 Ibid., p. 3.
5 Rukmini Callimachi, 'Turkey, a conduit for fighters joining ISIS, begins to feel its wrath', *New York Times*, 29 June 2016. Available at http://www.nytimes. com/2016/06/30/world/middleeast/turkey-a-conduit-for-fighters-joining-isis-begins-to-feel-its-wrath.html.
6 Frank Gardner, 'Will a Turkish border deal block IS recruits?', *BBC News*, 28 August 2015. Available at http://www.bbc.co.uk/news/world-middle-east-34060925.
7 Barçın Yinanç, 'Turkey pursuing triple aim in debate over Mosul', interview with Hasan Köni, *Hürriyet Daily News*, 24 October 2016. Available at http:// www.hurriyetdailynews.com/turkey-pursuing-triple-aim-in-debate-over-mosul. aspx?PageID=238&NID=105268&NewsCatID=352.
8 Verda Özer, 'Does Turkey want to take Mosul?', *Hürriyet Daily News*, 15 October 2016. Available at http://www.hurriyetdailynews.com/does-turkey-want-to-take-mosul.aspx?pageID=449&nID=104987&NewsCatID=466.
9 Author's translation.
10 Ahmet Kaya's acceptance of the award is available to watch at https://www. youtube.com/watch?v=tgWXVWFz59M.

1. The Kurdish Issue: Made in Turkey

1 Serhun Al, 'Barış ve Çatışma Arasında: Türkiye ve Ortadoğu'da Kürt Dünyasını Anlamlandırmak', İzmir Economy University (February–May 2016). Available at https://serdargunes.files.wordpress.com/2015/08/baris-ve-catisma-arasc4b1nda-turkiye-ve-ortadoguda-kurt-dunyasini-anlamlandirmak.pdf.
2 Martin van Bruinessen, 'Erken 21. Yüzyılda Kürt Kimlikleri ve Kürt Milliyetçilikleri', in Elçin Aktoprak and A. Celil Kaya (eds), *21. Yüzyılda Milliyetçilik: Teori ve Siyaset* (Istanbul: İletişim Yayınları, 2016), pp. 349–73.
3 Malcolm Sutton, 'An index of deaths from the conflict in Ireland', Conflict Archive on the Internet (CAIN) (2010). Available at http://cain.ulst.ac.uk/sutton/.
4 TBMM, 'Terör ve şiddet olayları kapsamında yaşam hakkı ihlallerini inceleme raporu' (the Turkish Parliament's Commision on Human Rights report on terror and violence) (2013). Available at https://www.tbmm.gov.tr/komisyon/insanhaklari/

belge/TERÖR%20VE%20ŞİDDET%20OLAYLARI%20KAPSAMINDA%20
YAŞAM%20HAKKI%20İHLALLERİNİ%20İNCELEME%20RAPORU.pdf.

5   According to Turkey's official statistics almanac (*Türkiye İstatistik Yıllığı*), produced by the State Institute of Statistics (Devlet İstatistik Enstitüsü), Turkey's GDP per capita in 2004 was US$2,146, whereas in Diyarbakır it was US$1,312.

6   Ahmet Özer, *Çözülemeyen Kürt Sorunu* [The Unresolved Kurdish Problem] (Istanbul: Hemen Kitap, 2012), pp. 22–3.

7   Hamit Bozarslan, 'Kurds and the Turkish state', in Reşat Kasaba (ed.), *The Cambridge History of Turkey* (New York: Cambridge University Press, 2008), p. 335.

8   Ibid., p. 336.

9   Erik J. Zürcher, *Turkey: A Modern History* (London and New York: I.B.Tauris, 2014), pp. 169–72.

10 Andrew Mango, 'Atatürk and the Kurds', *Middle Eastern Studies* 35/4 (1999), pp. 1–25.

11 Ayşe Hür, 'Kürtlere Özerklik Sözü Verdi mi?', *Taraf*, 19 December 2010. *Taraf* was shut down by the authorities, but a copy of the article is available at http://www.cafrande.org/osmanlidan-bugune-kurtler-ve-devlet-kurtlere-ozerklik-sozu-verildi-mi-ayse-hur//.

12 Gerard Chaliand, *A People without a Country: The Kurds and Kurdistan* (London: Zed Books, 1993), p. 47.

13 Tolga Korkut, 'Öcalan: It has taken a long time but it will be good', *Bianet*, 17 August 2009. Available at http://bianet.org/english/other/116508-Öcalan-it-has-taken-a-long-time-but-it-will-be-good.

14 Othman Ali, 'The Kurds and the Lausanne peace negotiations, 1922–23', *Middle Eastern Studies* 33/3 (1997), p. 521.

15 Ezgi Başaran, 'Devlet beni şahin diye pazarlıyor', interview with Emine Ayna, *Radikal*, 28 July 2011. Available at http://www.radikal.com.tr/yazarlar/ezgi-basaran/devlet-beni-sahin-diye-pazarliyor-1057907/.

16 Zürcher, *Turkey: A Modern History*.

17 Martin van Bruinessen, 'Genocide in Kurdistan? The suppression of the Dersim Rebellion in Turkey (1937–38) and the chemical war against the Iraqi Kurds (1988)', in George J. Andreopoulos (ed.), *Genocide: Conceptual and Historical Dimensions* (Philadelphia: University of Pennsylvania Press, 1994), pp. 141–54. Also available at http://www.hum.uu.nl/medewerkers/m.vanbruinessen/publications/Bruinessen_Genocide_in_Kurdistan.pdf.

18 Taken from the Turkish parliamentary archives. Available at https://www.tbmm.gov.tr/tutanaklar/TUTANAK/TBMM/d03/c001/tbmm03001014.pdf.

19 Mesut Yeğen and Dilek Kurban, 'Adaletin kıyısında "zorunlu" göç sonrasında', TESEV Yayınları, 2012.

20 Andrew Mango, 'Turks and Kurds', *Middle Eastern Studies* 30/4 (2006), p. 983.

21 Muhsin Batur, 'Anılar ve Görüşler' [Memoirs and views], *Milliyet*, 1985, quoted in van Bruinessen, 'Genocide in Kurdistan?', p. 4.

22 Ayşe Gül Altınay, *The Myth of the Military-Nation: Militarism, Gender, and Education in Turkey* (New York: Springer, 2004), p. 38.

23 Sabiha Gökçen, *Atatürk'ün İzinde Bir Ömür Böyle Geçti*, p. 125, cited in Altınay, *The Myth of the Military-Nation*, p. 58.

24 Ezgi Başaran, 'Dersim'den CHP kadar DP de sorumlu', interview with Hüsamettin Cindoruk, *Radikal*, 28 November 2011. Available at http://www.radikal.com.tr/yazarlar/ezgi-basaran/dersimden-chp-kadar-dp-de-sorumlu-1070843/.

25 Zürcher, *Turkey: A Modern History*, p. 138.
26 Reha Mağden, 'Turgut Özal'ın "Kürt meselesi" yorumu', interview with Turgut Özal, *Aktüel*, 18 October 1992. Available at http://www.aktuel.com.tr/dergi/2013/10/10/turgut-ozalin-kurt-meselesi-yorumu.
27 Cengiz Çandar, *Mezopotamya Ekspresi* (Istanbul: İletişim Yayınları, 2014).
28 'Öcalan'la görüşmesi sonu oldu', interview with Feyzi İşbaşaran, *Radikal*, 15 June 2012. Available at http://www.radikal.com.tr/turkiye/ocalanla-gorusmesi-sonu-oldu-1091199/.
29 Feroz Ahmad, *Turkey: The Quest for Identity* (London: Oneworld Publications, 2014), p. 163.
30 Ezgi Başaran, 'Devlet Kürtleri ne asimile etti, ne inkar etti sadece bilinçli olarak göz ardı etti', interview with Metin Heper, *Hürriyet*, 12 October 2008. Available at http://www.hurriyet.com.tr/devlet-kurtleri-ne-asimile-etti-ne-ink-r-etti-sadece-bilincli-olarak-goz-ardi-etti-10094707.
31 Paul White, *The PKK: Coming Down from the Mountains* (London: Zed Books, 2015), p. 16.
32 Ergun Aydınoğlu, *Fis Köyünden Kobane'ye Kürt Özgürlük Hareketi* (Istanbul: Versus, 2014), p. 38.
33 Bozarslan, 'Kurds and the Turkish state', p. 346.
34 Selin Yeleser, *The Revolutionary Eastern Cultural Hearths (1969–1971): A Turning Point in the Formation of the Kurdish Left in Turkey* (Saarbrücken: LAP Lambert Academic Publishing, 2012).
35 White, *The PKK*, p. 17.
36 Selim Çürükkaya, 'PKK'yi Kimler Kurdu? 1', *Ma'diya*, 17 April 2012. Available at http://madiya.net/index.php?option=com_content&view=article&id=512:pkk-yi-kimler-kurdu&catid=40:portreler&Itemid=59.
37 Ezgi Başaran, 'Demokratik özerklik ilanının hiçbir anlamı yok', interview with Tarık Ziya Ekinci, *Radikal*, 18 July 2011. Available at http://www.radikal.com.tr/yazarlar/ezgi-basaran/demokratik-ozerklik-ilaninin-hicbir-anlami-yok-1056689/.
38 Hasan Kaya, *Doğunun Elçisi'nden Yüce Divan'a Şerafettin Elçi* (Ankara: Fanos Yayınları, 2012), p. 74.
39 Selim Çürükkaya, 'PKK yi Kimler Kurdu 8', *Ma'diya*, 16 April 2012. Available at http://madiya.net/index.php?option=com_content&view=article&id=532:pkk-yi-kimler-kurdu-8&catid=40:portreler&Itemid=59.
40 David McDowall, *A Modern History of the Kurds* (London and New York: I.B.Tauris, 2003), p. 422.
41 Ibid., p. 423.
42 Altan Tan, *Hz. İbrahim'in Ayak İzlerinde Ortadoğu* (Istanbul: Çıra, 2016), p. 367.
43 Abdullah Öcalan, '1978 PKK Kuruluş Kongresi konuşması', *İlk Konuşmalar*, *Weşanen Serxwebun* 91, 1998, p. 141.
44 'Going up to the mountains' or 'heading for the mountains' are euphemisms for joining the PKK.
45 Ezgi Başaran, 'Çözüm için Kürtleri tatmin, Türkleri de ikna etmek lazım', interview with Şerafettin Elçi, *Radikal*, 6 February 2012. Available at http://www.radikal.com.tr/yazarlar/ezgi-basaran/cozum-icin-kurtleri-tatmin-turkleri-de-ikna-etmek-lazim-1077830/.
46 Ruşen Çakır, 'Yoktan var olan Kürt hareketi ile vardan yok olan Türk solu', *Vatan*, 7 February 2014. Available at http://www.gazetevatan.com/rusen-cakir-607569-yazar-yazisi-yoktan-var-olan-kurt-hareketi-ile-vardan-yok-olan-turk-solu/.

47 Also known as strappado, this is a form of torture in which the victim's hands are tied behind their back and they are then suspended by a rope attached to the wrists.

48 Quoted in Hasan Cemal, *Kürtler* (Istanbul: Doğan Kitap, 2003), p. 30.

49 Ibid., p. 31.

50 Quoted in Jenna Krajeski, 'Turkey's museum of shame', *Foreign Policy*, 30 December 2011. Available at http://foreignpolicy.com/2011/12/30/turkeys-museum-of-shame/.

51 Ezgi Başaran, 'Öcalan sıralamayı değiştirdi, çekilmeyi bir adım öne aldı', interview with Remzi Kartal, *Radikal*, 16 April 2013. Available at http://www.radikal.com.tr/yazarlar/ezgi-basaran/ocalan-siralamayi-degistirdi-cekilmeyi-bir-adim-one-aldi-1129686/.

52 Şeyhmus Diken, *Sırrını Surlarına Fısıldayan Şehir: Diyarbakır* (Istanbul: İletişim Yayınları, 2002), p. 28.

53 McDowall, *A Modern History of the Kurds*, p. 427.

54 Ahmad, *Turkey: The Quest for Identity*, p. 164.

55 Vera Eccarius-Kelly, *The Militant Kurds: A Dual Strategy for Freedom* (Santa Barbara, CA: Praeger Publishers, 2012), p. 111.

56 Turkish Ministry of Defence, Turkish military and police forces sources, 2011.

57 Global IDP Database, 'Profile of internal displacement: Turkey (compilation of the information available in the Global IDP Database of the Norwegian Refugee Council)'. Available at http://www.internal-displacement.org/assets/library/Europe/Turkey/pdf/Turkey+-July+2003.pdf.

58 TBMM 10/25 Esas Sayılı Meclis Araştırması Komisyonu Raporu (1996). Available at https://www.tbmm.gov.tr/sirasayi/donem20/yil01/ss532.pdf.

59 Eccarius-Kelly, *The Militant Kurds*, p. 121.

60 Ibid., p. 156.

61 Öcalan's lawyers were prosecuted for being members of a terrorist organization.

62 'Abdullah Öcalan – özgür kadın'. Available at https://www.a-ocalan-ozgurkadin.info/2-10-2015-mektubu-1999-mektupları/.

63 Abdullah Öcalan, 'Democratic modernity: era of woman's revolution', official PKK website. Available at http://www.pkkonline.com/en/index.php?sys=article&artID=235.

64 Deniz Erdoğan, 'Female fighters of PKK', *Uno Sguardo al femminile*, 12 November 2014. Available at http://www.unosguardoalfemminile.it/wordpress/?p=6115.

65 Eric W. Schoon, 'The paradox of legitimacy: resilience, successes, and the multiple identities of the Kurdistan Workers' Party in Turkey', *Social Problems* 62/2 (2015) p. 62.

66 'KCK Yürütme Konseyi üyesi Duran Kalkan ANF'ye konuştu', *Sol*, 27 February 2013. Available at http://haber.sol.org.tr/devlet-ve-siyaset/kck-yurutme-konseyi-uyesi-duran-kalkan-anfye-konustu-haberi-68892.

67 Thomas L. Friedman, 'When the necessary is impossible', *New York Times*, 30 March 2016. Available at http://www.nytimes.com/2016/03/30/opinion/when-the-necessary-is-impossible.html?_r=0.

68 İmralı Notları – *Demokratik Kurtuluş ve Özgür Yaşamı İnşa* (Neuss: Mezopotamya Yayınları, 2014), p. 239.

69 Murray Bookchin, *The Ecology of Freedom: The Emergence and Dissolution of Hierarchy* (Chico, CA: AK Press, 2015).

70 'KCK Sözleşmesi'. Available at https://tr.wikisource.org/wiki/KCK_Sözleşmesi.

71 Derya Bayır, 'The role of the judicial system in the politicide of the Kurdish opposition', in Cengiz Güneş and Welat Zeydanlıoğlu (eds), *The Kurdish Question*

in Turkey: New Perspectives on Violence, Representation and Reconciliation (London: Routledge, 2013), p. 33.

72   Ezgi Başaran, 'Gerçek 2. Cumhuriyet şimdi başladı', interview with Fırat Anlı, *Radikal*, 23 April 2013. Available at http://www.radikal.com.tr/yazarlar/ezgi-basaran/gercek-2-cumhuriyet-donemi-simdi-basladi-1126507/.

73   PKK Tüzüğü. Available at https://rojbas2.wordpress.com/pkk-tuzugu/.

74   Abdullah Öcalan, 'Önderlik gerçekliği ve PKK deniyimi', *Weşanen Serxwebun* 55/1 (1992), p. 144.

75   Eccarius-Kelly, *The Militant Kurds*, p. 112.

76   Ezgi Başaran, 'Çözüm olsun ben iş bulurum', interview with Murat Karayılan on Qandil Mountain, *Radikal*, 27 April 2013. Available at http://www.radikal.com.tr/yazarlar/ezgi-basaran/cozum-olsun-ben-is-bulurum-1131279/.

77   Başaran, 'Gerçek 2. Cumhuriyet şimdi başladı'.

78   Rengin Arslan, '68. günde açlık grevleri sona erdi', BBC Turkey, 18 November 2012. Available at http://www.bbc.com/turkce/haberler/2012/11/121118_hunger_strike_ends_update.shtml.

79   Ezgi Başaran, 'Silahsızlanma iyi planlanmazsa PKK radikalleşir', interview with Prof. Abbas Vali, *Radikal*, 4 February 2013. Available at http://www.radikal.com.tr/yazarlar/ezgi-basaran/silahsizlanma-iyi-planlanmazsa-pkk-radikallesir-1119805/.

80   Vahap Coşkun, 'Process of resolution: gains and dangers', Democratic Progress Institute, 2015. Available at http://www.democraticprogress.org/wp-content/uploads/2015/10/VAHAP-COSKUN-Report-Summer-2015.pdf.

81   Recep Tayyip Erdoğan, speech in the Turkish parliament, 26 February 2013.

82   A reputable company called KONDA conducted a poll in 30 cities involving 2,650 people in May 2013. The results are available at http://t24.com.tr/haber/kondanin-son-anketi-cozum-surecine-destek-yuzde-813e-ulasti,229284.

83   'Erdoğan'ın açıkladığı çözüm süreci anketi', *Ensonhaber*, 27 March 2013. Available at http://www.ensonhaber.com/erdoganin-acikladigi-cozum-sureci-anketi-2013-03-27.html.

84   Trevor Payne, 'Kurdistan: revolution at a critical juncture', in Eddie Abrahams (ed.), *The New Warlords: from the Gulf War to the Recolonisation of the Middle East* (London: Larkin Publications, 1994), p. 144.

85   'İşte Tahir Elçi'nin son sözleri', *Hürriyet*, 28 November 2015. Available at http://www.hurriyet.com.tr/video/iste-tahir-elci-nin-son-sozleri-123208.

2. Kurds in New Turkey

1   Cihan Tuğal, *The Fall of the Turkish Model: How the Arab Uprisings Brought Down Islamic Liberalism* (London and New York: Verso, 2016), p. 35.

2   Zeyno Baran, *Torn Country: Turkey between Secularism and Islamism* (Stanford: Hoover Institution Press, 2010), p. 36.

3   A Kurdish Islamist theologian who wrote a Qur'anic *tefsir* (exegesis) called the *Risale-i Nur Collection*. His followers are called the Nur movement, or Nurcular.

4   Quoted in Kemal Göktaş, 'Paradaki simge', *Cumhuriyet*, 7 August 2016. Available at http://www.cumhuriyet.com.tr/haber/yazi_dizileri/580490/Paradaki_simge.html.

5   Latif Erdoğan, *Şeytanın Gülen Yüzü* (Istanbul: Turkuvaz Kitap, 2016), pp. 127, 164–5.

6   Göktaş, 'Paradaki simge'.

7   Turkish Parliament Investigation Commission on FETÖ and July 15 Coup. Available at http://t24.com.tr/files/20161222094641_yeni-duzeltilmis-rapor-15.12. 2016.pdf.

8   Fethullah Gülen terrorist organization list of charges, prepared by the Mersin state prosecution and admitted by Mersin 2. Criminal Court in August 2015.

9   Fethullah Gülen list of charges, Ankara, 1999. Available at http://docplayer.biz. tr/5798308-Fethullah-gulen-davasi-iddianamesi.html.

10 Joshua D. Hendrick, Gülen: The Ambiguous Politics of Market Islam in Turkey and the World (New York: NYU Press, 2014), p. 61.

11 Joshua Landis, 'Public intellectual or public enemy', The Conversation, 8 August 2016. Available at https://theconversation.com/fethullah-gulen-public-intellectual-or-public-enemy-62887.

12 Helen Rose Ebaugh and Dogan Koc, 'Funding Gülen-inspired good works: demonstrating and generating commitment to the movement', fgulen.com, 27 October 2007. Available at http://gulenconferences.com/wp-content/uploads/2014/04/Prcd-Ebaugh-and-Koc.pdf.

13 Sibel Edmonds, 'Did you know: the King of Madrasas now operates 100 charter schools in the US?', Newsbud, 20 October 2010. Available at http://www.newsbud. com/2010/10/20/did-you-know-the-king-of-madrasas-now-operates-over-100-charter-schools-in-the-us/.

14 Fethullah Gülen, Fasıldan Fasıla-1, 1995. Available at http://odatv.com/fethullah-gulen-yahudiler-hakkinda-ne-dusunuyor-1012121200.html.

15 'Fethullah Gülen, the Jews, and hypocrisy', Balyoz Davası ve Gerçekler [blog], 5 November 2012. Available at https://balyozdavasivegercekler.com/2012/11/05/fethullah-gulen-the-jews-and-hypocrisy/.

16 Edip Asaf Bekaroğlu, 'The ambiguity of Turkish secularism', Critical Muslim 16 (2015), p. 32.

17 'Gömlek kavgası', Milliyet, 22 May 2003. Available at http://www.milliyet.com. tr/2003/05/22/siyaset/asiy.html.

18 'Erdoğan: Din üzerinden siyasete karşıyız', Hürriyet, 10 January 2004. Available at http://www.hurriyet.com.tr/erdogan-din-uzerinden-siyasete-karsiyiz-38556005.

19 Ezgi Başaran, 'AKP İslamcılığı bozmadı, zaten "moral olarak çökmüş İslamcı döküntüleriyle" kuruldu', interview with Hamza Türkmen, Radikal, 13 July 2015. Available at http://www.radikal.com.tr/yazarlar/ezgi-basaran/akp-islamciligi-bozmadi-zaten-moral-olarak-cokmus-islamci-dokuntuleriyle-kurul-1395973/.

20 Yüksel Taşkın, AKP Devri: Türkiye Siyaseti, İslamcılık, Arap Baharı (Istanbul: İletişim Yayınları, 2013).

21 'Genelkurmay'dan çok sert açıklama', Hürriyet, 29 April 2007. Available at http:// www.hurriyet.com.tr/genelkurmaydan-cok-sert-aciklama-6420961.

22 Ayşegül Usta, Fırat Alkaç ve Özge Eğrikar, 'Ergenekon Davasında tahliye dalgası', Hürriyet, 10 March 2014. Available at http://www.hurriyet.com.tr/ergenekon-davasinda-tahliye-dalgasi-25978971.

23 Ezgi Başaran, 'PKK böyle çekilecek', Radikal, 26 April 2013. Available at http:// www.radikal.com.tr/yazarlar/ezgi-basaran/pkk-boyle-cekilecek-1131137/.

24 Quoted in Hasan Cemal, 'Türk askeri düşmanımız değil', T24, 24 May 2013. Available at http://t24.com.tr/yazarlar/hasan-cemal/turk-askeri-dusmanimiz-degil-turk-analarinin-acilarini-paylasiyoruz,6751.

25 Ezgi Başaran, 'Kürtlere haklarını salam taktiğiyle veremezsiniz', interview with Hugh Pope, Radikal, 27 September 2012. Available at http://www.radikal.com.

tr/yazarlar/ezgi-basaran/kurtlere-haklarini-salam-taktigiyle-veremezsiniz-1101812/.

26 H. Akın Ünver, 'Turkey's Kurdish question, the United States and Europe', in Fevzi Bilgin and Ali Sarahan (eds), *Understanding Turkey's Kurdish Question* (Plymouth: Lexington Books, 2013), p. 198.

27 Ezgi Başaran, 'Çözüm için Kürtleri tatmin, Türkleri de ikna etmek lazım', interview with Şerafettin Elçi, *Radikal*, 6 February 2012. Available at http://www.radikal.com.tr/yazarlar/ezgi-basaran/cozum-icin-kurtleri-tatmin-turkleri-de-ikna-etmek-lazim-1077830/.

28 Ezgi Başaran, '"Anadilde özel okul" neoliberal aklın bir sonucu', interview with Fatma Gök, *Radikal*, 7 October 2013. Available at http://www.radikal.com.tr/yazarlar/ezgi-basaran/anadilde-ozel-okul-neoliberal-aklin-bir-sonucu-1154350/.

29 Ezgi Başaran, 'Demokrasisiz barış olur ama Kürtlerin istediği bu mu?', interview with Cengiz Aktar, *Radikal*, 18 March 2013. Available at http://www.radikal.com.tr/yazarlar/ezgi-basaran/demokrasisiz-baris-olur-ama-kurtlerin-istedigi-bu-mu-1125567/.

30 Tuğal, *The Fall of the Turkish Model*, p. 93.

31 '-22 derecede Kürt sorunu tartıştı', *Sabah*, 25 December 2002. Available at http://arsiv.sabah.com.tr/2002/12/25/s1902.html.

32 '"Kürt sorunu benim sorunum"', BBC Turkey, 12 August 2005. Available at http://www.bbc.co.uk/turkish/news/story/2005/08/050812_turkey_kurds.shtml.

33 'Kürt açılımını başlattık', *Hürriyet*, 23 July 2009. Available at http://www.hurriyet.com.tr/kurt-acilimini-baslattik-12129354.

34 'Erdoğan'dan BDP'ye sert eleştiri', *Hürriyet*, 30 April 2011. Available at http://www.hurriyet.com.tr/erdogandan-bdpye-sert-elestiri-17676072.

35 '"Kürt sorunu yok, PKK sorunu var"', TRT Haber, 15 July 2011. Available at http://www.trthaber.com/haber/gundem/kurt-sorunu-yok-pkk-sorunu-var-2535.html.

36 'Erdoğan'ın "Kürt sorunu yoktur" açılımında geldiği son nokta: "Var" diyen ayrımcıdır', *Diken*, 28 April 2015. Available at http://www.diken.com.tr/erdoganin-kurt-sorunu-yoktur-aciliminda-geldigi-son-nokta-var-diyen-ayrimcidir/.

37 Ezgi Başaran, 'En büyük Kürt partisi kim açıklıyorlar (2)', interview with Mesut Yeğen, *Radikal*, 26 May 2015. Available at http://www.radikal.com.tr/yazarlar/ezgi-basaran/en-buyuk-kurt-partisi-kim-acikliyorlar-2-1365448/.

38 Those cities are Adıyaman, Ağrı, Batman, Hakkâri, Şırnak, Bingöl, Diyarbakır, Mardin, Tunceli, Urfa, Van and Kars.

39 Başaran, 'En büyük Kürt partisi kim açıklıyorlar (2)'.

40 Ibid.

41 Ezgi Başaran, 'Ümmetçi kalınabilseydi Kürt sorunu çözülürdü', interview with Altan Tan, *Radikal*, 11 July 2001. Available at http://www.radikal.com.tr/yazarlar/ezgi-basaran/ummetci-kalinabilseydi-kurt-sorunu-cozulurdu-1055824/.

3. Kurdish Peace and the New Deep State

1 '2010'da Türkiye', SETAV Analiz, January 2011. Available at https://www.setav.org/2010da-turkiye/.

2 Özgür Herekol, 'Cemaat–AKP kavgası ve Kürtler', *Nerinaazad*, 12 January 2014. Available at http://www.nerinaazad.com/columnists/ozgur_herekol/cemaat-akp-kavgasi-ve-kurtler.

3   Ezgi Başaran, 'Gülen cemaati ve liberaller sayesinde AKP "ılımlı İslamcı" olarak algılandı', interview with Prof. Yüksel Taşkın, *Radikal*, 14 July 2015. Available at http://www.radikal.com.tr/yazarlar/ezgi-basaran/gulen-cemaati-ve-liberaller-sayesinde-akp-ilimli-islamci-olarak-algilandi-1396521/.

4   Ezgi Başaran, 'Zekâmı ölçmeye makine dayanmaz', interview with Necmettin Erbakan, *Radikal*, 2 January 2011. Available at http://www.radikal.com.tr/politika/zekmi-olcmeye-makine-dayanmaz-1034839/.

5   Doğan Koç, 'The Hizmet movement and the Kurdish question', in Fevzi Bilgin and Ali Sarahan (eds), *Understanding Turkey's Kurdish Question* (Plymouth: Lexington Books, 2013), p. 186.

6   The Turkey branches of the Kimse Yok Mu Foundation were shut down following the 15 July 2016 coup attempt.

7   Ezgi Başaran, 'Biz dindarlar Kürtlerin ıstırabını hissetmedik', interview with Cemal Uşşak, *Radikal*, 10 October 2011. Available at http://www.radikal.com.tr/yazarlar/ezgi-basaran/biz-dindarlar-kurtlerin-istirabini-hissetmedik-1065858/.

8   Mustafa Akyol, 'Is Gülen movement against peace with PKK?', *Al-Monitor*, 22 May 2013. Available at http://www.al-monitor.com/pulse/originals/2013/05/gulen-movement-peace-process-pkk.html.

9   A platform of Kurdish associations and movements founded in 2011 that has proclaimed democratic self-government.

10 Helin Alp, '"Erdoğan çözüm istiyor ancak projesi yok"', interview with Hatip Dicle, Al Jazeera, 21 May 2014. Available at http://www.aljazeera.com.tr/al-jazeera-ozel/erdogan-cozum-istiyor-ancak-projesi-yok.

11 *İmralı Notları – Demokratik Kurtuluş ve Özgür Yaşamı İnşa* (Neuss: Mezopotamya Yayınları, 2015), p. 421.

12 AK Group, 'Illegal tape alleges secret PKK talks', Gatestone Institute, 15 September 2011. Available at https://www.gatestoneinstitute.org/2426/illegal-tape-alleges-secret-pkk-talks.

13 Ezgi Başaran, 'Çözüm olsun ben iş bulurum', interview with Murat Karayılan on Qandil Mountain, *Radikal*, 27 April 2013. Available at http://www.radikal.com.tr/yazarlar/ezgi-basaran/cozum-olsun-ben-is-bulurum-1131279/.

14 The leaked tape of Oslo talks, 2012. Available at https://vimeo.com/51264002.

15 *İmralı Notları*, p. 376.

16 Ezgi Başaran, 'Bir annenin Habur yolculuğu ve Kandil gardırobu', 'Elif Uludağ's letter', *Radikal*, 22 March 2012. Available at http://www.radikal.com.tr/yazarlar/ezgi-basaran/bir-annenin-habur-yolculugu-ve-kandil-gardirobu-1082542/.

17 Ezgi Başaran, interview with Lord Alderdice, 2 April 2016, Oxford, unpublished.

18 Chris Kutschera, 'The secret Oslo talks that might have brought peace to Turkey', *The Middle East Magazine*, December 2012. Available at http://www.chris-kutschera.com/A/Oslo.htm.

19 Cemil Bayık interview, ANF, 1 June 2010. No link available.

20 Kutschera, 'The secret Oslo talks'.

21 According to informal statistics maintained by the Crisis Group (11 September 2012), since the 12 June 2011 parliamentary elections 711 people had been killed by mid-August 2012, including 222 soldiers, police and village guard militias, 405 PKK fighters and 84 civilians. This is four times more deaths than in 2009 and far more than the annual figures in 2000–4, when the PKK was implementing a unilateral ceasefire.

22 Ezgi Başaran, 'Kürtlere haklarını salam taktiğiyle veremezsiniz', interview with Hugh Pope, *Radikal*, 27 September 2012. Available at http://www.radikal.com.tr/yazarlar/ezgi-basaran/kurtlere-haklarini-salam-taktigiyle-veremezsiniz-1101812/.

23 Murat Yetkin, 'Umutlar solmasın', interview with Zübeyir Aydar, *Radikal*, 29 March 2013. Available at http://www.radikal.com.tr/yazarlar/murat-yetkin/umutlar-solmasin-1127121/.

24 'İşte İmralı görüşmesinin tutanaklarının tam metni!', T24, 28 February 2013. Available at http://t24.com.tr/haber/iste-imralidaki-gorusmenin-tutanaklari, 224711.

25 ANF News Agency, 'Karayılan'dan mektup', *Taraf*, 8 October 2011. *Taraf* was shut down by the authorities, but a copy of the article is available at http://www.yenihayatnews.com/news/?p=7809.

26 'Sakine Cansız ve 2 kadın PKK'lıya AK Parti'den ilk yorum', *Ensonhaber*, 10 January 2013. Available at http://www.ensonhaber.com/sakine-cansiz-ve-2-kadin-pkkliya-ak-partiden-ilk-yorum-2013-01-10.html.

27 Soren Seelow, 'Assassinat de militantes kurdes à Paris: la justice souligne l'implication des services secrets turcs', *Le Monde*, 23 July 2015. Available at http://www.lemonde.fr/police-justice/article/2015/07/23/assassinat-de-militantes-kurdes-a-paris-la-justice-pointe-l-implication-des-services-secrets-turcs_4694801_1653578.html.

28 Banu Güven, interview with Cemil Bayık, IMC TV, 10 March 2015. Available to watch at https://www.youtube.com/watch?v=FezWb5XB5qc.

29 Ahmet Şık, 'Ya Apo Kandil'e ya biz İmralı'ya', interview with Cemil Bayık, *Cumhuriyet*, 14 March 2015. Available at http://www.cumhuriyet.com.tr/haber/turkiye/231247/Ya_Apo_Kandil_e_ya_biz_imrali_ya.html.

30 Zübeyir Aydar interview, *Libération*, 14 January 2013. Available at http://www.liberation.fr/planete/2013/01/13/le-meurtre-des-trois-kurdes-ne-sert-pas-le-gouvernement-turc_873717.

31 Kayhan Karaca, 'Cenazeler Diyarbakır'a gönderilecek', Firat News Agency, 14 January 2013. Available at http://anfmobile.com/guncel/zubeyir-aydar-suikast-planlaryny-acyklady.

32 Duran Kalkan interview, Firat News Agency, 4 January 2014. No video link is available, but the text version can be read at http://rojevakurdistan.org/roeportaj/12339-kalkan-paris-katliam-aydnlatlrsa-coezuemuen-oenue-aclr.

33 Uğur Dündar, interview with İlker Başbuğ, *Arena* (TV show), Kanal D, 5 July 2010. Available to watch at https://www.youtube.com/watch?v=87SsWSK5dWE.

34 Med Nuce TV, 28 April 2013. No link available.

35 'Karayılan: 2013'te hazırdık, önderliğe "Savaş istiyoruz" diyemedik, hata ettik', T24, 17 June 2015. Available at http://t24.com.tr/haber/karayilan-2013te-hazirdik-onderlige-savas-istiyoruz-diyemedik-hata-ettik,299958.

36 Gareth H. Jenkins, 'One step from the brink: Turkey's Kurdish peace process edges closer to collapse', *The Turkey Analyst* 6/13 (2013). Available at https://www.turkeyanalyst.org/publications/turkey-analyst-articles/item/58-one-step-from-the-brink-turkey's-kurdish-peace-process-edges-closer-to-collapse.html.

37 Ezgi Başaran, 'IRA sorununu çözen beyin Jonathan Powell'dan 10 maddede kalıcı barış', interview with Jonathan Powell, *Radikal*, 10 April 2013. Available at http://www.radikal.com.tr/yazarlar/ezgi-basaran/ira-sorununu-cozen-beyin-jonathan-powelldan-10-maddede-kalici-baris-1128863/.

38 Selin Ongun, '"Feryat ediyorum, başaramadık Türkiye'ye yazık, hepimize yazık..."', interview with Hatip Dicle, *Cumhuriyet*, 18 January 2016. Available at http:// www.cumhuriyet.com.tr/koseyazisi/465446/_Feryat_ediyorum__basaramadik_ Turkiye_ye_yazik__hepimize_yazik..._.html.

39 Ezgi Başaran, 'Öcalan sıralamayı değiştirdi, çekilmeyi bir adım öne aldı', interview with Remzi Kartal, *Radikal*, 16 April 2013. Available at http://www.radikal.com.tr/yazarlar/ ezgi-basaran/ocalan-siralamayi-degistirdi-cekilmeyi-bir-adim-one-aldi-1129686/.

4. The PKK Embraces the World

1 Peshmerga is the Kurdish name given to the military force of Iraqi Kurdistan. It means 'the one who confronts death'.

2 The word *'medya'* refers to the Med Empire, the only Kurdish state ever to have existed.

3 Nadir Gergin, Hacı Duru and Hakan Cem Çetin, 'Profile and life span of the PKK guerrillas', *Studies in Conflict & Terrorism* 38/3 (2015), pp. 219–32.

4 Ezgi Başaran, 'Öcalan'ınki gerçekten şartsız barış mı?', *Radikal*, 22 March 2013. Available at http://www.radikal.com.tr/yazarlar/ezgi-basaran/ocalaninki-gercekten-sartsiz-bir-baris-mi-1126195/.

5 'Turkey and the PKK: saving the peace process', International Crisis Group report no. 234, 6 November 2014. Available at https://www.crisisgroup.org/europe-central-asia/western-europemediterranean/turkey/turkey-and-pkk-saving-peace-process.

6 Bejan Matur, *Dağın Ardına Bakmak* (Istanbul: Timaş Yayınları, 2011), p. 39.

7 Ibid., p. 47.

8 Kurdish word for 'friend'.

9 Quoted in Ezgi Başaran, 'PKK böyle çekilecek', *Radikal*, 26 April 2013. Available at http://www.radikal.com.tr/yazarlar/ezgi-basaran/pkk-boyle-cekilecek-1131137/.

10 Cengiz Kapmaz, *Öcalan'ın İmralı Günleri* (Istanbul: İthaki Yayınları, 2011), p. 87.

11 Murat Karayılan, *Bir Savaşın Anatomisi* (Diyarbakır: Aram Yayınları, 2014), p. 352.

12 'Eski PKK'lı Fırat, Kandil'in korkusunu anlattı', Melik Fırat interview, *Akşam*, 28 March 2013. Available at http://www.aksam.com.tr/guncel/eski-pkkli-firat-kandilin-korkusunu-anlatti/haber-181466.

13 Murat Karayılan, interview, Med Nuce TV, 11 May 2013. Available to watch at https://www.youtube.com/watch?v=zHqIQVy3VmE.

14 Ezgi Başaran, 'Çözüm olsun ben iş bulurum', interview with Murat Karayılan on Qandil Mountain, *Radikal*, 27 April 2013. Available at http://www.radikal.com. tr/yazarlar/ezgi-basaran/cozum-olsun-ben-is-bulurum-1131279/.

15 Quoted in 'Turkey and the PKK: saving the peace process', p. 18.

16 Onur Burçak Belli and Özlem Topçu, '"Erdoğan ist der wahre Kalif"', interview with Cemil Bayık, *Die Zeit*, 1 January 2015. Available at http://www.zeit.de/2014/52/ pkk-recep-tayyip-erdogan-islamischer-staat-cemil-bayik.

17 Interview by ICG, June 2014. Available at https://d2071andvip0wj.cloudfront. net/turkey-and-the-pkk-saving-the-peace-process.pdf.

18 Jose Miguel Calatayud, '"Just a few looters": Turkish PM Erdogan dismisses protests as thousands occupy Istanbul's Taksim Square', *The Independent*, 2 June 2013. Available at http://www.independent.co.uk/news/world/europe/just-a-few-looters-turkish-pm-erdogan-dismisses-protests-as-thousands-occupy-istanbuls-taksim-square-8641336.html.

19 'Erdoğan Berkin Elvan'ı terörist ilan etti annesini de yulahattı', *Cumhuriyet*, 14 March 2014. Available at http://www.cumhuriyet.com.tr/video/video/50743/Erdogan_Berkin_Elvan_i_terorist_ilan_etti_annesini_de_yuhalatti.html.

20 '"Dindar bir gençlik yetiştirmek istiyoruz"', *Hürriyet*, 1 February 2012. Available at http://www.hurriyet.com.tr/dindar-bir-genclik-yetistirmek-istiyoruz-19819295.

21 Hülya Karabağlı, 'BDP'li Baluken'den Cumhurbaşkanı'nın sözlerine destek', T24, 3 June 2013. Available at http://t24.com.tr/haber/bdpli-balukenden-cumhurbaskaninin-sozlerine-destek,231232.

22 Ezgi Başaran, '"Öcalan'ın Gezi konusunda bize eleştirisi oldu"', interview with Ahmet Türk, *Radikal*, 29 July 2013. Available at http://www.radikal.com.tr/yazarlar/ezgi-basaran/ocalanin-gezi-konusunda-bize-elestirisi-oldu-1143839/.

23 'White Turk' is a term first used by the late journalist Ufuk Güldemir in his 1992 book *Teksas Malatya* to describe people who were uneasy with the presidency of Turgut Özal. The term is usually used to describe Turkish people who come from a Kemalist ideology and are in a higher income bracket.

24 Some of the tweets and social media comments on the uprisings can be read at http://www.yuksekovahaber.com.tr/haber/turkler-kurtleri-anlamaya-basladi-102872.htm.

25 'KCK: Geri çekilmeyi durdurduk', *Evrensel*, 9 September 2013. Available at https://www.evrensel.net/haber/67365/kck-geri-cekilmeyi-durdurduk.

26 Gareth H. Jenkins, 'One step from the brink: Turkey's Kurdish peace process edges closer to collapse', *The Turkey Analyst* 6/13 (2013). Available at https://www.turkeyanalyst.org/publications/turkey-analyst-articles/item/58-one-step-from-the-brink-turkey's-kurdish-peace-process-edges-closer-to-collapse.html.

27 'Erdoğan'ı kızdıran kostere binemiyor', *Taraf*, 15 October 2013. *Taraf* was shut down by the authorities, but a copy of the article is available at http://gazeteport.com/haber/index.php?id=148273.

28 'We can think about the presidency. We can support Mr Tayyip's presidency. We can align with the AKP about the presidency.' Özel Dosya, 'İşte İmralı görüşmesinin tutanaklarının tam metni!', T24, 28 February 2013. Available at http://t24.com.tr/haber/iste-imralidaki-gorusmenin-tutanaklari,224711.

29 Selahattin Demirtaş, 'Önce koster bozuktu, şimdi Başbakan bozuk' ('Once the boat was broken, now the Prime Minister is'), speech to the Turkish Assembly HDP group, 12 February 2013. Available to watch at https://www.youtube.com/watch?v=4KDbtZMq9uI.

30 Ezgi Başaran, 'Öcalan, süreci böyle tanımladı: Lunaparktaki rodeo atı gibi, hareket ediyor, ilerlemiyor', interview with Pervin Buldan, *Radikal*, 21 September 2013. Available at http://www.radikal.com.tr/politika/ocalan-sareci-boylye-tanimladiilunaparktaki-rodeo-ati-gibi-hareket-ediyor-il-1151849/.

31 Başaran, 'Çözüm olsun ben iş bulurum', interview with Murat Karayılan: 'A video message would also be a good thing, but this face-to-face meeting should not be a bargaining point. Really, for all of our friends to be convinced, and in the interests of overcoming obstacles, it would be much more constructive if the leadership were able to talk to a group of friends directly. We are not bringing this up to create a problem; there is a real need for it. For instance, we have now started a process. Towards the midpoint or near the end, a meeting like this would greatly relieve us, you know. These kinds of things, besides being a necessity, also have a political meaning.'

32 Ezgi Başaran, 'IRA sorununu çözen beyin Jonathan Powell'dan 10 maddede kalici

barış', interview with Jonathan Powell, *Radikal*, 10 April 2013. Available at http://
www.radikal.com.tr/yazarlar/ezgi-basaran/ira-sorununu-cozen-beyin-jonathan-
powelldan-10-maddede-kalici-baris-1128863/.

33   'Kalkan: Öcalan'la doğrudan görüşmeliyiz', *Bianet*, 11 June 2014. Available at
http://bianet.org/bianet/siyaset/156341-kalkan-ocalan-la-dogrudan-gorusmeliyiz.

34   Alexander Christie-Miller, 'War is easy, peace is hard: the collapse of Turkey's
Kurdish peace process', *The White Review*, October 2015. Available at http://www.
thewhitereview.org/features/war-is-easy-peace-is-hard-the-collapse-of-turkeys-
kurdish-peace-process/.

35   'Turkey and the PKK: saving the peace process', International Crisis Group report.

36   'Baskın Oran akil adam heyetinde yok', *Gerçek Gündem*, 17 October 2014. Available
at http://www.gercekgundem.com/guncel/77849/baskin-oran-akil-adam-
heyetinde-yok.

5. Syria and the Kurdish Peace

1   Zilan's real name and the name of the news outlet he worked for have been
changed to protect his family.

2   Interview with Zilan, June 2016, unpublished.

3   Ezgi Başaran, 'Muhatap "Kürt Akil Adamlar" olabilir mi?', *Radikal*, 2 September
2012. Available at http://www.radikal.com.tr/yazarlar/ezgi-basaran/muhatap-
kurt-akil-adamlar-olabilir-mi-1098942/.

4   Ezgi Başaran, '"Öcalan'ın Gezi konusunda bize eleştirisi oldu"', interview with
Ahmet Türk, *Radikal*, 29 July 2013. Available at http://www.radikal.com.tr/
yazarlar/ezgi-basaran/ocalanin-gezi-konusunda-bize-elestirisi-oldu-1143839/.

5   Fehim Taştekin, *Rojava: Kürtlerin Zamanı* (Istanbul: İletişim Yayınları, 2016), p. 129.

6   Ibid., p. 130.

7   The Adana Agreement was signed on 20 October 1998 between the Syrian and
Turkish governments. Its goal was to establish cooperation in opposing the PKK.

8   Ezgi Başaran, 'Çözüm sürecinden sonra Suriye muhalefetiyle iletişim arttı',
interview with Salih Müslim, *Radikal*, 15 April 2013. Available at http://
www.radikal.com.tr/yazarlar/ezgi-basaran/cozum-surecinden-sonra-suriye-
muhalefetiyle-iletisim-artti-1129519/.

9   Ibid.

10   Ezgi Başaran, 'Çözüm olsun ben iş bulurum', interview with Murat Karayılan on
Qandil Mountain, *Radikal*, 27 April 2013. Available at http://www.radikal.com.
tr/yazarlar/ezgi-basaran/cozum-olsun-ben-is-bulurum-1131279/.

11   Ibid.

12   Arwa Ibrahim, 'Analysis: Turkey's regional policy and the Kurdish peace process',
Middle East Eye, 1 September 2015. Available at http://www.middleeasteye.net/
fr/news/analysis-turkeys-regional-policy-and-kurdish-peace-process-675325380.

13   'Kurdish fighters aren't terrorists', *Bloomberg*, 20 August 2014. Available at https://
www.bloomberg.com/view/articles/2014-08-20/kurdish-fighters-aren-t-terrorists.

14   Cale Salih and Mutlu Civiroglu, 'Analysis: Could support for the "other" Kurds
stall Islamic State?', BBC, 25 August 2014. Available at http://www.bbc.co.uk/
news/world-middle-east-28925179.

15   Elizabeth Griffin, 'These remarkable women are fighting ISIS. It is time you
know who they are', *Marie Claire*, 30 September 2014. Available at http://www.
marieclaire.com/culture/news/a6643/these-are-the-women-battling-isis/.

16 Ahmet Topal, '"PYD, DAEŞ'ten çok daha tehlikeli"', *Sabah*, 19 June 2015. Available at http://www.sabah.com.tr/gundem/2015/06/19/pyd-daesten-cok-daha-tehlikeli-1434663598.

17 Yüksel Temel, 'PYD 'nin kaos planı son anda önlendi', *Sabah*, 20 June 2015. Available at http://www.sabah.com.tr/gundem/2015/06/20/pydnin-kaos-plani-son-anda-onlendi.

18 'DAEŞ destekli Kobani oyunu – ISIS-backed Kobani game', *Akşam*, 26 June 2015.

19 'Hedef Türkiye' ('Turkey is the target'), *Yeni Şafak*, 26 June 2015.

20 'PYD-DAEŞ elele, hedef Türkiye' ('PYD-ISIS hand in hand, Turkey is the target'), *Star*, 26 June 2015.

21 Taştekin, *Rojava*, p. 226.

22 Chase Winter, 'Turkey's strained Kurdish peace process', *EKurd Daily*, 12 December 2013. Available at http://ekurd.net/mismas/articles/misc2013/12/turkey4876.htm.

23 'Erdoğan: Kobani düştü düşecek!', *Habertürk*, 7 October 2014. Available at http://www.haberturk.com/gundem/haber/997321-erdogan-kobani-dustu-dusecek.

24 *İmralı Notları – Demokratik Kurtuluş ve Özgür Yaşamı İnşa* (Neuss: Mezopotamya Yayınları, 2015), p. 179.

25 Galip Dalay, 'What is next for Turkey's Kurdish peace process?', Al Jazeera, 29 July 2015. Available at http://www.aljazeera.com/indepth/opinion/2015/07/turkey-kurdish-peace-process-150729074358423.html.

26 Robert Fisk, 'Syria's road from jihad to prison', *The Independent*, 1 September 2012. Available at http://www.independent.co.uk/voices/commentators/fisk/robert-fisk-syrias-road-from-jihad-to-prison-8100749.html.

27 Ezgi Başaran, 'Esad sonrası topraktan yeni silahlar çıkarılacak', interview with Robert Fisk, *Radikal*, 5 September 2012. Available at http://www.radikal.com.tr/yazarlar/ezgi-basaran/esad-sonrasi-topraktan-yeni-silahlar-cikarilacak-1099255/. During the publishing of this book, Fisk mentioned another possibility regarding these explosives. He had travelled to Sweden and visited the explosives factory where the items came from. It turned out to be a fireworks factory which manufactured illuminations for Volvo trucks. The Swedish company had told Fisk that the items were fitted to all Volvo trucks, including vehicles for export – and had thus made their way to Syria over several years. According to Fisk, when al-Nusra and others discovered the firework 'safety' packs in new Volvo lorries, they used them to blast their way through the walls of houses in urban fighting. Fisk also told me that 'this doesn't in any way diminish Turkey's real involvement in armed groups in Syria, the evidence of the gendarmerie raids, and of the prisoner I spoke to in the Damascus jail'.

28 'Paralel Savcı MİT TIR'larını elleriyle aradı', *Yeni Şafak*, 24 January 2015. Available at http://www.yenisafak.com/gundem/paralel-savci-mit-tirlarini-elleriyle-aradi-2068827.

29 The radical Salafist group has ties to al-Qaeda, since it had commanders such as Abu Khaled al-Soury, who fought alongside al-Qaeda founder Osama bin Laden and was close to its current chief, Ayman al-Zawahiri.

30 Fehim Taştekin, 'Turkish military says MIT shipped weapons to al-Qaeda', *Al-Monitor*, 15 January 2015. Available at http://www.al-monitor.com/pulse/originals/2015/01/turkey-syria-intelligence-service-shipping-weapons.html.

31 Ibid.

32 Humeyra Pamuk and Nick Tattersall, 'Exclusive: Turkish intelligence helped ship arms to Syrian Islamist rebel areas', Reuters, 21 May 2015. Available at

http://www.reuters.com/article/us-mideast-crisis-turkey-arms-idUSKBN0O61L 220150521.

33 'Turkey sends weapons to Daesh terrorists in Syria under the disguise of "humanitarian aid convoys"', *Global Research*, 2 April 2016. Available at http://www.globalresearch.ca/turkey-sends-weapons-to-daesh-terrorist-in-syria-under-the-disguise-of-humanitarian-aid-convoys/5518065.

34 Adam Lidgett, 'Russia–Turkey crisis: Moscow says US drone footage shows ISIS tankers crossing into Turkey', *International Business Times*, 12 May 2015. Available at http://www.ibtimes.com/russia-turkey-crisis-moscow-says-us-drone-footage-shows-isis-tankers-crossing-turkey-2212946.

35 'Kilis'te taksi durakları artıyor', *Kilis Postası*, 26 November 2014. Available at http://www.kilispostasi.com/kilis-te-taksi-duraklari-artiyor/1207690/.

36 'Canlı bomba listesindeki Tatar: Sınırdan IŞİD için açılan yoldan gittik', *Evrensel*, 21 October 2015. Available at https://www.evrensel.net/haber/263279/canli-bomba-listesindeki-tatar-sinirdan-isid-icin-acilan-yoldan-suriyeye-gectik.

37 'Bir cihatçının itirafları: IŞİD, Türkiye sınırında çok rahat biçimde hareket ediyor', *Birgün*, 8 July 2015. Available at http://www.birgun.net/haber-detay/bir-cihatcinin-itiraflari-isid-turkiye-sinirinda-cok-rahat-bicimde-hareket-ediyor-84332.html.

38 '"Demirtaş'a suikast için IŞİD ekip gönderdi"', *Birgün*, 14 October 2014. Available at http://www.birgun.net/haber-detay/demirtas-a-suikast-icin-isid-ekip-gonderdi-92276.html.

39 İdris Emen, 'Adıyaman – Suriye cihat hattı', *Radikal*, 29 September 2013. Available at http://www.radikal.com.tr/turkiye/adiyaman-suriye-cihat-hatti-1152993/.

40 Ezgi Başaran, 'Yeni bombalı saldırı tahmin ettiğimizden yakın', *Radikal*, 23 July 2015. Available at http://www.radikal.com.tr/yazarlar/ezgi-basaran/yeni-bombali-saldiri-tahmin-ettigimizden-yakin-1401811/.

6. No Presidency, No Peace

1 Ezgi Başaran, 'Hükümetin yerinde olsam ben de BDP'den kurtulmak isterdim', interview with Selahattin Demirtaş, *Radikal*, 27 October 2013. Available at http://www.radikal.com.tr/yazarlar/ezgi-basaran/hukumetin-yerinde-olsam-ben-de-bdpden-kurtulmak-isterdim-1157549/.

2 Ezgi Başaran, 'Kürt Ulusal Kongresi niye erteleniyor? Kürtler arası güç savaşı, Erdoğan ve Barzani işbirliği', interview with Prof. Abbas Vali, *Radikal*, 5 September 2013. Available at http://www.radikal.com.tr/yazarlar/ezgi-basaran/kurt-ulusal-kongresi-niye-erteleniyorkurtler-arasi-guc-savasi-erdogan-ve-barz-1149360/.

3 Başaran, 'Hükümetin yerinde olsam ben de BDP'den kurtulmak isterdim'.

4 Ibid.

5 Serpil Çevikcan, 'Başbakan Erdoğan'ın başdanışmanı Yalçın Akdoğan, Milliyet'e konuştu', interview with Yalçın Akdoğan, *Milliyet*, 7 June 2014. Available at http://www.milliyet.com.tr/-padisahlik-yorumlari-afak-ve/siyaset/ydetay/1893708/default.htm.

6 Bülent Arınç, press conference at the Turkish General Assembly, 25 November 2014. Available to watch at http://www.milliyet.com.tr/Milliyet-Tv/video-izle/Bulent-Arinc--Ocalan-i-itibarsiz-hale-getirmek-istiyorsunuz-2pSSbL5KbRpM.html.

7 Abdülkadir Selvi, 'Kandil, Öcalan'a direniyor', *Yeni Şafak*, 16 February 2015. Available at http://www.yenisafak.com/yazarlar/abdulkadirselvi/kandil,-ocalan'a-direniyor-2007900.

8   International Crisis Group interview, member of government-appointed 'Wise Persons' delegation, Ankara, June 2014. 'Turkey and the PKK: saving the peace process', International Crisis Group report no. 234, 6 November 2014. Available at https://www.crisisgroup.org/europe-central-asia/western-europemediterranean/turkey/turkey-and-pkk-saving-peace-process.

9   In the course of a dialogue in İmralı with HDP co-chair Selahattin Demirtaş, Abdullah Öcalan talked about Osman Öcalan and his comrade Nizamettin Taş, who both split from the PKK and formed another party, as an example of betrayal. *Aydinlik Gazetesi*, 17 August 2013. Available at https://26august.wordpress.com/2014/09/01/imrali-tutanaklari-aydinlik/.

10   Orhan Miroğlu, 'Kandil Apo'ya "evet" diyerek reddediyor', interview with Osman Öcalan, *Star*, 1 December 2014. Available at http://www.star.com.tr/yazar/kandil-apoya-evet-diyerek-reddediyor-yazi-974221/.

11   'Akdoğan'dan Demirtaş'a Brütüs göndermesi', *Hürriyet*, 31 May 2015. Available at http://www.hurriyet.com.tr/akdogandan-demirtasa-brutus-gondermesi-29131997.

12   'Akdoğan: Öcalan'ı diri diri gömdüler', BBC Turkey, 3 November 2015. Available at http://www.bbc.com/turkce/haberler/2015/11/151103_yalcin_akdogan_ocalan.

13   Akif Beki, 'Cumhurbaşkanı Erdoğan: İmralı Kandil kopuk', *Hürriyet*, 2 March 2015. Available at http://www.hurriyet.com.tr/cumhurbaskani-erdogan-imrali-kandil-kopuk-28333582.

14   'Turkey and the PKK: saving the peace process', International Crisis Group report.

15   'KCK: Silah bırakma iradesi bize ait', Al Jazeera, 12 June 2015. Available at http://www.aljazeera.com.tr/haber/kck-silah-birakma-iradesi-bize-ait.

16   Besê Hozat, 'Yeni süreç, devrimci halk savaşı sürecidir', *Özgür Gündem*, 15 July 2015. Available at http://www.ozgur-gundem.com/yazi/133642/yeni-surec-devrimci-halk-savasi-surecidir.

17   *İmralı Notları – Demokratik Kurtuluş ve Özgür Yaşamı İnşa* (Neuss: Mezopotamya Yayınları, 2015), p. 276.

18   Ibid., p. 372.

19   Ruşen Çakır, 'İmralı iyi, Kandil kötü' diye diye...', *Habertürk*, 22 October 2014. Available at http://www.haberturk.com/yazarlar/rusen-cakir-2302/1001929-imrali-iyi-kandil-kotu-diye-diye.

20   Ibid.

21   Ezgi Başaran, 'Öcalan, süreci böyle tanımladı: Lunaparktaki rodeo atı gibi, hareket ediyor, ilerlemiyor', interview with Pervin Buldan, *Radikal*, 21 September 2013. Available at http://www.radikal.com.tr/politika/ocalan-sareci-boylye-tanimladilunaparktaki-rodeo-ati-gibi-hareket-ediyor-il-1151849/.

22   *İmralı Notları*, p. 332.

23   Ayla Jean Yackley, 'Kurdish Obama challenges perceptions with Turkish presidential bid', Reuters, 9 August 2014. Available at http://www.reuters.com/article/us-turkey-election-kurds-idUSKBN0G90CI20140809.

24   *İmralı Notları* (October 2015), p. 357.

25   'Demirtaş'a Kobani olayları soruşturması', *Milliyet*, 31 July 2015. Available at http://www.milliyet.com.tr/demirtas-a-kobani-olaylari/siyaset/detay/2095151/default.htm.

26   Burcu Karakaş, 'Dolmabahçe'de tarihi açıklama', *Milliyet*, 1 March 2015. Available at http://www.milliyet.com.tr/dolmabahce-de-tarihi-aciklama/siyaset/detay/2021055/default.htm.

27 Ali Bayramoğlu, 'The process of resolution: from politics to arms', Democratic Progress Institute, 10 November 2015. Available for download at http://www.democratic progress.org/publications/the-process-of-resolution-from-politics-to-arms-4/.

28 'Erdoğan: Silah bırakma çağrısı çok çok önemli', *Rûdaw*, 28 February 2015. Available at http://www.rudaw.net/NewsDetails.aspx?pageid=108976.

29 Ibid.

30 'Erdoğan hükümete sert çıktı: İzleme Heyeti'ne karşıyım, harberleri gazeterlerden okuyorum!', T24, 20 March 2015. Available at http://t24.com.tr/haber/cumhurbaskani-erdogan-ukrayna-ziyareti-oncesi-konusuyor,291016.

31 'Bülent Arınç'tan İzleme Heyeti açıklaması', *Hürriyet*, 21 March 2015. Available at http://www.hurriyet.com.tr/bulent-arinctan-izleme-heyeti-aciklamasi-28515718. Deputy Prime Minister Arınç continued with the same topic on CNN Türk TV on 30 January 2016: 'In the Dolmabahçe meeting, they agreed on everything from the seating plan to who will talk and how. I know that the president was also aware. Yalçın Akdoğan also told me back then that he had informed the president.'

32 'Erdoğan, Dolmabahçe'yi de 10 maddeyi de eleştirdi', President Erdoğan's statement, 22 March 2015. Available at http://www.aljazeera.com.tr/haber/erdogan-dolmabahceyi-de-10-maddeyi-de-elestirdi.

33 'Erdoğan: Kürt sorunu yoktur Kürtlerin bazı sorunları vardır' ['There is no Kurdish problem'], *Sabah*, 2 May 2015. Available at http://www.sabah.com.tr/gundem/2015/05/02/erdogan-kurt-sorunu-yoktur-kurtlerin-bazi-sorunlari-vardir.

34 'İmralı delegation: AKP wants to end the peace process and start war', ANF, 19 May 2015. Available at http://www.anfenglish.com/news/imrali-delegation-akp-wants-to-end-the-process-and-start-war.

35 *İmralı Notları*, p. 368.

36 Ibid.

37 Ibid.

38 HDP delegation–Prime Minister Davutoğlu meeting, 10 September 2014.

39 Yıldıray Oğur, 'Şimdi söz sırası kronolojide', *Türkiye Gazetesi*, 11 August 2015. Available at http://www.turkiyegazetesi.com.tr/yazarlar/yildiray-ogur/587467.aspx.

40 Ezgi Başaran, 'Devlet beni şahin diye pazarlıyor', interview with Emine Ayna, *Radikal*, 28 July 2011. Available at http://www.radikal.com.tr/yazarlar/ezgi-basaran/devlet-beni-sahin-diye-pazarliyor-1057907/.

41 'Erdoğan vows to transform entire political system, again demands "400 MPs"', *Hürriyet Daily News*, 30 April 2015. Available at http://www.hurriyetdailynews.com/Erdoğan-vows-to-transform-entire-political-system-again-demands-400-mps--.aspx?pageID=238&nid=81780.

42 Ezgi Başaran, interview with Selahattin Demirtaş, Brussels, June 2016, unpublished.

43 Ibid.

44 Ibid.

45 Ibid.

46 Ibid.

47 Ezgi Başaran, 'HDP co-chair Demirtaş reveals details of peace process', interview with Selahattin Demirtaş, *Hürriyet Daily News*, 28 July 2015. Available at http://www.hurriyetdailynews.com/hdp-co-chair-demirtas-reveals-details-of-peace-process-.aspx?PageID=238&NID=86041&NewsCatID=338.

48 Ibid.

49 'Turkey faces snap elections as coalition talks fail', Al Jazeera, 13 August 2015.

Available at http://www.aljazeera.com/news/2015/08/turkey-coalition-government-150813123140443.html.

50   'Turkey vs. ISIS and PKK: a matter of distinction', Bipartisan Policy, July 2015. Available at http://cdn.bipartisanpolicy.org/wp-content/uploads/2016/07/BPC-Turkey-ISIS-PKK.pdf.

51   ISIS's first attack in Ankara was on 10 October, 20 days prior to the snap election held on 1 November 2015.

52   'Erdoğan'dan Dağlıca açıklaması', *Hürriyet*, 6 September 2015. Available at http://www.hurriyet.com.tr/erdogandan-daglica-aciklamasi-30002984.

7. What Do Kurds Want?

1   Mahmut Bozarslan, 'Why PKK shifted to urban warfare', *Al-Monitor*, 29 March 2016. Available at http://www.al-monitor.com/pulse/originals/2016/03/turkey-why-pkk-carry-clashes-cities.html.

2   Ezgi Başaran, interview with Selahattin Demirtaş, London, October 2016, unpublished.

3   '"Alarming" reports of major violations in south-east Turkey – UN rights chief', UN News Centre, 10 May 2016. Available at http://www.un.org/apps/news/story.asp?NewsID=53895#.V_UJ3TKZM_U.

4   Didem Özel Tümer, '"Hendeğin bilançosu: Nüfusun %22'si göç etti"', AlJazeera, 11 January 2016. Available at http://www.aljazeera.com.tr/al-jazeera-ozel/hendegin-bilancosu-nufusun-22si-goc-etti.

5   Edip Tekin, '"355 bin kişi terörden göç etti"', *Hürriyet*, 27 February 2016. Available at http://www.hurriyet.com.tr/355-bin-kisi-terorden-goc-etti-40061270.

6   'Cizre gözlem raporu', Turkey Human Rights Foundation, 31 March 2016. Available at http://tihv.org.tr/wp-content/uploads/2016/04/Cizre-Gözlem-Raporu_31-Mart2016.pdf.

7   Ibid.

8   A dish of vine leaves stuffed with meat and rice is called *sarma* in Turkish. It is a very much loved traditional Turkish food.

9   Rojin Akın and Funda Danışman, *Bildiğin Gibi Değil: 90'larda Güneydoğu'da Çocuk Olmak* (Istanbul: Metis Yayınları, 2011), p. 50.

10   *Küçük Kara Balıklar: Türkiye'nin Güneydoğusu'nda Çocuk Olmak* [documentary film], Drama Istanbul, 2014. Available to watch at at https://vimeo.com/108880966.

11   Ibid.

12   Celal Başlangıç, 'Cumhurbaşkanının yanından PKK'ye giden yol gittikçe kısalıyor', *Gazete Duvar*, 28 October 2016. Available at http://www.gazeteduvar.com.tr/yazarlar/2016/10/28/cumhurbaskaninin-yanindan-pkkye-giden-yol-gittikce-kisaliyor/.

13   Ayla Albayrak, 'Urban warfare escalates in Turkey's Kurdish-majority southeast', *Wall Street Journal*, 19 August 2015. Available at https://www.wsj.com/articles/urban-warfare-escalates-in-turkeys-kurdish-majority-southeast-1440024103.

14   This interview was conducted in September 2015 by sending questions to Qandil Mountain through trusted sources and receiving answers via the same route. Several other sources confirm that Murat Karayılan himself answered my questions.

15   'Duran Kalkan'dan itiraf: Cizre'de hata yaptık', *Kurdistan Post*, 25 February 2016. Available at http://www.kurdistan-post.eu/tr/siyaset/duran-kalkandan-itiraf-cizrede-hata-yaptik.

16 İmralı Notları – Demokratik Kurtuluş ve Özgür Yaşamı İnşa (Neuss: Mezopotamya Yayınları, 2015), p. 402.

17 Kanat Atkaya, 'Devlet "düşman", aileler "hain" BDP "light"', Hürriyet, 3 March 2012. Available at http://www.hurriyet.com.tr/devlet-dusman-aileler-hain-bdp-light-20046457.

18 Ezgi Başaran, 'Gerçek 2. Cumhuriyet şimdi başladı', interview with Fırat Anlı, Radikal, 25 March 2013. Available at http://www.radikal.com.tr/yazarlar/ezgi-basaran/gercek-2-cumhuriyet-donemi-simdi-basladi-1126507/.

19 Ezgi Başaran, 'Kürtlerin Gezi'deki bir ağaç kadar değeri yokmuş diyorlar', interview with Ayhan Bilgen, Radikal, 13 October 2014. Available at http://www.radikal.com.tr/yazarlar/ezgi-basaran/kurtlerin-gezideki-bir-agac-kadar-degeri-yokmus-diyorlar-1218402/.

20 A coffee house where men can talk, drink coffee and tea and play card games or backgammon. Even the smallest villages have a kahvehane, as it is a hub of social life.

21 Bahar Baser, Diasporas and Homeland Conflicts: A Comparative Perspective (London: Routledge, 2015), p. 185.

22 Abdullah Öcalan, Kürdistan – Devrim Manifestosu (Neuss: Mezopotamya Yayınları, 2012), p. 597.

23 Pınar Öğünç, 'Kürtler demokratik özerklikle ne istiyor (1): "Devletin el değiştirmesiyle özgürlük, adalet gelmiyor"', interview with Demir Çelik, Radikal, 28 April 2014. Available at http://www.radikal.com.tr/yazarlar/pinar-ogunc/kurtler-demokratik-ozerklikle-ne-istiyor-1devletin-el-degistirmesiyle-ozg-1188942/.

24 Ezgi Başaran, 'Demokratik özerklik ilanının hiçbir anlamı yok', interview with Tarık Ziya Ekinci, Radikal, 18 July 2011. Available at http://www.radikal.com.tr/yazarlar/ezgi-basaran/demokratik-ozerklik-ilaninin-hicbir-anlami-yok-1056689/.

25 DTK, HDP official website, 2011. Available at http://en.hdpeurope.com/?page_id=912.

26 'Draft Submission for a Democratic Autonomous Kurdistan', January 2011. Available at http://demokratischeautonomie.blogsport.eu/files/2012/10/DTK.engl_.pdf.

27 'DTK'dan "öz yönetim" deklarasyonu!', Milliyet, 27 December 2015. Available at http://www.milliyet.com.tr/dtk-sonuc-bildirgesinde-gundem-2170231/.

28 Mehmet Acet, 'Erdoğan'ın hükümete gösterdiği yeni hedef', Yeni Şafak, 10 October 2016. Available at http://www.yenisafak.com/yazarlar/mehmetacet/Erdoğanin-hukumete-gosterdigi-yeni-hedef-2033391.

29 Ezgi Başaran, 'Silahsızlanma iyi planlanmazsa PKK radikalleşir', interview with Prof. Abbas Vali, Radikal, 4 February 2013. Available at http://www.radikal.com.tr/yazarlar/ezgi-basaran/silahsizlanma-iyi-planlanmazsa-pkk-radikallesir-1119805/.

30 Joost Jongerden, Ahmet Hamdi Akkaya and Bahar Şimşek, İsyandan İnşaya: Kürdistan Özgürlük Hareketi (Ankara: Dipnot Yayınları, 2015), p. 169.

31 Rafael Taylor, 'The new PKK: unleashing a social revolution in Kurdistan', ROAR Magazine, 17 August 2014. Available at https://roarmag.org/essays/pkk-kurdish-struggle-autonomy/.

32 Fehim Taştekin, Rojava: Kürtlerin Zamanı (Istanbul: İletişim Yayınları, 2016), p. 414.

33 Öcalan, Kürdistan, p. 518.

34 Murray Bookchin, The Ecology of Freedom: The Emergence and Dissolution of Hierarchy (Chico, CA: AK Press, 2015).

35 Sardar Saadi, 'Rojava revolution: building autonomy in the Middle East', ROAR Magazine, 25 July 2014. Available at https://roarmag.org/essays/rojava-autonomy-syrian-kurds/.

36 'The Constitution of the Rojava Cantons'. Available at https://civiroglu.net/the-constitution-of-the-rojava-cantons/.

37 Oso Sabio, *Rojava: An Alternative to Imperialism, Nationalism, and Islamism in the Middle East* (Oso Sabio, lulu.com, 2015).

38 Arzu Demir, *Devrimin Rojava Hali* (Istanbul: Ceylan Yayınları, 2015), p. 101.

39 Nilgün Yıldız, 'Senin de bir komünün olsun', *Özgür Gündem*, 1 September 2014. Available at http://ozgur-gundem.com/haber/117673/senin-de-bir-komunun-olsun.

40 Ibid.

41 Taylor, 'The new PKK'.

42 SAMER ISIS Report, 2015. Available at http://www.ssamer.com/Rapor_Detay-Samer_ISİS_Report-1026-1003.html.

43 Ezgi Başaran, interview with Harriet Allsopp, Oxford, November 2016, unpublished.

44 Ibid.

45 Amnesty International, 'Syria: "We had nowhere to go" – forced displacement and demolitions in northern Syria', 13 October 2015. Available to download at https://www.amnesty.org/en/documents/mde24/2503/2015/en/.

46 Richard Spencer, 'Syrian Kurds accused of ethnic cleansing and killing opponents', *Telegraph*, 18 May 2016. Available at http://www.telegraph.co.uk/news/2016/05/18/syrian-kurds-accused-of-ethnic-cleansing-and-killing-opponents/.

47 Taştekin, *Rojava*, p. 152.

48 Oso Sabio, *Rojava*.

49 Yasin Duman, *Rojava: Bir Demokratik Özerklik Deneyimi* (Istanbul: İletişim Yayınları, 2016), p. 199.

50 Ibid., p. 100.

51 *İmralı Notları*, p. 276.

8. The Coup Attempt that Shook Turkey

1 Uğur Ergan, 'Genelkurmay'dan darbe iddialarına yanıt', *Hürriyet*, 31 March 2016. Available at http://www.hurriyet.com.tr/genelkurmaydan-darbe-iddialarina-yanit-40078557.

2 An attack by ISIS militants at Istanbul Atatürk Airport claimed 45 lives and injured 236 on 29 June 2016.

3 'Mahçupyan: Laikler darbeye karşı durmasaydı iktidar çöker, iç savaş çıkardı', T24, 23 August 2016. Available at http://t24.com.tr/haber/mahcupyan-laikler-darbeye-karsi-durmasaydi-iktidar-coker-ic-savas-cikardi,356404.

4 Enis Şenerdem, 'Andy-Ar araştırması: Halkın çoğunluğu darbe girişiminden Gülen'i sorumlu tutuyor; siyasetteki ılımlı havanın devamını istiyor' ['Andy-Ar research: the majority of people hold Gülen responsible for the coup attempt; want to keep the moderate atmosphere in politics'], 26 July 2016. Available at http://t24.com.tr/haber/andy-ar-arastirmasi-halkin-cogunlugu-darbe-girisimiden-guleni-sorumlu-tutuyor-siyasetteki-ilimli-havanin-devamini-istiyor,351987.

5 Joshua Hendrick, 'Fethullah Gülen: public intellectual or public enemy?', *The Conversation*, 8 August 2016. Available at https://theconversation.com/fethullah-gulen-public-intellectual-or-public-enemy-62887.

6 'İlker Başbuğ'dan çok konuşulacak açıklamalar: darbe girişiminin arkasında 3 grup var', *Hürriyet*, 2 August 2016. Available at http://www.hurriyet.com.tr/ilker-basbug-darbenin-arkasinda-3-grup-var-40178184.

7   'Başbakan Yardımcısı Tuğrul Türkeş: 15 Temmuz darbesi farklı grupların müşterek
     hareketi olabilir', CNN Turk, 13 August 2016. Available at http://www.cnnturk.
     com/video/turkiye/basbakan-yardimcisi-tugrul-turkes-15-temmuz-darbesi-farkli-
     gruplarin-musterek-hareketi-olabilir.

8   '15 Temmuz'a nasıl gelindi, darbe girişimi neden önlenemedi, cemaatin rolü ne?',
     T24, 8 December 2016. Available at http://t24.com.tr/haber/15-temmuza-nasil-
     gelindi-darbe-girisimi-neden-onlenemedi-cemaatin-rolu-ne,375602.

9   'Ahmet Şık: Türkiye yazarı hükümetin darbe girişimini önceden bildiğini yazdı',
     T24, 10 November 2016. Available at http://t24.com.tr/haber/ahmet-sik-turkiye-
     yazari-hukumetin-darbe-girisimini-onceden-bildigini-yazdi,370079.

10   'TSK, darbe girişimine katılan personel sayısını açıkladı', NTV, 27 July 2016.
     Available at http://www.ntv.com.tr/turkiye/tsk-darbe-girisimine-katilan-personel-
     sayisini-acikladi,ns92udU75k2vw-1OlEK4gQ.

11   Translated testimony of General Hulusi Akar, Robert Amsterdam & Partner LLP,
     28 July 2016. Available at https://robertamsterdam.com/translated-testimony-
     of-gen-hulusi-akar/.

12   Several photographs of aide-de-camp Levent Türkkan indicate that ill-treatment
     and most probably torture may have accompanied the testimony procedure.

13   Mesut Hasan Benli, 'Top Turkish commander's aide admits allegiance to Gülenists',
     Hürriyet Daily News, 20 July 2016. Available at http://www.hurriyetdailynews.
     com/Default.aspx?pageID=238&nID=101851&NewsCatID=341.

14   Ibid.

15   Berrin Koyuncu-Lorasdağlı, 'The prospects and pitfalls of the religious nationalist
     movement in Turkey: the case of the Gülen movement', Middle Eastern Studies
     46/2 (2010), pp. 221–34.

16   Filiz Canyaş and Orkunt Canyaş, 'The interplay between formal and informal
     institutions in Turkey: the case of the Fethullah Gülen community', Middle Eastern
     Studies 52/2 (2016), pp. 280–94.

17   Ibid.

18   Sedat Ergin, 'O albaylar gitti darbeciler geldi', Hürriyet, 22 July 2016. Available at
     http://sosyal.hurriyet.com.tr/yazar/sedat-ergin_308/o-albaylar-gitti-darbeciler-
     geldi_40164262.

19   Ahmet Hakan, '"Ordu içindeki Fethullahçi general ve albayları isim isim biliyorum"',
     interview with Ahmet Zeki Üçok, Hürriyet, 5 April 2016. Available at http://sosyal.
     hurriyet.com.tr/yazar/ahmet-hakan_131/ordu-icindeki-fethullahci-general-ve-
     albaylari-isim-isim-biliyorum_40082175.

20   Ezgi Başaran, interview with retired general Ahmet Yavuz, August 2016,
     unpublished.

21   'Fethullah Gülen'den "darbe" açıklaması: Erdoğan'a yanıt verdi', Cumhuriyet, 16
     July 2016. Available at http://www.cumhuriyet.com.tr/haber/turkiye/568596/
     Fethullah_Gulen_den__darbe__aciklamasi__Erdogan_a_yanit_verdi.html.

22   İlker Başbuğ, 15 Temmuz öncesi ve sonrası (Istanbul: Doğan Kitap, 2016), p. 23.

23   Yavuz Selim Demirağ, İmamların Öcü-Türk Silahlı Kuvvetlerinde Cemaat Yapılanması
     (Istanbul: Kırmızı Kedi Yayınevi, 2015), quoted in Başbuğ, 15 Temmuz öncesi ve
     sonrası, p. 28.

24   Başbuğ, 15 Temmuz öncesi ve sonrası, p. 29.

25   İmralı Notları – Demokratik Kurtuluş ve Özgür Yaşamı İnşa (Neuss: Mezopotamya
     Yayınları, 2015), p. 206.

26   Ibid., p. 265.

27 Murat Somer, 'Understanding Turkey's democratic breakdown: old vs. new and indigenous vs. global authoritarianism', *Southeast European and Black Sea Studies* 16/4 (2016). Available at http://dx.doi.org/10.1080/14683857.2016.1246548, p. 6.

28 Yener Dönmez, 'Cemaatten kim geldi de geri çevirdik', *Yeni Akit*, 23 November 2013. Available at http://www.yeniakit.com.tr/haber/cemaatten-kim-geldi-de-geri-cevirdik-7500.html.

29 Samuel E. Finer, *The Man on Horseback: The Role of the Military in Politics* (Piscataway, NJ: Transaction Publishers, 2002).

30 Yaprak Gürsoy, *Between Military Rule and Democracy: Regime Consolidation in Greece, Turkey, and Beyond*, Michigan University Press, forthcoming.

31 Ezgi Başaran, interview with Dr Yaprak Gürsoy, St Antony's College, Oxford University, November 2016, unpublished.

32 Ibid.

33 Yüksel Taşkın, 'Darbe atlatıldı: Şimdi nereye?', *Birikim* 328–9 (2016), p. 17.

34 Edward Newman and Oliver Richmond (eds), *Challenges to Peacebuilding: Managing Spoilers During Conflict Resolution* (Tokyo, New York and Paris: United Nations University Press, 2006), pp. 1–3.

35 'Cumhurbaşkanı Erdoğan: Bedelini ağır ödeyecekler', *Hürriyet*, 16 July 2016. Available at http://www.hurriyet.com.tr/cumhurbaskani-erdogan-bedelini-agir-odeyecekler-37309724.

36 'Cumhurbaşkanı Erdoğan: Biz bunu Amerikalı dostlarımıza hala anlatamadık', speech by Recep Tayyip Erdoğan, *Habertürk*, 22 September 2016. Available at http://www.haberturk.com/gundem/haber/1300358-cumhurbaskani-erdogan-biz-bunun-amerikali-dostlarimiza-hala-anlatamadik.

37 Figures taken from https://turkeypurge.com.

38 Figures taken from engelliweb.com, which has now been shut down by the Turkish government.

39 Ayla Albayrak and Joe Parkinson, 'Turkey's government forms 6,000-member social media team', *Wall Street Journal*, 16 September 2016. Available at https://www.wsj.com/articles/turkeys-government-forms-6000member-social-media-team-1379351399?tesla=y.

40 'Demokrasi ve Şehitler Mitingi'ne "şov" diyen Sıla'nın konserleri iptal ediliyor', *Diken*, 11 August 2016. Available at http://www.diken.com.tr/demokrasi-ve-sehitler-mitingine-sov-diyen-silanin-konserleri-iptal-edildi/.

41 Ezgi Başaran, 'Sürtük olmak bu kadar kolaysa çaresine bakalım', interview with Hazal Peker and Hangül Özbey, *Radikal*, 7 March 2012. Available at http://www.radikal.com.tr/yazarlar/ezgi-basaran/surtuk-olmak-bu-kadar-kolaysa-caresine-bakalim-1080960/.

42 'Ahmet Türk tutuklandı!', T24, 24 November 2016. Available at http://t24.com.tr/haber/ahmet-turk-tutuklama-talebiyle-mahkemeye-sevk-edildi,372749.

43 'Goodbye, "Republic"', *The Economist*, 5 November 2016. Available at http://www.economist.com/news/europe/21709586-flagship-secular-newspaper-hit-purges-spread-goodbye-republic.

44 Özgür Altuncu, 'Duygun Yarsuvat'tan devlet çöker uyarısı', DHA [news agency], 1 November 2016. Available at http://arsiv.dha.com.tr/duygun-yarsuvattan-devlet-coker-uyarisi_1367815.html.

45 Daron Acemoğlu and James A. Robinson, *Why Nations Fail: The Origins of Power, Prosperity and Poverty* (London: Profile Books, 2013).

46 Daron Acemoğlu, blog. Available at http://whynationsfail.com/blog/2013/10/29/ what-are-institutions.html.

47 Ezgi Başaran, 'Basına baskının derin ekonomik bedelleri olur', interview with Daron Acemoğlu, *Radikal*, 5 May 2014. Available at http://www.radikal.com.tr/ yazarlar/ezgi-basaran/basina-baskinin-derin-ekonomik-bedelleri-olur-1190254/.

48 Somer, 'Understanding Turkey's democratic breakdown', p. 11.

49 Ibid., pp. 9–10.

50 'Ahmet Altan: CHP tabanı bize Ergenekon ve Balyoz'dan, AKP "diktatör" dediğimiz için bize kızgın, bu yüzden yalnızız', T24, 15 November 2016. Available at http:// t24.com.tr/haber/ahmet-altan-chp-tabani-ergenekon-ve-balyozdan-akp-diktator-dedigimiz-icin-bize-kizgin-bu-yuzden-yalniziz,370761.

51 International Referendum Observation Mission, Republic of Turkey – Constitutional Referendum, 16 April 2017. Available at http://www.osce.org/odihr/elections/ turkey/311721?download=true.

Conclusion: The Kurdish Issue Goes Global

1 Seyit's real name has been changed for security and business purposes.

2 Quoted in Karen Kaya, 'Turkish commanders discuss counterterrorism strategies and lessons learned from 25 years of fighting the PKK', *Small Wars and Insurgencies* 23/3 (2012), p. 530.

3 Ibid., p. 538.

4 Cihan Tuğal, *The Fall of the Turkish Model: How the Arab Uprisings Brought Down Islamic Liberalism* (London and New York: Verso, 2016), pp. 83–94.

5 '"'Şangay Beşlisi'ne alın AB'yi unutalım"', *Hürriyet*, 26 January 2013. Available at http://www.hurriyet.com.tr/sangay-beslisine-alin-abyi-unutalim-22448548.

6 Serkan Demirtas, 'UK envoy: Gülen may be behind failed coup attempt', *Hürriyet*, 30 July 2016. Available at http://www.hurriyetdailynews.com/uk-envoy-gulen-may-be-behind-the-coup.aspx?PageID=238&NID=102258&NewsCatID=510.

7 Constanze Letsch, 'US drops weapons and ammunition to help Kurdish fighters in Kobani', *The Guardian*, 20 October 2014. Available at https://www.theguardian. com/world/2014/oct/20/turkey-iraqi-kurds-kobani-isis-fighters-us-air-drops-arms.

8 'Erdoğan'dan ABD'ye: Senin ortağın ben miyim, Kobani'deki teröristler mi?', T24, 7 February 2016. Available at http://t24.com.tr/haber/erdogandan-abdye-senin-ortagin-ben-miyim-kobanideki-teroristler-mi,327166.

9 Nate Schenkan, 'What happens in Turkey doesn't stay in Turkey', *Foreign Policy*, 7 November 2016. Available at http://foreignpolicy.com/2016/11/07/what-happens-in-turkey-doesnt-stay-in-turkey/.

10 Mustafa Akyol, 'Is Russia pulling Turkey away from the West?', *Al-Monitor*, 7 October 2016. Available at http://www.al-monitor.com/pulse/en/originals/2016/10/ turkey-russia-urges-ankara-desert-west.html.

11 Uğur Ergan and Selçuk Şenyüz, 'YPG: Şah Fırat Operasyonu'na destek verdik', *Hürriyet*, 23 February 2015. Available at http://www.hurriyet.com.tr/ypg-sah-firat-operasyonuna-destek-verdik-28271808.

Further Reading

Turkish-language sources

Akın, Rojin Canan and Funda Danışman, *Bildiğin Gibi Değil: 90'larda Güneydoğu'da Çocuk Olmak* [*It Is Not the Way You Know: Being a Child in the 90s in the South-East*] (Istanbul: Metis Yayınları, 2011).

Aktan, Hamza, *Kürt Vatandaş* [*The Kurdish Citizen*] (Istanbul: İletişim Yayınları, 2012).

Alpay, Necmiye and Hakan Tahmaz (eds), *Barış Açısını Savunmak* [*Advocating for Peace*] (Istanbul, Metis Yayınları, 2015).

Anter, Musa, *Hatıralarım* [*My Memories*] (Diyarbakır: Aram Yayınları, 2011).

Aydınoğlu, Ergun, *Fis Köyünden Kobanê'ye Kürt Özgürlük Hareketi* [*From Fis Village to the Kobane Kurdish Freedom Movement*] (Istanbul, Versus, 2014).

Başaran, Ezgi, *Barış Bir Varmış Bir Yokmuş* [*Once upon a Time Peace*] (Istanbul: Doğan Kitap, 2015).

Başbuğ, İlker, *Terör Örgütlerinin Sonu* [*End of Terrorist Organizations*] (Istanbul: Remzi Kitabevi, 2011).

———, *15 Temmuz öncesi ve Sonrası* [*Before and After 15 July*] (Istanbul: Doğan Kitap, 2016).

Batur, Muhsin, *Anılar ve Görüşler* [*Memories and Opinions*] (Istanbul: Milliyet Yayınları, 1985).

Beşikçi, İsmail, *Doğu Mitinglerinin Analizi* [*Analysis of the Eastern Rallies*] (Istanbul: İsmail Beşikçi Vakfı Yayınları, 2014).

Bila, Fikret, *Komutanlar Cephesi* [*The Generals' Front*] (Istanbul: Detay Yayıncılık, 2007).

Bozarslan, Hamit, *Ortadoğu: Bir Şiddet Tarihi* [*The Middle East: A History of Violence*] (Istanbul: İletişim Yayınları, 2010).

Çağlayan, Handan, *Kürt Kadınların Penceresinden* [*From the Window of the Kurdish Women*] (Istanbul: İletişim Yayınları, 2013).

Çakır, Ruşen, *Türkiye'nin Kürt Sorunu* [*Turkey's Kurdish Problem*] (Istanbul: Metis Yayınları, 2004).

———, *100 Soruda Erdoğan – Gülen Savaşı* [*War between Erdogan and Gülen in 100 Questions*] (Istanbul: Metis Yayınları, 2016).

Çandar, Cengiz, *Mezopotamya Ekspresi* [*Mesopotamian Express*] (Istanbul: İletişim Yayınları, 2014).

Cemal, Hasan, *Kürtler* [*The Kurds*] (Istanbul: Everest Yayınları, 2014).

Demir, Arzu, *Devrimin Rojava Hali* [*Revolution's Rojava State*] (Istanbul: Ceylan Yayınları, 2015).

Demirağ, Yavuz Selim, *İmamların Öcü-Türk Silahlı Kuvvetleri'nde Cemaat Yapılanması* [*The Revenge of the Imams: The Gülen Movement's Infiltration into the Turkish Army*] (Istanbul: Kırmızı Kedi Yayınevi, 2015).

Diken, Şeyhmus, *Sırrını Surlarına Fısıldayan Şehir: Diyarbakır* [*The City That Whispers Its Secrets to Its Walls: Diyarbakır*] (Istanbul: İletişim Yayınları, 2002).

Duman, Yasin, *Rojava: Bir Demokratik Özerklik Deneyimi* [*Rojava: An Experiment in Democratic Autonomy*] (Istanbul: İletişim Yayınları, 2016).

Ekinci, Tarık Ziya, *Türkiye'nin Kürt Siyasetine Eleştirel Yaklaşımlar* [*Critical Approaches to Turkey's Kurdish Politics*] (Istanbul: Cem Yayınevi, 2004).

Fırat, Nuri, *Politikanın Kürtçesi* [*The Politics of Kurdish*] (Istanbul: Everest Yayınları, 2015).

Genelkurmay Belgelerinde Kürt İsyanları 2 [*Kurdish Uprisings in the Turkish Army's Documents 2*] (Istanbul: Kaynak Yayınları, 2011).

Gökçen, Sabiha, *Atatürk'ün İzinde Bir Ömür Böyle Geçti* [*A Lifetime Has Passed Following Ataturk*] (Ankara: Türk Hava Kurumu Yayınları, 1982).

Güller, Mehmet Ali, *Hükümet PKK Görüşmeleri 1986–2011* [*Meetings of the Government and the PKK 1986–2011*] (Istanbul: Kaynak Yayınları, 2015).

Heper, Metin, *Devlet ve Kürtler* [*The State and the Kurds*] (Istanbul: Doğan Kitap, 2008).

İmralı Notları – Demokratik Kurtuluş ve Özgür Yaşamı İnşa [*Imrali Notes: Democratic Emancipation and Building of a Free Life*] (Neuss: Mezopotamya Yayınları, 2015).

Işık, İbrahim S., *A'dan Z'ye Kürtler: Kişiler – Kavramlar – Kurumlar* [*Kurds from A to Z: People – Concepts – Institutions*] (Istanbul: Nubihar, 2013).

Jongerden, Joost and Ahmet Akkaya, *PKK Üzerine Yazılar* [*Writings on the PKK*] (Istanbul: Vate Yayınevi, 2015).

———, Bahar Şimşek, *İsyandan İnşaya – Kürdistan Özgürlük Hareketi* [*From Uprising to Rebuilding: The Kurdistan Freedom Movement*] (Ankara: Dipnot, 2015).

Kapmaz, Cengiz, *Öcalan'ın İmralı Günlükleri* [*Imralı Journals*] (Istanbul: İthaki Yayınları, 2011).

Karakaş, Ercan, *Kürt Sorunu – Sosyal Demokratik Yaklaşımlar – CHP ve SHP'nin Kürt Sorunu Raporları* [*The Kurdish Problem: Social Democratic Approaches: The CHP and SHP's Kurdish Problem Reports*] (Istanbul: Kalkedon, 2009).

Karayılan, Murat, *Bir Savaşın Anatomisi* [*Anatomy of a War*] (Diyarbakır: Aram Yayınları, 2014).

Kaya, Hasan, *Doğunun Elçisi'nden Yüce Divan'a – Şerafettin Elçi* [*From Ambassador of the East to the High Court: Şerafettin Elçi*] (Ankara: Fanos Yayınları, 2012).

Matur, Bejan, *Dağın Ardına Bakmak* [*Looking beyond the Mountain*] (Istanbul: Timaş Yayınları, 2011).

Öcalan, Abdullah, *Kürdistan – Devrim Manifestosu* [*Kurdistan: Revolutionary Manifesto*] (Neuss: Mezopotamya Yayınları, 2012).

Özdağ, Ümit, *PKK ile Pazarlık* [*Bargaining with the PKK*] (Ankara: Kripto, 2013).

Özer, Ahmet, *Çözülemeyen Kürt Sorunu* [*The Unresolved Kurdish Problem*] (Istanbul: Hemen Kitap, 2012).

Saraçoğlu, Cenk, *Şehir, Orta Sınıf ve Kürtler* [*The City, Middle Class and Kurds*] (Istanbul: İletişim Yayınları, 2011).

Sönmez, Mustafa, *Kürt Sorunu ve Demokratik Özerklik* [*The Kurdish Problem and Democratic Autonomy*] (Ankara: Nota Bene, 2012).

Tan, Altan, *Hz. İbrahim'in Ayak İzlerinde Ortadoğu* [*The Middle East in the Footprints of Abraham*] (Istanbul: Çıra, 2016).

Taşkın, Yüksel, *AKP Devri: Türkiye Siyaseti, İslâmcılık, Arap Baharı* [*Era of the AKP: Turkish Politics, Islamism, the Arab Spring*] (Istanbul: İletişim Yayınları, 2013).

Taştekin, Fehim, *Rojava: Kürtlerin Zamanı* [*Rojava: Time of the Kurds*] (Istanbul: İletişim Yayınları, 2016).

Tejel, Jordi, *Suriye Kürtleri: Tarih, Siyaset ve Toplum* [*Syria's Kurds: History, Politics and Society*] (Istanbul: Intifada Yayınları, 2015).

Uğur, Hasan Atilla, *Öcalan'ı Nasıl Sorguladım – İşte Gerçekler* [*How I Interrogated Öcalan: The Reality*] (Istanbul: Kaynak Yayınları, 2011).

Vali, Abbas, *Kürt Tarihi Kimliği ve Siyaseti* [*Kurdish History and Politics*] (Istanbul: Avesta Yayınları, 2013).

Yeğen, Mesut, *Devlet Söyleminde Kürt Sorunu* [*The Kurdish Problem in State Rhetoric*] (Istanbul: İletişim Yayınları, 2015).

———, *Son Kürt İsyanı* [*The Last Kurdish Uprising*] (Istanbul: İletişim Yayınları, 2016).

Yıldırım, Kadri, *Kürt Tarihi ve Coğrafyası – 1: Rojava* [*Kurdish History and Geography – 1: Rojava*] (Istanbul: Şemal Medya, 2015).

Yurtçiçek, Bayram, *Kürt İsyanları Bedirhan Bey'den Dersim'e* [*Kurdish Uprisings from Bedirhan Bey to Dersim*] (Istanbul: Kaynak Yayınları, 2016).

English-language sources

Abrahams, Eddie (ed.), *The New Warlords: From the Gulf War to the Recolonisation of the Middle East* (London: Larkin Publications, 1994).

Ahmad, Feroz, *Turkey: The Quest for Identity* (London: Oneworld Publications, 2014).

Allsopp, Harriet, *The Kurds of Syria* (London: I.B.Tauris, 2014).

Altınay, Ayşe Gül, *The Myth of the Military-Nation: Militarism, Gender, and Education in Turkey* (New York: Springer, 2004).

Baser, Bahar, *Diasporas and Homeland Conflicts: A Comparative Perspective* (London: Routledge, 2015).

Bilgin, Fevzi and Ali Sarihan (eds), *Understanding Turkey's Kurdish Question* (Plymouth: Lexington Books, 2013).

Bozarslan, Hamit, 'Kurds and the Turkish State', in Reşat Kasaba (ed.), *The Cambridge History of Turkey* (New York: Cambridge University Press, 2008), pp. 333–56.

Caban, Dana, *Kurds: A Nation Frozen In Time* (Bloomington, IN: Author House, 2009).

Chaliand, Gerard, *A People without a Country: The Kurds and Kurdistan* (London: Zed Books, 1993).

Eccarius-Kelly, Vera, *The Militant Kurds: A Dual Strategy for Freedom* (Santa Barbara, CA: Praeger Publishers, 2012).

Gunter, Michael M., *The Kurds: A Modern History* (Princeton, NJ: Markus Wiener Publishers, 2016).

Hendrick, Joshua D., *Gülen: The Ambiguous Politics of Market Islam in Turkey and the World* (New York: NYU Press, 2014).

Knapp, Michael, Anja Flach and Ercan Ayboga, *Revolution in Rojava: Democratic Autonomy and Women's Liberation in Syrian Kurdistan* (London: Pluto Press, 2016).

Kreyenbroek, Philip G. and Stefan Sperl (eds), *The Kurds: A Contemporary Overview* (London: Routledge, 2015).

McDowall, David, *A Modern History of the Kurds* (London and New York: I.B.Tauris, 2003).

Newman, Edward and Oliver Richmond (eds), *Challenges to Peacebuilding: Managing Spoilers during Conflict Resolution* (Tokyo, New York and Paris: United Nations University Press, 2006)

Öcalan, Abdullah, 'Democratic modernity: era of woman's revolution', official PKK website. Available at http://www.pkkonline.com/en/index.php?sys=article&artID=235.

Özcan, Ali Kemal, *Turkey's Kurds: A Theoretical Analysis of the PKK and Abdullah Öcalan* (London: Routledge, 2012).

Phillips, David L., *The Kurdish Spring: A New Map of the Middle East* (Piscataway, NJ: Transaction Publishers, 2015).

Romano, David, *The Kurdish Nationalist Movement: Opportunity, Mobilization and Identity* (Cambridge: Cambridge University Press, 2006).

Romano, David and Mehmet Gurses (eds), *Conflict, Democratization, and the Kurds in the Middle East: Turkey, Iran, Iraq, and Syria* (London: Palgrave Macmillan, 2014).

Sabio, Oso, *Rojava: An Alternative to Imperialism, Nationalism, and Islamism in the Middle East* (Oso Sabio, lulu.com, 2015).

Tuğal, Cihan, *The Fall of the Turkish Model: How the Arab Uprisings Brought Down Islamic Liberalism* (London and New York: Verso, 2016).

Turkey–Kurdish Regional Government Relations after the U.S. Withdrawal from Iraq: Putting the Kurds on the Map? (Carlisle, PA: Strategic Studies Institute and US Army College Press, 2014).

White, Paul, *The PKK: Coming Down from the Mountains* (London: Zed Books, 2015).

Zürcher, Erik J., *Turkey: A Modern History* (London and New York: I.B. Tauris, 2014).

Index